"I'm delighted to endorse the philosophy behind this series. Here sounds out the voice not of the scholar in the study but of the scholar in the pulpit. The authors are all able teachers who regularly expound God's living Word to his people. May this rich material give us 'patterns of preaching' that will not only feed the flock, but, by God's grace, change the church."

    R. C. Lucas, Retired Rector, St. Helen's Church, Bishopsgate, London, England

"This series will minister to a pastor's soul and provide him with an immense resource for his preaching, and it will minister to the parishioner wonderfully in personal Bible study. The reader will be filled with fresh thoughts about our Lord as well as joyful encouragement for himself."

    The late **Kenneth N. Taylor,** translator, *The Living Bible*

"It is a pleasure to commend this series of homiletical commentaries. They fill an enormous vacuum that exists between the practical needs of the pastor/teacher and the critical exegetical depth of most commentaries. With this series, evangelicalism may now claim its own William Barclay. While remaining true to the text and its original meaning, Dr. Hughes helps us face the personal, ethical, theological, and practical questions that the text wants us to answer in the presence of the living God and his illuminating Holy Spirit."

    Walter C. Kaiser Jr., President Emeritus and Distinguished Professor of Old Testament and Ethics, Gordon-Conwell Theological Seminary

"This is no dry and ponderous commentary, but a unique window into the feelings, the textures, the teachings, the times, the very hearts of the New Testament writers."

    Frank E. Peretti, author, *This Present Darkness*

Books in the PREACHING THE WORD Series:

Unless otherwise indicated, all volumes are by R. Kent Hughes

1 & 2 THESSALONIANS

The Hope of Salvation

James H. Grant Jr.

R. Kent Hughes, General Editor

WHEATON, ILLINOIS

1 & 2 Thessalonians

Copyright © 2011 by James H. Grant Jr.

Published by Crossway
        1300 Crescent Street
        Wheaton, Illinois 60187

Cover banner by Marge Gieser

Art direction: Keane Fine

First printing, 2011

Printed in the United States of America

ISBN 13: 978-1-4335-0544-7

ISBN 10: 1-4335-0544-4

ISBN PDF: 978-1-4335-0545-4

ISBN Mobipocket: 978-1-4335-0546-1

ISBN ePub: 978-1-4335-2255-0

Library of Congress Cataloging-in-Publication Data

Grant, James H., 1976–
    1 & 2 Thessalonians : the hope of salvation / James H. Grant Jr.;
R. Kent Hughes, general editor.
      p. cm. (Preaching the Word)
    Includes bibliographical references and index.
    ISBN 978-1-4335-0544-7 (hc)
    1. Bible. N.T. Thessalonians—Commentaries. I. Hughes, R. Kent.
II. Title. III. Title: First and second Thessalonians. IV. Series.
BS2725.53.G73   2011
227'.8107—dc22   2010024838

Crossway is a publishing ministry of Good News Publishers.

T S		2 0	1 9	1 8	1 7	1 6	1 5	1 4	1 3	1 2	1 1
1 5	1 4	1 3	1 2	1 1	1 0	9	8	7	6	5	4	3	2	1

In memory of my father,
J. Harold Grant Sr. (1949–2007),
who is currently asleep in Christ, awaiting the resurrection.

Grief has not been without hope,
for we believe Jesus will return,
uniting us together in the resurrection,
to be with the Lord and glorify him always.

This is good news indeed.

*Now may the God of peace himself sanctify you
completely, and may your whole spirit and
soul and body be kept blameless at
the coming of our Lord Jesus Christ.
He who calls you is faithful; he will surely do it.*
1 THESSALONIANS 5:23–24

*Now may our Lord Jesus Christ himself, and
God our Father, who loved us and gave us eternal
comfort and good hope through grace,
comfort your hearts and establish them in
every good work and word.*
2 THESSALONIANS 2:16–17

Contents

A Word to Those Who Preach the Word

There are times when I am preaching that I have especially sensed the pleasure of God. I usually become aware of it through the unnatural silence. The ever-present coughing ceases, and the pews stop creaking, bringing an almost physical quiet to the sanctuary — through which my words sail like arrows. I experience a heightened eloquence, so that the cadence and volume of my voice intensify the truth I am preaching.

There is nothing quite like it — the Holy Spirit filling one's sails, the sense of his pleasure, and the awareness that something is happening among one's hearers. This experience is, of course, not unique, for thousands of preachers have similar experiences, even greater ones.

What has happened when this takes place? How do we account for this sense of his smile? The answer for me has come from the ancient rhetorical categories of *logos*, *ethos*, and *pathos*.

The first reason for his smile is the *logos* — in terms of preaching, God's Word. This means that as we stand before God's people to proclaim his Word, we have done our homework. We have exegeted the passage, mined the significance of its words in their context, and applied sound hermeneutical principles in interpreting the text so that we understand what its words meant to its hearers. And it means that we have labored long until we can express in a sentence what the theme of the text is — so that our outline springs from the text. Then our preparation will be such that as we preach, we will not be preaching our own thoughts about God's Word, but God's actual Word, his *logos*. This is fundamental to pleasing him in preaching.

The second element in knowing God's smile in preaching is *ethos* — what you are as a person. There is a danger endemic to preaching, which is having your hands and heart cauterized by holy things. Phillips Brooks illustrated it by the analogy of a train conductor who comes to believe that he has been to the places he announces because of his long and loud heralding of them. And that is why Brooks insisted that preaching must be "the bringing of truth through personality." Though we can never perfectly embody the truth we preach, we must be subject to it, long for it, and make it as much a part of our ethos as possible. As the Puritan William Ames said, "Next to the Scriptures, nothing makes a sermon more to pierce, than when it comes out of the inward affection of the heart without any affectation." When a preacher's *ethos* backs up his *logos*, there will be the pleasure of God.

Last, there is *pathos* — personal passion and conviction. David Hume, the Scottish philosopher and skeptic, was once challenged as he was seen going to hear George Whitefield preach: "I thought you do not believe in the gospel." Hume replied, "I don't, but he does." Just so! When a preacher believes what he preaches, there will be passion. And this belief and requisite passion will know the smile of God.

The pleasure of God is a matter of *logos* (the Word), *ethos* (what you are), and *pathos* (your passion). As you preach the Word may you experience his smile — the Holy Spirit in your sails!

R. Kent Hughes

Acknowledgments

I want to thank R. Kent Hughes for the opportunity to contribute to the Preaching the Word series and my friend Justin Taylor for introducing us. I am indebted to my congregation, Trinity Reformed Church, for the call to preach the gospel to them every Sunday. I also want to thank Ted Griffin for his work in editing this volume. He is a fine editor-theologian, and this book is better because of his work.

My wife, Brandy, should receive a special thank you. She encouraged me throughout this process, especially as our family grew from two children (Macy and Trey) to four (Nate and Addie). She deserves more honor than words can express, and together we agreed to dedicate this volume to my father, J. Harold Grant, Sr., who entered into the presence of the Lord in January 2007. I started this series in the summer of 2008, and through it the Lord comforted our hearts and established us in the gospel.

Series Abbreviations

ABC	Anchor Bible Commentary
BECNT	The Baker Exegetical Commentary on the New Testament
ICC	International Critical Commentary
IVPNT	The IVP New Testament Commentary Series
NICNT	The New International Commentary on the New Testament
NIGTC	The New International Greek Text Commentary
NIVAC	The NIV Application Commentary
NTC	New Testament Commentary
PNTC	The Pillar New Testament Commentary

1

Listening to Paul's Conversation

Introduction to 1 Thessalonians

Have you ever stepped into the middle of a conversation only to find yourself lost in the discussion? If you are supposed to participate in the conversation, then you have to be "filled in" on the background. If the conversation continues and no one provides this information, you have to fill in the background for yourself. You have to figure out what they are talking about and why this topic is important.

When we read one of Paul's letters, we are walking in on a conversation that has already started, and we have to catch up with the discussion. Calvin Roetzel calls this a "conversation in context."[1] The conversation is taking place with a particular group of people in a particular city. For our purposes, we will be examining Paul's letters to the church in Thessalonica, a church he first planted with the help of Silas and Timothy. In order to get our bearings, we are going to set the stage for the whole first letter with an overview of Paul's main "talking points" with this church. We are going to set the stage in two areas — the background of this letter and its actual contents.

THE BACKGROUND FOR THIS CHURCH PLANT

Luke explains some of the background in Acts 17. Paul arrived in Thessalonica after a difficult ministry in Philippi that saw him placed in jail. In spite of that suffering, when Paul was released from prison he continued his ministry by heading to Thessalonica, but those trials continued to follow Paul. After establishing the church in Thessalonica, Paul had to leave quickly when a

mob dragged some of the Christian leaders before the magistrates of the
city. This mob claimed that the Christians were against the decrees of Caesar
because they were claiming allegiance to another king, a man named Jesus.

Although Paul left Thessalonica quickly, we know that he continued to
communicate with this young Christian church, even before he wrote this
first letter. Paul was concerned about the spiritual growth and strength of
these young Christians; so he decided to send Timothy back to Thessalonica.
In chapter 3 of 1 Thessalonians Paul says, "Therefore when we could bear
it no longer, we were willing to be left behind at Athens alone, and we sent
Timothy, our brother and God's coworker in the gospel of Christ, to establish and exhort you in your faith, that no one be moved by these afflictions"
(vv. 1–3).

After Timothy visited the church, he reunited with Paul in Corinth and
provided an update on the situation in Thessalonica. According to Paul,
Timothy brought back "the good news of your faith and love and reported
that you always remember us kindly and long to see us, as we long to see
you" (1 Thessalonians 3:6). Timothy also brought Paul up to speed on the
issues facing the Thessalonians, so Paul could continue to teach them and
instruct them in the Christian faith.

From a certain perspective, my role as a preacher is similar to the role
of Timothy. I am going to catch you up, as best I can, on the conversation
that Paul is having with this church in Thessalonica. We cannot do this perfectly, but we can do it well enough to understand parts of this conversation. But as we listen in on this conversation between Paul and the church
in Thessalonica, we are not just spectators. We are not just listening in on
something that happened almost two thousand years ago. We are not just
doing history. Instead we are part of this conversation. We must see ourselves in this story, seek to understand this conversation, and learn what Paul
is saying to us. In a very real way Paul is talking as much to us as he was to
them. As Paul tells them about events in his life, his desires and concerns for
them, he is at the same time instructing all of us in Christian doctrine and
practice, both in terms of personal issues related to individual Christians as
well as of issues related to the church and the ministry.[2]

A CONVERSATION ABOUT MINISTRY AND THE CHURCH

The first topic we notice is a conversation about ministry and the church.
Now this might seem like a given, but we have to remind ourselves of this.
We are listening to a conversation between a church and a man who was an
apostle, a church planter, a pastor, and a teacher. So this is an opportunity to
see how Paul approached ministry. We see his great concern for this church
and for these Christians.

Paul gives us some insight into his view of ministry in chapter 2: "But though we had already suffered and been shamefully treated at Philippi, as you know, we had boldness in our God to declare to you the gospel of God in the midst of much conflict" (v. 2). Paul says that although he suffered, he still came to declare the gospel to them. In the face of obstacles and opposition, he proclaimed the Word of God. But he continues:

> For our appeal does not spring from error or impurity or any attempt to deceive, but just as we have been approved by God to be entrusted with the gospel, so we speak, not to please man, but to please God who tests our hearts. For we never came with words of flattery, as you know, nor with a pretext for greed — God is witness. Nor did we seek glory from people, whether from you or from others, though we could have made demands as apostles of Christ. (2:3–6)

Do you see what Paul is saying? His desire in ministry was not to flatter them, but to please God. And as he pleased God, he would help these Christians grow.

Is this not the case in the ministry? Paul is explaining to us the fundamental reality of a God-centered approach to ministry and the church. He could not enter into the task of church planting by flattering people; he could not do it out of a self-centered sense of glory. If he did, he would not be serving and benefiting them. Instead he had to serve them by following and pleasing the Lord.

Paul also describes his ministry toward them as being "gentle . . . like a nursing mother taking care of her own children" (2:7). What an important view of pastoral ministry: the pastor is like a nursing mother taking care of her own children. That kind of gentleness should characterize all pastors, and this is a rebuke to me and to others who lead Christ's church when we do not look at our congregation as children to be nurtured and led in the faith. So we see two perspectives that complement each other in Paul's approach to the ministry. A pastor must approach the church with authority and conviction, not trying to flatter people and please them. But along with authority and conviction, the pastor must also display gentleness and nurture.

A CONVERSATION ABOUT SUFFERING AND PERSECUTION

How would you like to walk in on a conversation between Paul and a church on the topic of suffering? That is precisely what we have here, and this is important for us, too, because suffering and trials make up a fundamental part of life that touches all of us. We struggle with suffering, and we often do not know how to handle it. This is a central reason why Paul wrote this letter — to help Christians face suffering in a Christ-centered way.

Immediately in chapter 1 we come across the issue of suffering. Paul says they received the word of God with much affliction, and that was imitating what had happened to him (v. 6). Both Paul and the church faced suffering, but the conversation about suffering and affliction runs through the whole book. Paul goes on to explain to us a central theological perspective about suffering in 2:14–16. Paul is encouraged that this church imitated other churches in the midst of their suffering, but he reminded them that those who hinder us are also "displeas[ing] God and oppos[ing] all mankind" because they are attempting to stop the message of salvation. But in their attempt to stop the gospel, Paul says, those who oppose the gospel are actually "fill[ing] up the measure of their sins" because "God's wrath has come upon them at last!"

In these verses we have Paul's theology of suffering and trials. We can call this "A Doctrine of Persecution and Suffering." Paul did two things. First, he explained to these Christians that their suffering was not a result of their sin. Instead they were in a long line of Christians who suffered under the cross: "For you suffered the same things from your own countrymen as they did from the Jews, who killed both the Lord Jesus and the prophets, and drove us out" (2:14, 15). Jesus suffered, the Jews suffered, Paul suffered, and now the Thessalonians suffered for the sake of the gospel.

Paul did not stop with the suffering of these Christians. He went on to explain to them that even those who oppose the gospel are not outside of God's power. On the contrary, they are currently under God's wrath because they reject the offer of salvation. If we misunderstand those two points, we will constantly struggle with God. A proper understanding of suffering and affliction involves a proper understanding of God, who he is, and what he is doing.

This is just as important for us now as it was for them then. When we suffer for our faith, or even if we just suffer from the typical trials and tribulations of this life, our normal response is that we are doing something wrong. Secretly we ask God, "What did I do? Why are you letting this happen to me?"

Paul will have none of that. He is changing our perspective on the issue of suffering. He is telling us to transform our minds, to approach suffering from a completely different perspective. How then should we view suffering and trials? First, we should expect that we are going to suffer. Suffering and trials should not surprise us. We must embrace the reality that through much suffering we must enter the kingdom of God. Second, we should realize that God calls us to persevere through it because we are not suffering under his wrath. As Christians, God's wrath was poured out on the cross, on his Son. We are suffering because we are bearing the cross that God has placed on us in this life to make us long for Heaven.

This is not the typical perspective on suffering that is predominant in the Christian world. In fact, some Christians would say that I have just given you a wrong view of suffering. I could imagine you having a conversation with someone about suffering, and you say, "The Scriptures tell us that we should expect to suffer. I was just reading something on 1 Thessalonians that explained how suffering can be redemptive and how God uses it to help us grow." And your friend responds by saying, "That is just wrong! Why would I want to suffer? I was just listening to someone preach about this on TV, and the preacher said that our problem is our attitude. We have the wrong attitude about life. We are not positive enough, and our problem is that we think we should suffer. Instead we should expect God to bless us."

That perspective on suffering is not Christian, but it is being taught in some churches. It is not the message we find in the Bible. Paul's view of suffering is summarized in Acts 14:22: "through many tribulations we must enter the kingdom of God." Paul's discussion on suffering with this church in Thessalonica will help us understand a Biblical approach to suffering.

A CONVERSATION ABOUT THE FUTURE AND CHRIST'S SECOND COMING

Perhaps this conversation about suffering brought up our next topic: the second coming of Jesus Christ. We have in both of Paul's letters to the church in Thessalonica an ongoing conversation about the second coming. This is one of the most prominent themes in 1 and 2 Thessalonians. It is mentioned in every chapter of this first letter (1:10; 2:19, 20; 3:13; 4:13–18; 5:1–11, 23, 24), and Paul continued this conversation in the second letter.

This church was asking very important questions about the future and the coming of Jesus Christ:

- What happens to those who die?
- What happens to those who are alive?
- What about those who do not believe?

Paul explains to us what to expect. At Jesus' future coming, the dead in Christ will rise and will be caught up along with the living to meet the Lord in the air (4:15–17). Unbelievers will be subject to God's wrath, but Christians will be delivered from God's wrath, inheriting salvation instead (1:10; 5:2–4, 9, 10). There is a lot to examine regarding the second coming of Christ, and God has blessed us with the opportunity to understand Paul's instructions to these Christians in Thessalonica.

A CONVERSATION ABOUT THE CHRISTIAN LIFE AND GODLINESS IN THIS WORLD

The final area I want examine in this overview is connected to all three previous topics, but specifically to the second coming. Those saints who are destined to be with Jesus in his second coming must be holy and blameless (3:11–4:8; 5:23). This is one reason why Paul concludes the book the way he does. Notice this in 5:12–22, where Paul tells us to love those who minister over us, be at peace among ourselves, admonish the idle, encourage the fainthearted, help the weak, and be patient with everyone. As we live this life and face evil, respond with love, continue to rejoice, and always pray, and as we give thanks in all circumstances, we will be following the will of God and holding fast to what is good. What helpful and practical advice!

Paul has charged us to live differently than the world, but he knows that this can seem impossible for Christians. Sometimes all the commands and instructions overwhelm us. We often think, *How can I possibly do all that?* Paul has some closing words for us: "Now may the God of peace himself sanctify you completely, and may your whole spirit and soul and body be kept blameless at the coming of our Lord Jesus Christ. He who calls you is faithful; he will surely do it" (1 Thessalonians 5:23, 24).

Do not get discouraged: God will do this work. He will sanctify you completely. God will keep your whole spirit and soul and body blameless at the coming of the Lord.

God is faithful; he will do it.

That is the gospel. The conversation that we are dropping in on is a conversation about the gospel and what it means for our lives. Let us believe that God is for us and that he will finish the work he has started, and let us attend to his revelation to us in his Word.

2

Christianity at Thessalonica

1 THESSALONIANS 1:1 AND ACTS 17:1–10

Church planting was a crucial aspect of Paul's ministry, but in recent years, especially in Western culture, the emphasis on planting churches has diminished. Instead of reduplicating, Western churches developed the attitude that if we build it, people will come. Thankfully, it looks as if that tide is shifting, and church planting has received more attention. The movement toward church planting goes by several names, but it is usually described as being missional, a term that means we are to be moving outward toward those around us. It is a movement that seeks to make the faith public and to duplicate the faith among people who are our neighbors.

This missional, church-planting direction has gained popularity, and although we should be encouraged by this, we should not jump into a ministry without understanding some of the aspects of what we are doing. Church planting takes work. It is important to know something of the location regarding a church plant. Will the church be planted in a major city like New York or Chicago? Or will the church be planted in a rural area like the mountains of Colorado or the plains of Kansas? A church plant in New York City is not going to be the same as a church plant in Memphis, and both of those will be different from the church that is planted in the midst of farms in the heart of the United States.

Church planters must know something of the city in which they are going to plant a church, but this is not new. As Paul went into new cities, he understood the area and the issues surrounding those cities. Each one of his letters was slightly different, not just because of the issues the churches faced but also because of their locations. The Christians in Rome faced a different world than the Christians in Thessalonica. So we must pause and consider some of the features of the city of Thessalonica.[1]

BACKGROUND

Paul was on his second missionary journey. He had received a vision from Jesus that a man of Macedonia was urging him, "Come over to Macedonia and help us" (Acts 16:9). So Paul took up the call of Jesus to push the gospel into areas we consider today as Europe. In order to preach the gospel to this area, Paul was traveling along the Via Egnatia, a Roman road that connected Greece to Byzantium (modern-day Istanbul), connecting what we know as Europe and Asia. Before this road was built, the journey would have taken three to four months by ship or five to six weeks by land. But once the Via Egnatia was finished, the journey took less than three weeks.[2]

As Paul traveled along this road, he came upon several key cities, and he brought the gospel to those areas. First he came to Philippi (Acts 16). While he was there, he faced a great deal of suffering and persecution, which resulted in Paul and Silas being thrown into prison. God miraculously got them out of prison through an earthquake, and in the process the Philippian jailer and his family became Christians. The church was established in Philippi, and Paul and Silas left to continue their work of the gospel.

Once Paul and Silas departed from Philippi, Luke picks up their journey in Acts 17 as they passed through Amphipolis and Apollonia. This journey would have been similar to traveling along the Gulf Coast from Pensacola, Florida, through Mobile, Alabama, on your way to New Orleans, Louisiana. Paul and Silas were traveling on this major road along the Aegean Sea, and they passed through these two cities before they came to the central city we know of as Thessalonica.

THE IMPORTANCE OF THESSALONICA

Thessalonica was important for several reasons, and its importance played a role in Paul's decision to stop in this city. We do not know if he stopped in Amphipolis and Apollonia to establish churches, but it is doubtful. Luke tells us no more than that he passed through those cities, but Paul did stop in Thessalonica, one of the largest cities in the Roman world with over one hundred thousand people. As a large city, it had a synagogue. Luke mentions this immediately in Acts 17. We know that on his missionary journeys Paul would make the synagogue his starting point for the gospel as he preached the good news "to the Jew first and also to the Greek" (Romans 1:16). But we also see something of the providence of God in this event because synagogues had been established in large cities after the Jewish dispersion. By placing Jewish synagogues throughout the Roman Empire, God was providing a means for the gospel to advance throughout the Greco-Roman world. Thessalonica was also at a strategic location. It was on that important road, the Via Egnatia. In terms we can understand, perhaps we could compare it to New York City, which has a central harbor, several important airports, central train locations, and the connection of several central interstates. Thessalonica was centrally located just like that. It was a key city of the region because it had fertile farmland, a good mining operation, and a great fishing industry from both the rivers and the sea. So important was the city that one of the writers of that time, Meletius, once said, "So long as nature does not change, Thessalonica will remain wealthy and fortunate."[3]

Thessalonica was a free city in the Roman world. Other cities did not have this privilege. In other locations the Roman Empire had military occupation forces and set up its own government, but not in Thessalonica. The Thessalonians controlled their own affairs and political situations, making them almost democratic, unlike any other city in that region. They had freedom from military occupation, and they could mint their own coins. That makes their political structure very important. In fact, this plays a role in our story. If we don't understand the political structure of the city, some of Acts 17 and 1 Thessalonians will not make much sense.

The political structure of Thessalonica had several different levels. The lowest level was the citizen assembly. This was a type of local government consisting of individual citizens meeting to make decisions. This is indicated in Acts 17:5 when Luke says that the mob tried to bring the Christians "out to the crowd." The word for "crowd" indicates the people assembled in a public place or, as some believe, the citizen assembly. When trouble came up, the mob wanted to bring Paul and Silas before this citizen assembly. Luke then says in verse 6 that the mob could not find them, so Jason and other Christians were brought before the city authorities. The word for "city authorities" here is a specific word referring to government leaders called politarchs.[4]

The politarchs were the upper level of government in Thessalonica. They had a very important role in that city, which is why Jason and some of the brethren were brought to them. These leaders, these politarchs, were responsible for the governing of the city, and if they could not keep everything going smoothly, they would be accountable to the Roman Empire. So they did everything possible to please the Roman Empire and its citizens. They were politically perceptive leaders, and for good reason: they didn't want to get into trouble and lose all the privileges of the city. Thessalonica had wonderful privileges because it was a free city, and these governors or politarchs were put in place to make sure the city didn't lose its privileges. If Thessalonica lost its status as a free city, there would be terrible consequences. Their income would go down as they would have to pay more taxes, as well as paying and housing Roman military officers. The economy would take a significant hit, and the freedom of the city would be at stake. If there were problems, the Roman Empire would come in and take all privileges away.

Not only did these politarchs govern the city as political authorities, they also had another very important role to play in Thessalonica: they led the people in certain aspects of religious worship.[5] This is far removed from our concept of church and state and the separation of the two. At that time you could not separate the political leaders from the worship of the city. The ruler or king was often worshipped alongside other gods. In the Egyptian world, the Pharaoh was considered a god with all the other gods. The same thing is true of the Roman Empire. Caesar was worshipped, and this worship bound the Roman Empire together and created solidarity, and the politarchs played an important role regarding this religious unity.

Because of Thessalonica's key location, it had a significant religious atmosphere. There were many temples and shrines within the city. In fact, the city was only fifty miles from Mt. Olympus, the home of the Greek gods such as Zeus. In order to travel to Mt. Olympus, worshippers would come by ship to the Thessalonica harbor or take the central Roman road, the Via Egnatia. Since Thessalonica was on a major road, and since it had a major harbor, these religious opportunities brought a lot of money. So Thessalonica catered to every kind of god in that world — Roman, Greek, Egyptian, and numerous others. But the most important religious ceremony of the city concerned the worship of the Roman emperor. This was called the Roman imperial cult.[6] This movement placed the Caesars and some members of his family within the realm of deity, and the Roman citizens were called upon to worship Caesar. This was an important element of freedom in cities like Thessalonica. As long as they paid homage to Caesar, as long as they worshipped and honored him, they would have very little trouble with the Roman Empire.[7]

The Roman imperial cult arose during the time of the early reign of Caesar Augustus, whose full name was Gaius Julius Caesar Augustus (he was known as Octavius). His great-uncle was Julius Caesar, and after Julius Caesar's assassination, young Octavius brought peace, prosperity, and security to the Roman Empire. In fact, the Romans would often say that Caesar Augustus brought the gospel with him, the good news. They would actually use the term for gospel: Caesar was the bringer of the gospel, and he was to be worshipped. So the Caesars who followed after him — Tiberius, Caligula, Claudius, and Nero to mention a few — all continued this Roman imperial cult.

So the leaders, the politarchs, of Thessalonica wanted to protect the rule of Caesar. To demonstrate their loyalty to Caesar, they would lead the people in worship, and in that worship they would remind the people of the great Kingdom of Caesar and the good news that he brought of peace and security and prosperity. Caesar's kingdom was one of peace and prosperity that would never end, it was claimed. It was into that environment that Paul came preaching his gospel, the gospel of Jesus Christ.

THE GOSPEL COMES TO THESSALONICA

When he arrived, Paul began in the synagogue. That was Paul's custom; the gospel went to the Jew first and then to the Greek. In his pattern of planting churches, he would initially preach to the Jews. Paul would walk into the synagogue and be recognized by his dress, and he would stand up and speak. Luke explains:

> And Paul went in, as was his custom, and on three Sabbath days he reasoned with them from the Scriptures, explaining and proving that it was necessary for the Christ to suffer and to rise from the dead, and saying, "This Jesus, whom I proclaim to you, is the Christ." (Acts 17:2, 3)

That is what Paul did. When he had the opportunity to speak, he would step up and remind the brothers about the promises that God had given to their forefathers about the coming Messiah. He would demonstrate that the Messiah had to come and suffer, perhaps appealing to Isaiah 53 or Psalm 22 or other Old Testament passages. Then he would argue that Jesus of Nazareth was the Messiah, that he fulfilled the promises of God.

THE RESULT OF THE GOSPEL

After Paul proclaimed that Jesus was the Messiah, "some of them were persuaded and joined Paul and Silas, as did a great many of the devout Greeks and not a few of the leading women" (Acts 17:4). So there were Jews in the same community with God-fearing Greeks, as well as prominent women from the city. Paul's message reached different groups of people, but this good news had now created a problem. Luke explains that some of the Jews were jealous, so they formed a mob and set the city in an uproar. They attacked the house of Jason, and their goal was to bring Paul and Silas out to the citizen assembly. When they could not find Paul and Silas to bring them before this local assembly, the mob decided to take Jason and some fellow Christians before the city authorities, the politarchs. It is very important that we see the charge brought against these Christians: "These men who have turned the world upside down have come here also, and Jason has received them" (Acts 17:6, 7).

Now we see why this is a problem. "This message is causing a disruption throughout the whole Roman Empire, and if we let them come here, they will disrupt our economy and freedom. If you rulers allow this, you will fall from power, and Rome will come down upon us and accuse us of treason." Further evidence that this is precisely what was taking place is found in verse 7: "They are all acting against the decrees of Caesar, saying that there is another king, Jesus."

Why would the rulers be troubled? Paul was proclaiming another King — Jesus, the Messiah — and this message was turning the world upside down.

Notice what Luke says in verse 8: "And the people and the city authorities were disturbed when they heard these things." This claim disrupted the pseudopeace of these city authorities, these politarchs. The leaders saw the implications of this message and realized what it meant. The gospel of Jesus was challenging the very core of that city — its worship of Caesar, its love of money, and its love of freedom. The gospel of King Jesus had "turned the world upside down." Paul's gospel about a King who died upon a cross to forgive our sins was challenging the rule and reign of Caesar. This gospel was so powerful that some of the prominent people in the city were now identifying with that King. They were picking up their crosses and following him, even if it cost them prominence in the city, even if it cost them money, even if it cost them freedom. This message was going against the very culture of that city. That church would have been tolerated as long as it did not disrupt the social order, but as soon as the church stepped into the middle of life, as soon as the church started tinkering with life in the city, people became nervous and worried.

The mob brought them before the politarchs, and the magistrates forced Jason and the Christians to post bond. This would have been a good behavior bond.[8] Perhaps the city made them guarantee that Paul and Silas would leave the city. We are not sure. Whatever was required, the next event described by Luke is that the Christians in Thessalonica sent Paul and Silas away by night. This might have been a result of the hostility toward Paul and Silas, and the Thessalonians were concerned for their friends. But Paul and Silas were also worried about these new Christians and this new church. As long as Paul and Silas stayed, there was a threat to that new church. So Paul left under the cloak of the dark night.

PAUL'S DEPARTURE AND HIS CONCERN

That was the situation facing the church when Paul left the city. He didn't know what was going to happen. The Christians were faced with a serious charge — treason against Caesar. And the charge had some truth to it. No, these Christians did not want to rebel against the rule of Caesar, but they would not worship him as the Lord. That was reserved for Jesus alone. In that way there was no other king but Jesus Christ. That was a difficult stance to take in the Roman Empire, and Paul knew that it would bring about suffering and affliction. Paul was concerned for their faith, and he did not want them to be moved by these afflictions. He told them during his time there that they were destined, as Christians, to suffer affliction as they picked up their crosses and followed Jesus (1 Thessalonians 3:1–4). When he could no longer endure it, he sent Timothy back to establish and exhort them in the faith.

Timothy was going to exhort and encourage these Christians as they faced these trials. He was going to remind them of Paul's teaching. Those who were caught up in the message of peace, security, and comfort that came from the Roman Empire would not receive their message. The message disrupts that kind of life, even today, so we must be prepared to suffer for the cause of the gospel. But Timothy was also going to report back to Paul about their faith because Paul feared that "somehow the tempter had tempted [them] and [his] labor would be in vain" (1 Thessalonians 3:5).

What does the tempter say? He tempts them to give up on Jesus. He tempts them to turn back to all they had left behind in the Roman world. But Paul knew this was a deadly game. We should be reminded of the word from the writer of Hebrews here. Describing those who are strangers and exiles on the earth, those who seek a homeland beyond this world, he states that if they think about the land they left, the world they left, "they would have had opportunity to return" (Hebrews 11:15). When that temptation arises, they must "desire a better country, that is, a heavenly one," and as they live this way, "God is not ashamed to be called their God, for he has prepared for them a city" (Hebrews 11:16).

OUR BATTLE IS AGAINST . . .

This is what the Christians faced in Thessalonica, but this is also what followers of Christ face today. This battle has not disappeared, and it will not go away. It is a constant battle that must be faced by all Christians. Some estimates show that over forty million Christians were killed in the twentieth century because of their faith.[9] All we have to do is look at the Middle East or China, and we will see areas where Christians must stand firm for their faith as they face the threat of death. In 2008 the Summer Olympics came to China, and the opening ceremony was unlike anything seen in Olympic history. The ceremony was awe inspiring to anyone who watched it, but behind all the pomp and ceremony is a conflict in China, a conflict between the church and the Communist government. An underground church exists in China, and the government will not permit its believers to worship Jesus Christ openly and freely. Christians are viewed as a threat to communism, and they are persecuted for their allegiance to the Lord Jesus Christ.[10]

This type of conflict has been with the church since the beginning. The claims of Jesus have withstood the power and threats of the Roman Empire, Muslim armies, the rise of Communism, and any number of other claims to power. In our time we have a slightly different challenge, a challenge called secularism. Many within the United States of America, both citizens and politicians, believe that Christians' faith should be kept out of the public square. Faith is considered a private matter, and it should not play a role in public interaction. This is just as much a challenge to our faith as was the challenge in Thessalonica.

The truth is: if we are Christians, our faith cannot be private. We cannot just be a Christian on Sunday or in the privacy of our homes as we pray. We must follow Jesus publicly. Our faith cannot be limited to our churches or our homes but must be displayed in various ways at work and in the day-to-day activities of our world. That could mean several things for us. Perhaps it means we need to be more open or more serious about our commitment to Christ. Perhaps it means we should reflect the justice and truth of God in our callings or vocations, or perhaps it means we should reflect the love and compassion of the gospel in our callings or vocations. Whether we are at church, at work, at home, or in any other public place, we are ambassadors for King Jesus. That is the call Christ has placed on us.

We need to be stirred up to remember that the kingdom of God transcends the governments of this world. Jesus is King over everything in this world. He sits in Heaven ruling at the right hand of God, and as Christians we are called to acknowledge that "of his kingdom there will be no end" (Luke 1:33). As Abraham Kuyper famously said in the climax of his inaugural address at the dedication of the Free University of Amsterdam, "There is not a square inch in the whole domain of our human existence over which Christ, who is Sovereign over *all*, does not cry: 'Mine!'"[11] There is not a single place where Christ does not touch our lives. We cannot privatize our faith. We cannot think that as long as we are reading our Bibles and praying and coming to church, we are doing enough. We cannot give in to a secular mind-set. Our faith must speak in the public square.

The message Paul brings to us through this book and this situation in Thessalonica is that we cannot live that way. We cannot accept it when others in our culture say they will tolerate the church as long as we keep everything private. To be truly missional, to be the kind of Christians Christ has called us to be, we must be salt and light. If we live that way, Jesus gives us a promise: as we acknowledge him before men, he will acknowledge us before his Heavenly Father (Matthew 10:32). Let us openly acknowledge our King!

3

What Is in a Greeting?

Have you ever considered what is in a greeting? Have you ever considered how you greet people, and how they greet you? We commonly say, "Hello!" or "How are you?" In a less formal environment, we might say, "Hey, it's good to see you." The same is true about letters and e-mails. We tend to be somewhat more formal in letters. If we write, "Dear Paul," we are approaching a matter in a formal way. On the other hand, if I write to you and say, "Greetings in Christ," I am communicating something to you. I am saying that we are together in Christ, and I greet you based on our unity in Christ.

No matter what the situation is, we are communicating a message with our greetings. Christians have understood this through the centuries and have often greeted one another in a unique way. Paul has a distinctively Christian way of communicating, and he begins his letter to this church in Thessalonica by writing, "Paul, Silvanus, and Timothy, to the church of the Thessalonians in God the Father and the Lord Jesus Christ: Grace to you and peace." What is Paul communicating in this greeting?

TYPICAL LETTER WRITING

We should realize that just as there are standards for letter writing today, there were also standards in Paul's day. If we write a letter, it usually follows this structure: a greeting, the body of the letter, a concluding farewell. Although ancient letter writing was similar to this structure, there are some important elements to consider. For example, the opening section followed a very specific pattern that had three elements: the sender, the recipient, and the greeting.[1] The apostle followed the usual pattern: "Paul to the Thessalonians, greetings!"

Paul stayed close to this typical pattern in his letter, but he did change some things, and when he changed things, it was important. If a Biblical writer changed things from what you would normally expect, he was trying to communicate something important, and what we find is that Paul was trying to communicate something important, something distinctly Christian in this greeting. We could say that Paul was attempting to "Christianize" the letter opening.[2] Instead of following the precise pattern, he added something significant. Usually the opening of a letter just said, "Greetings." Notice that at the end of verse 1, Paul said two things in his greeting: "grace . . . and peace." Paul was communicating more to this church in those two words than we often stop to consider. What does he mean by "grace" and "peace"?

WHAT IS GRACE?

Grace is foundational to a proper understanding of Christian salvation, and it is an important word to Paul since he uses it over one hundred times. Most of the time we define grace as a gift, and that is true. Grace is a gift, and it comes from God. But we can press on to a deeper understanding of it. We will examine grace in a twofold way.

First, it means that we are in right standing with God. This would imply that at one time we were not in right standing with God. According to Paul in Ephesians 2:3, God considers humanity to be "children of wrath." Because of the rebellion of Adam and Eve in the Garden of Eden, we are disobedient children and are under God's judgment, but the gift of grace means that we have moved from this wrath to a position of favor with God. We have moved from wrath to grace, and Paul says in Romans that we "stand" in this grace (Romans 5:2). Grace is therefore part of God's saving activity, his action in sending Christ to die in our place and putting us "in Christ."

Second, grace is not only God's gift of salvation for us in Christ, to move us from wrath to favor, from enemies to friends, but grace is also part of God's work for us in the ongoing process of salvation and redemption. Grace continues to come to us throughout the Christian life. Paul explains in 1 Corinthians 15:10, "But by the grace of God I am what I am, and his grace toward me was not in vain. On the contrary, I worked harder than any of them, though it was not I, but the grace of God that is with me." In other words, grace not only placed Paul in a right standing with God, but it also empowered him to live and minister and obey.

WHAT IS PEACE?

The other word Paul uses is "peace." Although Paul is writing in Greek, he is still a Hebrew, and it would be wise for us to reflect on the Hebrew idea of peace, which is the word *shalom*. When you find the word *peace* in the Bible, the writer is not simply talking about some inner peace or tranquillity. The Hebrew word *shalom* is also not just about the absence of conflict. Instead *shalom* is about wholeness and well-being. The word not only reflects an individual's relationship with God but the relationship of the whole community to God and to each other.[3]

A helpful way to think about peace from a Biblical perspective is to see it in contrast to sin. Sin has messed everything up in this world. Sin has devastated not only our actions but also our consciences; sin has destroyed our relationships not only with God but also with each other. *Shalom* (" peace") is a word that describes how God is going to set all those things right. *Shalom* is a word that describes the way things are supposed to be. So when you hear Paul talk about "peace," think of *shalom*.[4]

Paul opened this letter with two very important words that describe the truth of the gospel in concise and precise ways. Both of these words have more depth than we can examine in one chapter, but Paul is going to unpack the meaning of these words throughout the whole letter, and we can see something more about them by looking at what immediately preceded these words: "To the church of the Thessalonians in God the Father and the Lord Jesus Christ." Although Paul did not explicitly tie grace and peace to God the Father and the Lord Jesus Christ in this passage as he did in all subsequent letters,[5] we can be sure that what is implied is that this grace and peace come from a heavenly source. They are not coming specifically from Paul. Paul is pronouncing this blessing from God. We often call this an apostolic greeting or an apostolic salutation. We mean that Paul was representing God. Paul was speaking the words of God to this church, and in this greeting Paul was saying that God's grace and peace rested on this church.

This greeting is similar to a benediction, the kind used at the end of worship services. The benediction is not a prayer because the preacher is not asking God for something. The benediction is from God, and God is sending you out from the worship service with his blessing. This is similar to what this greeting is doing. This greeting is from God, and God is speaking to us through Paul. In this opening greeting Paul is not praying. Paul is not asking God for anything. Instead God is giving us something. He is giving us grace and peace. God is declaring his grace and peace to us.

Since grace and peace come from God, notice what it does: it transforms our relationships. First, it transforms our relationship with God. We can now call God our Father. Grace has put us in a right standing with God. We have peace with him and are adopted into his family, so we call him Father. We should not take for granted the unbelievable reality that we can call the God of the universe "our Father." We are expressing a relationship in that language, and we are part of God's family not because of something we did but because God chose to adopt us into his family through his grace.

Second, grace and peace have transformed our relationship to Jesus.

Notice the full expression of his name: "the Lord Jesus Christ." "Jesus" is his name. "Lord" and "Christ" are his titles. It is not accidental that Jesus was his name. It means "Savior" or "the Lord is salvation." But his titles also express our new relationship to him. As Lord, he is our King and Ruler. He is a sovereign. He protects and defends us. The title *Christ* means "anointed" and is another word for Messiah. As our Messiah, he is our Savior, our Great High Priest. He is the one who makes atonement for our sins. He is the one who bridges the gap between us and God.

Our new relationship with Jesus works like this: our King and Priest, Jesus, is the one who brings us grace and peace so that we might be able to call God Father. The importance of grace and peace is lost if it is simply coming from Paul. Grace and peace only mean something if they come from God first. So our relationship with God has been transformed into knowing him as Father, and our relationship with Jesus has been transformed into knowing him as our King and Savior. But grace and peace also transform our relationships with each other. Notice that this is the other part of Paul's greeting. Is Paul the only person mentioned at the beginning of this letter? Notice again the people listed in verse 1: Paul, Silvanus (Silas), and Timothy. All three of them are connected to the church of the Thessalonians, that is "in God the Father and the Lord Jesus Christ."

Grace and peace create a new reality, a new ordering of human relationships. In this new community called the church, people are bound together in God the Father and in the Lord Jesus Christ. We are united to Jesus and to God our Father, which means we are united to each other. We should consider this from the opposite perspective. Paul didn't say, "Grace to you Gentiles, and *shalom*-peace to you Jews." Grace is not just for Gentiles, and peace is not just for Jews. The whole community receives grace and peace because we are not only in a new relationship with God and his Son Jesus, but we are in a new relationship with each other.

That should mean that there is no division in this new community. There is no division between Jew and Gentile, no division between slave and free, no division between male and female. Paul is probably indicating that unity by including Silas (Silvanus) and Timothy in the greeting. Paul does not always do this, but at this point he is emphasizing that the gospel brings us together as the people of God.

Why would Paul add Silas and Timothy here? Perhaps there are two reasons for the inclusion of these two men. First, Paul is showing the importance of unity in spite of our individual backgrounds. God brought Paul and Silas and Timothy together, and he was doing the same in Thessalonica with different individuals. In Acts 17:4 we notice that "a great many of the devout Greeks and not a few of the leading women" were part of this church. That means that people from different social and economic backgrounds are bound together because of their connection to Jesus Christ.

This seems to be a powerful expression of unity and solidarity in the face of the persecution that was coming upon the church in Thessalonica. This persecution was coming from leaders in the city. In Acts 17, after Paul preached the gospel in Thessalonica, some of the Jews opposed Paul and these new Christians, and they brought some of them before the city authorities and said, "These men who have turned the world upside down have come here also, and Jason has received them, and they are all acting against the decrees of Caesar, saying that there is another king, Jesus" (vv. 6, 7). And "the people and the city authorities were disturbed" when they heard about this (v. 8).

Think about this for a moment. When the whole city of Thessalonica has turned against you because you believe in King Jesus, you need to be reminded that a new reality is taking place. A day is coming when the new heavens and the new earth will be revealed, and in that day we will rejoice in our common fellowship and in our unity with one another.

Paul, as an apostle, is in a unique position to speak God's blessing to us, and ministers are in a unique position to speak God's blessing to others, in a worship service through the opening greeting and the benediction. Nevertheless, we should be more mindful of our own greetings to each other and to other people. We know the truth of the gospel. We know the promise of forgiveness. God has forgiven all of our sins; he has taken care of our greatest problem through his Son Jesus Christ. He has promised that there will come a day when he will wipe away every tear from our eyes.

As Christians, we need to live, right now, out of that future reality. We must live in such a way that we are reflecting that heavenly hope, and we can often do it in simple ways by being intentional with our greetings. When we depart from one another, let us say, "The Lord bless you" or "The Lord be with you." We can do it in letters and memos by signing off, "Grace and peace."

We should consider the way we greet each other, and our greetings and conversations should reflect something of our hope in the gospel. We should be able to greet each other with blessings, because our Lord Jesus Christ has secured the greatest blessing for us: we have grace and peace from God, who is our Father.

That is good news, and that good news should change the way we relate to this whole world. May we go into the world bearing the grace and peace of God our Father and the Lord Jesus Christ. Amen.

4

The Importance of Thankfulness

1 Thessalonians 1:2–5

Would it surprise you to learn that the pagans of the Greek and Roman world prayed? Christianity was not born into a world like ours, a world that separates one's public life from one's private religious life. Christianity was born into a world that was very religious. In our time, pagans are generally people who are not religious, but that was not the case in Paul's world. Pagans were religious people who worshipped many gods in numerous temples and shrines. They would worship and pray and offer sacrifices, and in many cases pagans were devoutly religious and ethical people. What made them pagans was the denial of the gospel. They did not know the true God and his Son Jesus Christ, but they still prayed. In fact, they prayed to all the gods that they could, and in some cases they would often include Jesus with the rest of their deities.

We can see some of this devotion in the letters from that time. The beginning of a letter often contained a prayer for the one to whom the letter was written. An example of this comes from a third-century B.C. letter: "Toubias to Apollonios, greeting. If you are well and if all our affairs and everything else is proceeding according to your will, many thanks to the gods."[1] These prayers would focus upon the prosperity of the person, and occasionally the writer would thank the person for something; but more often than not, their prayer and thanksgiving focused on good health.

It is important to contrast the prayers of these religious pagans with the prayers of Paul because in almost all of Paul's prayers, he was not concerned about the physical health of the church. But he was concerned about their spiritual health. And Paul was usually more intentional about his opening prayer. Paul's opening prayers and thanksgivings would have at least three main functions.[2] First, they served a pastoral function — to express his love for the people. Second, they served as a challenge to the readers to live up to the prayer or thanksgiving. Finally, they served to foreshadow what Paul was going to say later in his epistle. In the case of this letter of 1 Thessalonians, Paul was thankful for their faith, love, and hope. What do our prayers look like? How do they compare to those of the Apostle Paul?

Prayer times in most evangelical churches are almost completely focused on physical health needs. "Pray for the health of my mom or my dad." Indeed, I have asked for that prayer request, and Paul asked for it on occasion, and there is nothing wrong with that. But when that is the primary request, we are missing something central in prayer. We are missing the spiritual dimension regarding our faith, and Paul can guide us to a deeper level of prayer concerning this matter.

What did Paul do in his prayer? The very first thing to notice in verse 2 is that Paul gave thanks to God for them. The overriding theme of Paul's prayer was thankfulness. What does it mean to be a thankful person? In some ways it simply means to be mindful of the blessings that are around you. Paul looked at what God had done in Thessalonica, and he gave thanks. We can identify several areas of thanksgiving. Paul opened by saying he was thankful for their "work of faith and labor of love and steadfastness of hope in our Lord Jesus Christ."

THE WORK OF FAITH

Paul was thankful for their "work of faith." Faith is receiving and resting on Christ alone for salvation.[3] By faith we receive what Christ has done for us. According to Hebrews 11:1, "Faith is the substance of things hoped for, the evidence of things not seen" (KJV). I grew up wondering what that meant until I heard someone explain that the word "substance" could be translated as "reality."[4] In other words, faith is the reality of the things for which you are hoping. Faith brings the reality of forgiveness to bear on your life. Faith brings the reality of the gospel into your world. When we bring the second phrase together with the first, we understand that faith is an "evidence" of the reality of the things we do not see. Faith witnesses to the reality of the heavenly world where Jesus reigns as King.

That kind of heavenly faith works. From the moment we trust in Christ, faith produces fruit in us. So the emphasis of this word "work" in 1 Thessalonians 1:3 is on the activity of faith. Faith is not something that is dead. It is alive. The focus here is on the activity or aliveness of faith, not the intensity of faith. John Calvin interprets it this way: "A rare energy of faith has shewn itself powerfully in you."[5] Faith is a new instinct that directs our attention to Heaven — to God's grace and holiness and sovereignty and glory. We see an immediate example of this faith toward the end of chapter 1, where Paul explained, "Your faith in God has gone forth everywhere, so that we need not say anything" (v. 8). Other Christians had heard of the Thessalonian believers' "work of faith," which included how they "turned to God from idols to serve the living and true God, and to wait for his Son from heaven" (vv. 9, 10). Their faith had produced fruit.

THE LABOR OF LOVE

Paul was not only thankful for the Thessalonian believers' "work of faith," he was also thankful for their "labor of love." It is important to realize that Paul was drawing a distinction between these two phrases. Although the English terms *work* and *labor* are similar, Paul was using two different Greek words here. The word for labor is *kopos*, which stresses intense labor or hard work. Although the importance of love is clear for the Christian faith, this particular expression in the context of 1 Thessalonians is not abundantly clear. Paul could be talking about their love for one another, which is explicitly what he said in his second letter: "the love of every one of you for one another is increasing" (2 Thessalonians 1:3). To love someone is hard work, and to demonstrate that love consistently toward a community of people who know each other's faults and failures is extremely difficult.

Perhaps we can be more specific with this phrase. Gordon Fee observes that Paul's opening words often foreshadow issues that he is going to address later.[6] In this case, their "labor of love" is anticipating the problem with work that Paul describes in 1 Thessalonians 4:9–12:

> Now concerning brotherly love you have no need for anyone to write to you, for you yourselves have been taught by God to love one another, for that indeed is what you are doing to all the brothers throughout Macedonia. But we urge you, brothers, to do this more and more, and to aspire to live quietly, and to mind your own affairs, and to work with your hands, as we instructed you, so that you may walk properly before outsiders and be dependent on no one.

In this passage Paul was connecting their love for one another with living quietly, minding their own affairs, and working hard with their hands. This is the opposite of what the "idle" or "disorderly" were doing as busybodies (see 1 Thessalonians 5:14 and 2 Thessalonians 3:6–15). "Labor of love" can certainly mean that we love one another as Christians just as the Thessalonians demonstrated their love for Paul in spite of the suffering caused by his message. But in a more specific way, they demonstrated their love for one another by actually doing what they were supposed to do with their manual labor.

THE STEADFASTNESS OF HOPE

We come to Paul's last virtue that he listed in remembrance of them — their "steadfastness of hope." This could also be translated as "endurance inspired by hope."[7] This statement indicates an endurance that happens throughout the Christian life as we are under trials or as we journey through the life of faith. This patient endurance is motivated or inspired by hope, and this hope is a confident hope. For Christians, hope is not just wishful thinking; it is not some general hopefulness. For the Christian, hope is a confident expectation that the future is in God's hands, and he is working all things for our good.

In the specific case of the believers at Thessalonica, they suffered for their faith, but they kept serving God and proclaiming the gospel while keeping their hope squarely focused upon Christ, because they believed that what Christ started at his resurrection he would finish at his return. This patient hope is articulated in chapters 4 and 5 when Paul turns his attention to the coming of the Lord Jesus Christ. Evidently some of the Christians in Thessalonica had lost some of their confident hope in the future. They were confused about what happens to those who die "in Christ." So Paul said,

> But we do not want you to be uninformed, brothers, about those who are asleep, that you may not grieve as others do who have no hope. For since we believe that Jesus died and rose again, even so, through Jesus, God will bring with him those who have fallen asleep. (1 Thessalonians 4:13, 14)

Paul was providing them with the confident ground of their hope: when Jesus returns, both the dead in Christ and those alive in Christ will receive their resurrected bodies. Our confident hope as Christians is on the sure promise that God will one day make all things new through Christ. This is precisely why faith looks to the things we cannot see. Faith binds itself to hope, and Paul is saying that our hope is in the future, the glory that is yet to come, the glory that will outlast the suffering. It is like this: in our present life we are called forward in hope, and that future, the hope we have, comes back into the present and encourages us to be patient as we run this race.

Paul was thankful for these spiritual virtues, and when he prayed for the Thessalonian believers, he remembered their work of faith, labor of love, and patience of hope. But there is another element of this prayer that we cannot ignore. We see this in verse 4: "For we know, brothers loved by God, that he has chosen you." This verse is connected to what we have seen in verse 3. The main verb is "we give thanks" (v. 2). Three points are connected to this main verb, each of which is a participle. It often doesn't show up in our

English translations, but if it did, it would be translated like this: "constantly mentioning" (v. 2), "remembering" (v. 3), and "knowing" (v. 4).[8] By doing this, Paul specifically ties verse 4 into his thanksgiving section.

PAUL'S ULTIMATE REASON FOR GIVING THANKS

Paul ties verse 4 into his prayer of thanksgiving because he wants us to understand the grace involved in our Christian life and the ultimate reason why we have faith, love, and hope: "God has chosen you." Paul provides the ultimate ground of all our thankfulness: God chose us to be his people, and God granted the Thessalonian believers the faith, love, and hope that we are witnessing in this letter, just as he grants us the faith, love, and hope that we see demonstrated in our own churches. Paul was thankful that he knew their "election of [by] God" (KJV). The word translated "election" is not a verb but a noun; however, it implies the action of God's choice, which is why the ESV translates it as "chosen" by God. We should understand this in the way that Paul uses it in 2:12: "We exhorted each one of you and encouraged you and charged you to walk in a manner worthy of God, who calls you into his own kingdom and glory." God called them into his own kingdom because he chose them.

The concept of election is often controversial. One theological tradition known as Arminianism argues that election is based on God's foreknowledge of events in the future. In other words, God elected those whom he knew would choose him. The other theological tradition known as Calvinism argues that election is of God's free choice, without regard for our future choices. We follow Jesus because he first chose us.[9] All of us fall somewhere in one of these two categories, or at least in some version of these two traditions. The doctrine of election has been debated for centuries and provided one of the best-known conflicts in the early church between St. Augustine and Pelagius. So we should not expect to solve this debate easily. But it is a reality that is mentioned right here in our passage, and as we preach through books of the Bible, we cannot avoid these hard passages.

We should observe how Paul uses this concept here. It seems that Paul has two goals in using this doctrine of election in his prayer of thanksgiving. First, Paul is saying that God's choice of these Thessalonians was the reason why they had faith, love, and hope. If we believe in the importance and reality of grace, we would not want it any other way! We would never want to say that God's choice of these Thessalonians was based on their own faith, love, and hope. If we do that, we turn these virtues into works that gain God's favor, and we certainly do not want to do that. So Paul was thankful that God chose these Christians and that God's choosing them produced the fruit of faith, love, and hope.

Paul is doing something else with this doctrine, and by understanding election in this way we can see how relevant it was for the Christians in Thessalonica. By calling these Christians elect, Paul was using language from the Old Testament, language usually used exclusively for Israel. The Old Testament background for election is crucial. Israel was God's elect, God's chosen people. But Paul was now applying that truth to this Gentile church in Thessalonica. They were now God's elect, God's chosen people. God's plan for the kingdom would now go forward through them. What was true of Israel is now true of the Church, those who believe in Messiah Jesus.[10]

We can see confirmation of this from the fact that Paul called them "beloved by God" (NASB). Paul was tying this church in Thessalonica to a central theme that runs through Scripture regarding God's love for his people. Israel was considered God's "beloved," the nation loved by God. When Jesus arrived on the scene in the Gospels, he was baptized by John the Baptist, and when he came out of the waters, God said, "You are my beloved Son; with you I am well pleased" (Mark 1:11). Jesus embodied this reality for us, and according to Paul in Ephesians 1:4, God chose us in Christ "before the foundation of the world, that we should be holy and blameless before him." The result of this will be "to the praise of the glory of His grace, which He freely bestowed on us in the Beloved" (v. 6, NASB). Our election is bound up and connected to Jesus Christ, and when we trust in him, we are adopted into God's family as beloved sons and daughters.

Paul is also pressing us to consider something else as we are thankful for God's election. It would also do us good to reflect on why God chose Israel, and hence understand why he chooses us. Did God choose Israel because they were so great? Was there anything in them that caused God to call Israel his elect, chosen people? According to Moses in Deuteronomy 7:6–8, God's choice of Israel was by grace alone:

> For you are a people holy to the LORD your God. The LORD your God has chosen you to be a people for his treasured possession, out of all the peoples who are on the face of the earth. It was not because you were more in number than any other people that the LORD set his love on you and chose you, for you were the fewest of all peoples, but it is because the LORD loves you and is keeping the oath that he swore to your fathers, that the LORD has brought you out with a mighty hand and redeemed you from the house of slavery, from the hand of Pharaoh king of Egypt.

Do not miss the glorious truth of this passage. God set his love upon them not because they were greater than other people but simply because the Lord loved them and had made a promise to Abraham, Isaac, and Jacob. God loved them because he chose to love them. This is the root of John's statement, "We love [God] because he first loved us" (1 John 4:19). And that is the basis of our election, as Paul says in 1 Thessalonians 1:4: we are chosen by God because we are loved by him. Paul was thankful that God placed his love upon this church by choosing them. These people in Thessalonica were not the greatest in number. They were not the great people of the city. Some were scorned for their faith, and some were dragged off to prison. But God chose them for his purpose.

Sometimes when we talk about election, we are tempted to leave it there in the eternal plan of God. But I want to caution you against that because when Paul talks about God's eternal work, he brings it to bear in history. Paul explains to these Christians that he knows they are elect, not because he can see into the eternal mind and plan of God, but because the gospel came to them in power and they believed. We see this in the connection between verses 4 and 5. Notice how this flows. Paul says in verse 4, "we know . . . that [God] has chosen you," but why? Verse 5 finishes the thought: "because our gospel came to you not only in word, but also in power and in the Holy Spirit and with full conviction." Paul knows that God chose them because the gospel came in power, in the Holy Spirit, and with full conviction.

Paul is using the doctrine of election to bring them assurance! How odd that is, at least to our way of thinking. The doctrine that often causes disputes in the Christian church is used by the Apostle Paul as a source of comfort. But remember, it is not comfort because we know the eternal plans and decrees of God. It is comfort because we see that plan unfolding before us in history. The Holy Spirit has brought the gospel to us, and we are following Jesus as disciples.

This is the main reason we should offer to God our sacrifice of thanksgiving. Yes, he has granted us faith that works, love that labors, and hope that is steadfast, but all this is true because he chose us to be his people. As you pray, remember the areas of first importance — spiritual growth and maturity and God's work in your life.

In our prayers and in our lives, let's be thankful to God for his grace in electing us, calling us, and working through us for the good of the gospel.

5

The Christian Doctrine of Imitation

1 THESSALONIANS 1:6–8

As Christians, we have to be mindful of the messages of our culture that compete with the gospel. We live in a culture that is overwhelmed with constant communication and media — e-mails, phones, text messages, social networking, blogs, movies, television, and any number of ways we communicate and entertain ourselves in life. One of the dominant messages coming from all these mediums is directly contrary to the gospel and the call of Jesus to take up our crosses and follow him. Our culture preaches to us a message of fulfillment and happiness. If you just imitate the people on TV, or if you imitate the athletic path, you can find fulfillment with money and fame, we are told. This message bombards us constantly and attempts to draw us into the world, holding out the hope of fulfillment and happiness in the same way that television stars and movie stars and athletic stars find their supposed happiness. Pursue your own happiness and fulfillment at all costs. If you do, you will be content.

We are often tempted to follow this path. We buy into the message and the promise of happiness in the American dream. We do not even pause to consider what we are doing as we follow these movie stars and athletes. We just imitate them. We try to dress like them and live like them and play like them. All of this is evidence of a strong sense of imitation in our culture. One example of this was the popularity of the basketball star Michael Jordan. He is considered not only one of the greatest basketball players of all time but also one of the greatest athletes. He would fly through the air, making incredible shots and dunks. One of the commercials about him had a catchy little song that used the phrase, "I wanna be like Mike." I can remember that song ringing in my ears as a teenager playing basketball, and the message was, if you want to be like Mike, buy a certain brand of tennis shoes. So my high school basketball team bought the Michael Jordan tennis shoes because we all wanted to "be like Mike."

Do not underestimate the power of imitation in our culture. We are living and breathing that air, and we need to realize that temptation. We are tempted to follow the path of famous people, and we are tempted to believe that if we just had enough money or if we just had the right home or the right car or the right job or the right spouse, we would be happy; everything would be OK.

But that is a lie. People who have great wealth admit it is never enough. In December 2007 Tom Brady was featured on a CBS *60 Minutes* interview. At the time, Brady was the quarterback of the New England Patriots, a three-time Super Bowl champion, and he had a contract worth millions of dollars a year. By our cultural standards, he had everything. But in the interview he said,

> Why do I have three Super Bowl rings and still think there's something greater out there for me? I mean, maybe a lot of people would say, "Hey man, this is what is." I reached my goal, my dream, my life. Me, I think, "God, it's got to be more than this." I mean this isn't, this can't be what it's all cracked up to be.[1]

Brady has reached his dream, a dream many of us share, whether we are talking about fame or fortune. But he says, "God, it's got to be more than this." The idea that if men imitate the athletes or women imitate the models they will be happy and fulfilled is a lie that is being fed to us, and we know it. In our most honest moments, we would confess what Tom Brady confessed. As Christians we should be much more cautious about the message of our culture because it is at odds with the gospel. Only as we follow the message of the gospel and hope in Christ will we be content in our circumstances.

We must not be tempted by the message of our culture and buy into its path of happiness, but we must also beware of another temptation, a temptation from the Christian world. This temptation is similar because it, too, uses the idea of imitation. Christians get caught up in their own message of imitation that is not very Biblical. What is that message? "Imitate me. I am spiritual, and if you do this you will be spiritual too." A Christian couple has a good marriage, so they decide to write a book about their experience. The book calls for you to copy and imitate their life because it is supposedly successful. If you imitate or follow their principles, you will have a successful marriage, it is claimed.

Or perhaps it is a successful ministry at a particular church. The leaders of that church write a book on their success or they have a seminar about how to grow a church. Hundreds of thousands of ministers read the books or attend the seminars, all trying to imitate that successful church. Then they bring those principles right back to their local churches. We seldom pause to consider that the principles might not apply to our particular locations.

You are probably more aware of this type of imitation. It is very seductive for Christians. The punch line might be, "Seven principles for making a marriage work." When did we start thinking there are only seven principles that make a marriage work? Or "Six tips for successful child raising." I don't know about you, but that hasn't worked for me. Or the claim might be, "Ten steps to financial success" or "Fifteen ways to grow your church." In following this course, I am afraid that the church has fallen into the trap of the world. "You will find happiness if you just follow these ten helpful steps." "You will have a great marriage because you will be like this model couple." "Your church will grow and be like . . . "

This concept of imitation has a significant history. *Aesop's Fables*, written as moral education for children, used it. The Greeks had a view of history that involved it too. Plato and Aristotle had theories involving imitation (mimesis). Plato wrote a treatise that encouraged people to follow him along the path of happiness. He had found it, and he was going to pass it along to others. This definition of imitation has a long tradition in Western civilization.

The Biblical notion of imitation is rooted in passages like 1 Thessalonians 1:6 where Paul call us to imitate him: "And you became imitators of us and of the Lord."[2] This little phrase "became imitators" is used by Paul about six or seven times in different epistles. He uses it later in 1 Thessalonians 2:14 when he says, "For you, brothers, became imitators of the churches of God in Christ Jesus that are in Judea." What exactly is Paul getting across with this language or doctrine of imitation?

Beginning in verse 2, Paul mentions the Thessalonian believers in his prayer. He is thankful for these Christians and their virtues — their work of faith, labor of love, and perseverance of hope. Paul is thankful that their faith directs all their actions, their love undertakes painfully difficult tasks, and their hope in the Lord's coming causes them to persevere despite the trials they experience. That moves us into verses 4, 5. Paul continued to express thanks because the Thessalonians were chosen by God, and he knew that God had chosen them for two reasons: the gospel came with the power of the Holy Spirit and with full conviction (v. 5), and they became imitators of Paul and his fellow workers and of the Lord (v. 6).

When he preached the gospel, it came to them with the power of the Holy Spirit. In other words, they believed. In spite of the opposition, they trusted the gospel. They did not turn away from the gospel, but they embraced it. Now that makes sense to us, right? The first work of the Holy

Spirit is to cause us to believe the message. We have at some point been convicted by the Holy Spirit, believed in the gospel, and made a profession of faith. That is how the gospel came to us with the power of the Holy Spirit. That phrase stresses the supernatural work of the Holy Spirit in the life of the Thessalonians because they believed and became Christians.

Paul, however, describes something else in verse 6: "you became imitators." This doctrine of imitation sometimes trips us up in the Christian life. Many have experienced the Holy Spirit's convicting them, but they do not realize that they must press on and grow in holiness. One way we grow in holiness is by seeing the example of an older and more mature Christian and following that example. So Paul says, "You became imitators of us [Paul, Silas, and Timothy] and of the Lord." The evidence of our election, according to Paul, is that we believe on Christ and we imitate other Christians.

As a good pastor, Paul not only spoke the word of God to them, but he gave them his life. He was like a father with his children, encouraging and exhorting them to walk in a manner that is worthy of God (1 Thessalonians 2:11, 12). When they heard the word of God, they accepted it as true (v. 13) and in the process became imitators of other churches in Judea that had suffered in a similar way (v. 14). So here is the pattern: they received the word, they believed it, they followed Jesus, and they suffered like Jesus and other Christians.

Another example is found in 2 Thessalonians 3:6–9. After commanding them to stay away from those who walk in a disorderly way, Paul explained that these Christians should imitate him and the other missionaries: "We were not idle when we were with you, nor did we eat anyone's bread without paying for it, but with toil and labor we worked night and day, that we might not be a burden to any of you. It was not because we do not have that right, but to give you in ourselves an example to imitate." Paul warned them against imitating the wrong people and encouraged them to imitate him. They knew the pattern of Paul's behavior, and they could look at specific examples of what Paul had done while he lived among them.

So on one level this doctrine of imitation is a pattern of faith and obedience that can be seen in other Christians. But we have to be careful here. Paul is not holding himself out as a super-Christian who has it all together and could give them seven steps to becoming the mature Christians they needed to be. Paul is not giving them principles here. His understanding of the Christian faith is more nuanced and profound than to give Christians seven steps on the road to maturity. His letters deal with weighty theological and ethical concerns, and when he appeals to this doctrine of imitation, we should see it in the context of his whole theology. When he talks about imitating Jesus, we cannot just go through the Gospels and pick out five things Jesus did. Paul is talking about the totality of our lives. Paul is describing who he is because of Christ and how his identity is bound up with Christ Jesus.

This doctrine of imitation, therefore, is connected to what we often call Paul's doctrine of union with Christ. Do you remember how Paul described the church at the beginning of this letter? "The church . . . *in* God the Father and the Lord Jesus Christ." That is our identity as Christians. We are in Jesus. Christian baptism is described as being baptized *into* the body of Christ. Our baptism connects us to Christ in a way that cannot be easily explained. We have God's Trinitarian name stamped upon us. This is so much the case that Paul said in verse 3 that the Thessalonian believers' actions ("work of faith and labor of love and steadfastness of hope") were evident in the sight of our God and Father. All of our works as Christians are done in the presence of God, not just because God is everywhere but because we are in the Father and in the Son. We are connected by faith to Jesus and so are described as being in Christ and living in the sight of God the Father.

Now look at what he says in verse 5. After he says that the gospel comes in word and power and much conviction, notice the last phrase: "You know what kind of men we proved to be among you for your sake." How do we know what kind of man Paul was among them? What did Paul prove to them? This is the passage that clues us in on how to imitate Paul and demonstrates for us what kind of man Paul was among them. Did Paul give them principles for a successful Christian life? Did he provide six goals for happiness? Is that what he says here? Was that what they were called to imitate?

In order to understand Paul's point, let's look back to Acts 17. We will find our answer there, and then we will confirm it in 1 Thessalonians 1:6, 7. Acts 17 is the record of Paul's first visit to this church. In light of Acts 17, what kind of man did Paul prove to be among these people? When he arrived in Thessalonica, he went to the synagogue and preached to them about Jesus. According to Luke, Paul explained and proved that it was necessary for the Christ to suffer and to rise from the dead, and he concluded by saying, "This Jesus, whom I proclaim to you, is the Christ" (v. 3). The message Paul came with was the message of the gospel. Luke says in verse 3 that Paul explained the sufferings of the Messiah. Paul taught the message of the gospel. That is the word they believed.

Notice Acts 17:5. Some of the Jews were not persuaded. They rallied a mob and attacked the Christians. When they could not find Paul and Silas, they brought Jason and some of the believers before the city authorities saying, "These men who have turned the world upside down have come here also, and Jason has received them, and they are all acting against the decrees of Caesar, saying that there is another king, Jesus" (vv. 6, 7). These Christians were disrupting their culture because they were bringing a different message. What was the message of that culture? *Look to Caesar. He will give you peace and prosperity, and he will bring you happiness. He will protect you and guard you. If you follow him and trust him and imitate other Roman citizens, everything will go well.*

Paul brought a different message. Paul came with a proclamation about imitating and following Jesus. Let's make this more personal. There was a man there named Jason. He believed in the gospel, and he hosted Paul at his house. What reward did Jason get for confessing Jesus and hosting a missionary? The message Paul brought to Jason didn't bring him fame and fortune with his community, and it did not bring him peace and happiness and security in this world. The message brought suffering and persecution. Jason was indeed imitating Paul, but he was imitating Paul in terms of suffering. What had been happening to Paul in Philippi followed him to Thessalonica, and then that suffering touched the new Christian Jason and he was brought before the city leaders.

We can push this even further. Jesus preached a message that disrupted his culture, and he suffered for it. Paul preached a message that disrupted the Roman culture, and he suffered for it, thus following Jesus. Jason accepted this message and was suffering for it, thus imitating Paul who was imitating Jesus. And what precisely is this message? Notice the end of verse 7: "there is another king, Jesus." This disturbed the rulers and the people and disrupted the city. This message was not popular. If you go with the message of the gospel into this world, it will not always be a popular message, and it will not be easy. Notice how the story ends in verse 10: they went away by night to Berea. Where is the happiness in being sent away in the dark of night?

I would submit to you that this is a crucial part of Paul's doctrine of imitation. Paul imitated Jesus by bringing the gospel to this city and by suffering for these people. Paul lived out his identity with Christ; Paul bore his own cross. When Christ was on this earth, he was rejected and put on the cross. Paul was rejected, too, and was called a fool. He had to leave town in the middle of the night so he would not be discovered and killed. Let me ask you: do you know of five principles to keep you from getting killed after preaching the gospel? I don't.

So what kind of man was Paul? Remember, that was our question. Paul said, "You know what kind of men we proved to be among you" (1 Thessalonians 1:5). What kind of man was Paul?

He was a man of the gospel. Paul saw the gospel as the center of his life. He was a man who focused on a kingdom other than the Roman Empire. He was a man who followed another king, not Caesar. He was a man who was not of this world. He preached a message of hope that didn't depend upon Caesar or the approval of various people in that community. Paul's hope was his approval by Christ. Paul lived in such a way that he reflected the reality of another world. Can you see this in Acts 17? Paul could not go into Thessalonica and be mistreated and live through that with joy unless he believed that the city would not last, unless he believed in a more abiding city. He glorified God by witnessing to the reality of the kingdom of God in the face of tribulations and trials.

Paul lived in such a way that he reflected the reality of another world. That is what kind of man Paul proved to be among them. Paul glorified God by witnessing to the reality of the kingdom of God in the face of the power of the Roman Empire. That is what Paul did in their presence. And guess what happened?

They became imitators of Paul. Consider chapter 1 of 1 Thessalonians in light of the background from Acts 17. Paul said, "And you became imitators of us and of the Lord, for you received the word in much affliction, with the joy of the Holy Spirit, so that you became an example to all the believers in Macedonia and in Achaia" (1 Thessalonians 1:6, 7). Do you see it? What happened according to verse 6? They became imitators of Paul and of the Lord by "receiv[ing] the word in much affliction, with the joy of the Holy Spirit."

We just saw this in Acts 17. Some of the Christians were brought before the city authorities and were persecuted. Yes, they imitated Paul as Paul imitated Jesus. But this imitation was an imitation of picking up their crosses and following Paul as Paul followed Jesus. This is what Paul is talking about. He is not talking about principles. He is talking about a way of life. As mentioned previously, baptism is an example of this new identity, this new life, and it is also an example of this call to suffering. When you see a baptism, you are witnessing the death of someone to the old world in order that they might be resurrected to a new life and follow Jesus. In baptism you die to your wants and desires and wishes, and your life is hidden with Christ in God.

That is what it means to be a Christian. You die to yourself and this old way of life in order to live in such a way that your hope transcends the struggles of this world. Your hope looks beyond the trials and tribulations of this world toward the promises of another world. Notice what Paul says in verse 6. I will confess that this verse is difficult, and in our cultural environment we might find it odd. Normal Americans do not talk this way: "you received the word in much affliction, with the joy of the Holy Spirit." Who would put affliction and joy side by side? That kind of language makes no sense if your hope is based on the promises of this world. The Thessalonian believers did not have much joy in relation to their circumstances in the Roman Empire.

Paul is talking about true joy, not the kind that is offered through television programs and movies or by politicians and athletes and models. Paul is offering joy unspeakable, a joy found in the gospel, in the work of the Holy Spirit. This joy comes from peace with God because our sins are forgiven. This is a joy that knows God will make all things right one day. This is a joy that knows God's kingdom will never end. This is a joy that could not be taken away from Paul or his companions when they were thrown in jail. This is a joy that cannot be taken away from us because we lost our jobs. This is a joy that is not dependent upon the ups and downs of an economy.

This is a joy that will see us through trials and tribulations, and even through death. There is no message in this world for the sting of death, and that is where the rubber meets the road for Christians. That is where our faith will be tested because the message of the gospel is a message that will bring hope in the face of death, and these Christians in Thessalonica could face death for the gospel.

This is why Paul says, "Imitate me as I imitate Jesus, even if that means picking up your cross and dying, because in doing so you are following your Savior, Jesus Christ." The Lord is working out his life in us, and the Lord's life is being reflected in our lives as we testify to the reality of a different world that is far beyond the joys and hopes and promises of this world. This is a heavenly joy and a heavenly hope, a hope that one day God will wipe away every tear from our eyes and make all things new. That is what Paul called them (and us) to imitate, and that is only possible because we have the good news of the gospel, the good news of a kingdom that will never end.

6

All of Life Is Repentance

1 THESSALONIANS 1:9–10

Mount Olympus is the highest mountain in Greece, and it was considered the home of the twelve Olympians who were the principal gods of the Greek world — Zeus, Hera, Athena, and Apollo to mention a few. That mountain was one of the most important religious sites, if not the most important religious site, in the Greek world, and it was just fifty miles outside of Thessalonica.

That kind of idolatry was prominent in Thessalonica. The city had a very religious atmosphere with temples and shrines everywhere, with temples to Greek gods, Egyptian gods, and a host of other foreign gods. You could worship any type of god you chose in that city, and the young Christians there had to face the temptation of idolatry at every turn. Some of them came out of that world into Christianity. They had to turn their backs on their community, their lives, their idols, and Paul was encouraged by their allegiance to Christ in the face of this temptation. He says toward the end of chapter 1 that others noticed "how you turned to God from idols to serve the living and true God" (v. 9).

Sometimes we are tempted to feel far removed from our brothers and sisters at Thessalonica. They had to face the worship of idols, and sometimes even the worship of Caesar. They had to repent of that sin and follow Jesus, but we don't face those struggles, do we? We don't have to face the temptation to bow down to idols . . . or do we?

We shouldn't be quick to think of idols only in terms of inanimate objects. Idolatry is far-reaching and comes to us in many ways. What Calvin observed long ago is no less true today: the human heart, our image-bearing and image-fashioning nature, is an idol factory. We have made idols of money and jobs. We have made idols of sex and power. We have made idols of sports and recreation. Tim Keller says:

> Sin isn't only doing bad things, it is more fundamentally making good things into ultimate things. Sin is building your life and meaning on anything, even a very good thing, more than on God. Whatever we build our life on will drive us and enslave us. Sin is primarily idolatry.[1]

All of these can take the place of Christ. We face idolatry just as much as our brothers and sisters in Thessalonica did. Not only do we, too, face idols, but we must respond to them in the same way — we must repent.

Repentance is a central aspect of the Christian faith, but Christians are often confused about repentance. How is repentance connected to the gospel and to the work of Christ? What does repentance have to do with the Christian life? Is it a one-time response? Or must we continue to repent for the rest of our Christian life?

The issue of repentance is crucial for Christians, whether in the first century or the twenty-first century. Repentance is at the heart of what it means to be Christians. It is one of the most basic aspects of the Christian life, so basic that a young child can repent. Because it is so basic, we often take it for granted and easily forget the importance of repentance for the Christian life. But repentance must not be taken for granted.

Before we leave the first chapter of 1 Thessalonians, we need to linger for a moment on Paul's final two verses of that chapter: "For they themselves report concerning us the kind of reception we had among you, and how you turned to God from idols to serve the living and true God, and to wait for his Son from heaven, whom he raised from the dead, Jesus who delivers us from the wrath to come." I want us to examine the importance of *turning to God from idols to serve the living and true God.* That means we are going to look at repentance and idolatry.

Why pause over this issue? Because this is something we all need to hear as Christians. Do you think this message is not for you because you fully understand repentance since you are a Christian? I hope that is not your response. One of the central goals of discipleship is not to give us new information all the time but to remind us of the aspects of the faith that we must continue to do and that we must not grow weary of doing well. Repentance is one of those areas in which we must continue to mature. We need to be reminded of the basic aspects of the faith.

Another reason to examine repentance concerns the confusion over this doctrine. When I first learned about repentance, I was told that it was a turning from sin to Christ. Although that is true, that doesn't quite get to the depth of repentance. Sometimes this description gives us the impression that repentance only happens once, at the moment of faith in Christ. Repentance is described as that initial moment of turning from sin or idols to Christ. This is true, but along the way in my Christian life I discovered a profound and important truth about repentance. Let me tell you how I came to understand this crucial doctrine.

Growing up, I was told that repentance was something you only had to do one time. If you *really* repented, then you would not commit that particular sin anymore. Needless to say, I struggled and struggled with this issue. It created several crisis moments for my faith. Here was the cycle: I would get angry, realize that I had sinned again, and repent. But then I would get angry again, and I would repent. I would get angry again, and I would repent. The cycle would keep repeating, and that would cause me to question whether or not I was really a Christian.

That cycle produced a great deal of doubt. I was told that if I really repented of my anger, then I would stop getting sinfully angry. Repentance means to turn away, so when I repented I thought I had turned away from my anger. But then I would get angry again. I concluded that I must not really be repenting. That would make me think that I wasn't saved. *I cannot be saved if I act like this.* Did you notice all the qualifications: if I *really* did this . . . if I *really* meant that . . . then I would *really* be saved. Perhaps you can identify with this struggle. Perhaps you have been down that road, and maybe you are still on that roller coaster. You sin and think that you cannot really be a Christian because if you really had repented, you would not keep sinning like this.

That is a misunderstanding of both sin and repentance. First, it is a very weak view of sin. I think of St. Anselm's famous line when he was dealing with the need of Christ's death, his substitutionary death for us. In his work *Cur Deus Homo (Why God Became Man)*, he sets about the task of demonstrating "How Great a Burden Sin Is," and in a dialogue with a character named Boso, Anselm remarks, "You have not yet considered what a heavy weight sin is."[2] This is profoundly true. Our sin is beyond our knowledge. So great is our sin that it sent God's Son to the cross. Ponder that for a moment. Our sin is so deep and so pervasive that the Son of God had to die in our place. We have not considered the depth of our sin; we have not considered that there are sins we will never confess because we never realized we sinned against someone in that particular way. We actually think that we can stop sinning, but the truth is that we cannot fully stop. The rest of our lives will be a struggle with sin. It will not go away until we get to Heaven. So we have a poor understanding of sin and the depth of idolatry in our hearts.

We cannot, however, stop there because we also have a misunderstanding of repentance. Sometimes we are tempted to think that repentance is a one-time event, that it is a silver bullet and if we just get it right, our struggle with sin will stop. Here is what we need to see as Christians: repentance is a continuous event. Repentance is ongoing, and we are to grow in our repentance as we grow in our faith. When Martin Luther posted his "Ninety-five Theses" on the church door at Wittenberg Cathedral, the issue of repentance was in the very first thesis: "Our Lord and Master Jesus Christ . . . willed the entire life of believers to be one of repentance."

This was a major breakthrough for Luther, and it was for me. I realized that repentance is the way we make progress in the Christian life. Tim Keller has a short article on this topic entitled, "All of Life Is Repentance." You will never get away from repentance because that is how Jesus designed the Christian life for your growth and maturity and holiness.

WHAT IS REPENTANCE?

According to Paul here, repentance involves turning away from dead idols and turning to the true and living God. This is a helpful and precise definition of repentance. Repentance is turning away from idolatry to the living and true God. One of the images you should have in your mind is that some of these Christians turned away from pagan temples and pagan sacrifices. They changed their course, turned around, and went to the location where the small church would meet. And if they slipped and went back to the temple, they would repent and come back to Jesus, acknowledging their sin.

It would be helpful to unpack the idea of repentance. The verb for repentance means "to turn." As I have already pointed out, repentance is more than a single experience. Repentance is rather complex because it encompasses the whole Christian life, but at its root, repentance is basically a change of heart and mind. It is a movement and a process in seeing things the way God sees them. One of the helpful descriptions of repentance comes from the *Westminster Shorter Catechism*. Question 87 says, "What is repentance unto life?"

> Answer: Repentance unto life is a saving grace, whereby a sinner, out of a true sense of his sin, and apprehension of the mercy of God in Christ, doth, with grief and hatred of his sin, turn from it unto God, with full purpose of, and endeavor after, new obedience.

The catechism breaks down repentance into several helpful categories.

First, we acknowledge that we are sinners. Through the grace of Christ and the work of the Holy Spirit, we have a true sense of our sin. We cannot skip this first point because some never get past it. When presented with the gospel, some will respond that they are not really that bad. *Sinner* is a strong word, and the person will not admit to being a sinner. If we cannot admit we are sinners, then we have not repented. Because of our sin, we are in deep trouble with God and, according to Paul, God's wrath is upon us. We should not forget that the root issue of repentance is an acknowledgment that a sin is indeed sin.

Second, we have a sense of grief and hatred of our sin. We have a sense of sorrow. Sin is foul and ugly. It is an offense to God. It does damage to a human soul. There should be moments in our lives when it comes crashing down on us how much our sin has hurt other people and caused damage to them, and that should create a sense of sorrow and grief. That doesn't necessarily mean we will shed tears, but we will have a deep sense of how wrong it is and how much we have hurt people and offended God.

Third, we turn from our sin unto God. There is a movement from the idol of sin toward the true and living God. You realize that the idols that you hold dear are dead. In the case of the Thessalonians, they had turned from the temples and the false gods, but those false gods represented things like wealth and happiness and fame. So a crucial part of repentance is the desire for God over everything else.

Fourth, in turning toward God we also have a new purpose of obedience to God. We desire to practice righteousness. We desire to please God. This last aspect of repentance, the desire to obey, or as the Catechism says, a "purpose of new obedience," is called the fruit of repentance in Scripture. In the third chapter of the Gospel of Luke, John the Baptist says that we must "bear fruits in keeping with repentance" (v. 8). Then he says, "Even now the axe is laid to the root of the trees. Every tree therefore that does not bear good fruit is cut down and thrown into the fire" (v. 9). John then goes on to be very specific. If you have extra food or clothing and someone is in need, be a giving person. If you are a tax collector, be an honest person. If you are a soldier (they were usually violent), be a gentle person. In each case, there is a true change. There is a turning from an idol (be it material possessions, money, or power) and a turning to God.

What is repentance? Repentance is a turning away from idols to the true and living God. The most concrete example of turning from idolatry for the Christians in Thessalonica concerned the worship of other gods. Thessalonica was on a harbor. If you were standing in that harbor, overlooking the water toward the southwest, you would see a large mountain appearing to rise out of the water. That mountain was Mount Olympus. This well-known mountain was in Greek mythology the home of the gods. So these people lived in the shadow of idolatry. To reject that world was a radical change.

Repentance is not a philosophy of life. Repentance involves an allegiance to Jesus as Lord and Christ. For the Thessalonian Christians, repentance meant a change of allegiance from Caesar to King Jesus. For new Christians, that initial moment might be very clear, but idolatry is deeper than simply going to a temple to worship a false god. Idolatry is something against which we all struggle. Idolatry is anything we put in place of God.

Idolatry happens in any area of life. Some of the idols of our life could be money, but it also could be our pride. Idolatry could be our desire for what we want. People make idols out of history and nature and economics and politics. Americans have made idols out of their country and their government. It is idolatry when we think the government will save us from catastrophes and trials. Do you think these Christians expected Caesar to come save them? Guess what — Caesar killed these Christians, and if the tide shifts in our country, there will be no hope with our government. We must be careful not to make an idol out of all these good things. Our only hope should be found in the Lord Jesus Christ.

The Lord Jesus provides meaning and direction for our lives. We are supposed to find our meaning and hope in Jesus, but sometimes we shift our hope to something else and thus create an idol. We are called to glorify and enjoy God in all things, but when we shift our focus to enjoy something other than God, it becomes an idol.

Why did Paul come preaching against these idols? A central reason is that idolatry is wrong, and it is an offense to the one true God. But Paul suggests another important reason in 1 Thessalonians 1. Paul came preaching against idols because they are dead. They do not provide true life. Notice the words of the psalmist:

> Their idols are silver and gold, the work of human hands. They have mouths, but do not speak; eyes, but do not see. They have ears, but do not hear; noses, but do not smell. They have hands, but do not feel; feet, but do not walk; and they do not make a sound in their throat. Those who make them become like them; so do all who trust in them. (Psalm 115:4–8)

In other words, whoever makes an idol or trusts in an idol is dead. The idol has no life and no hope. The psalmist goes on to say in verse 9, "O Israel, trust in the LORD! He is their help and their shield." An idol will not be your help and shield. Only the one true God can do that.

This is precisely the reason why Paul describes God in the way that he does. Did you see it in our text? He describes the Lord as "the living and true God" (1 Thessalonians 1:9). God is alive. He is real. And he has given us promises and hope for this life. But sadly, we forsake the true and living God and turn to idols for our happiness.

That phrase "the living and true God" comes from the prophets. Every time the people turned to idols, the prophets warned them, "You are turning from the living and true God, the only source of life." Paul was drawing his message from the prophets, particularly Jeremiah. That prophet was railing against the nations when his book started, and in chapter 2 he made this tremendous statement:

> Be appalled, O heavens, at this; be shocked, be utterly desolate, declares the LORD, for my people have committed two evils: they have forsaken

me, the fountain of living waters, and hewed out cisterns for themselves, broken cisterns that can hold no water. (Jeremiah 2:12, 13)

Jeremiah called them to repent of two evils: they had forsaken God, the fountain of living waters, and they had made idols for themselves, idols described as clay pots that hold no water. Do you see the contrast? The idols do not hold water. Only the one true and living God provides living water that quenches our thirst. These are the two evils that Paul is describing in 1 Thessalonians 1. These Christians provided a picture of true repentance: they turned from empty clay pots, empty temples and shrines, and they turned to the one true God, the only source of joy, who provides living water.

We must find our hope and our trust in God's promises, the forgiveness of sins, and the hope of the future. Our hope for the future is bound up in our God. In fact, the most significant hope we have is in his Son, Jesus Christ. God has given Jesus to us as a testimony of his promises and our hope for the future. Look at verse 10: we are called "to wait for his Son from heaven, whom he raised from the dead, Jesus who delivers us from the wrath to come." Paul says that as we turn from idols to serve the living and true God, we are called to wait patiently for the return of Christ. After we repent, the direction of our faith is future oriented. Only at the return of Christ will our salvation be complete and our hope be fulfilled. Only at that time will repentance stop. Only then will all the idols in our life be destroyed, and this is why we long for Christ's return. Christ and the gospel are central to the Christian life.

Now look at that last little phrase: Jesus "delivers us from the wrath to come." That word "delivers" should not be translated as a present tense verb, which does not get across the meaning intended by Paul. It is a continuous verb and thus should read, "who is delivering us from the wrath to come." Paul says that Christ is continuing to deliver us, even at this moment, from the wrath to come. Why does Paul say it like that?

The way the gospel is often preached, once we have had some experience of turning to God or repentance, we are safe, we are saved, we are in. I have heard well-meaning Christians say, "If you prayed the prayer, you know that you are a Christian." That kind of mind-set is on shaky ground because it views salvation only through a past experience as opposed to grounding salvation on the work of Jesus. It is simply not true that once you say a prayer or have a certain kind of experience you are in. It is not true that once the Thessalonians turned from idols they were automatically safe and secure.

Do you know why this is shaky ground? Because the very next week they would go back to their jobs and their daily lives and would face the temptation of the temple and the shrines, the idols and the offerings. This is no different from our experiences. We face temptations again on Monday morning after we experience a message from the Lord on Sunday. We must be prepared for the ongoing battle of the Christian life. But we are often tempted to say, "Life is hard. I have too much going on to worry about my commitments to the church and worship. I cannot devote my attention to God's Word." But if we go down that road, if we do not continue to persevere in the faith, we are headed toward death.

These Thessalonians had to keep turning to Christ for the rest of their lives, and so do we. They had to be continually delivered by Jesus through repentance and faith. Here we are taught that the salvation that comes from Jesus is a moment-by-moment salvation. Jesus is delivering us each moment of our Christian life. He is delivering us right now from the wrath that is to come.

Please don't misunderstand what I am saying. Our salvation is not based on our own works, but this great salvation does produce good works because Jesus Christ leads his people into righteousness and eternal life. He works repentance into us. We need not fear this work of repentance, and we need not dread it. Yes, it can be bitter for a while. Confessing our sins to God and confessing our sins to a brother or sister is difficult. It is often painful to repent and actually change.

But of all people, Christians should not fear repentance because Jesus has forgiven all our sins and provided us with his righteousness. Our final salvation does not rest on how good we are or how much we have changed. It rests upon the Lord Jesus Christ. Jesus provides forgiveness and righteousness, and Jesus is continually at work to deliver us from the wrath to come. He never stops this work, and that is why the message of the gospel is such good news, and that is why we are called to repent. We must stop trying to find our hope and joy in all the things of this world apart from Christ. Rather, let us repent of those idols and turn to Jesus, and Jesus will continually deliver us from the wrath to come.

7

Union with Christ and the Christian Life

1 THESSALONIANS 2:1–12

At the Desiring God 2008 National Conference,[1] Sinclair Ferguson participated in a panel discussion with other speakers, and Justin Taylor asked Ferguson, "Can you say something about the importance of the doctrine of union with Christ? Any resources you recommend on this subject?" A portion of Ferguson's response was very helpful to me in regard to this passage. He said:

> [You begin to] understand that from the moment you become a Christian you are someone who has died to sin and been raised to a newness of life. You are somebody over whose life the dominion of the power of sin has been broken. You begin to learn to interpret your life in terms of what God says about you because you are united to Christ instead of interpreting the gospel in terms of where you are in your struggle.

Ferguson is talking about our union with Christ, and this doctrine is an important but neglected reality of the Christian life. It is so crucial that Paul begins this letter highlighting this: "Paul, Silvanus, and Timothy, to the church of the Thessalonians in God the Father and the Lord Jesus Christ: Grace to you and peace" (1 Thessalonians 1:1). The church is in union with God the Father and the Lord Jesus Christ. As Ferguson says, we must learn to interpret our life in terms of what God says about us because we are united to Christ. Paul is encouraging the Thessalonian church to look at their situation in light of this reality and not in light of their suffering and trials.

This doctrine of union with Christ is pervasive in Paul's writings. He sees union with Christ as a core doctrine of the Christian faith and as a crucial aspect of what it means to grow as a Christian. As John Murray explains, "Union with Christ is . . . the central truth of the whole doctrine of salvation. . . . It is not simply a phase of the application of redemption; it underlies every aspect of redemption."[2] Paul makes some astounding claims regarding the Christian's union with Christ:

> So you also must consider yourselves dead to sin and alive to God in Christ Jesus. Let not sin therefore reign in your mortal body, to make you obey its passions. (Romans 6:11, 12)

> Therefore, if anyone is in Christ, he is a new creation. The old has passed away; behold, the new has come. (2 Corinthians 5:17)

> I have been crucified with Christ. It is no longer I who live, but Christ who lives in me. And the life I now live in the flesh I live by faith in the Son of God, who loved me and gave himself for me. (Galatians 2:20)

> . . . in Christ Jesus you are all sons of God, through faith. (Galatians 3:26)

> Blessed be the God and Father of our Lord Jesus Christ, who has blessed us in Christ with every spiritual blessing in the heavenly places. (Ephesians 1:3)

> In him we have redemption through his blood, the forgiveness of our trespasses, according to the riches of his grace. (Ephesians 1:7)

> In him we have obtained an inheritance. (Ephesians 1:11)

This is only a sampling of Paul's emphasis on our union with Christ. Paul uses the expression "in Christ" (*en Christo*), together with its cognate expressions such as "in the Lord" (*en Kyrio*) or "in him" (*en auto*), over 160 times in his epistles.[3] This is such a central part of Paul's theology that Ferguson concludes his interview by saying, "The whole of the Christian life is stamped with participation in Christ."

We are going to take Paul's example in 1 Thessalonians 2 and examine it in light of this doctrine of union with Christ by asking this question: how does Paul live out this truth? To put it the way Sinclair Ferguson did, how does Paul interpret his life in terms of what God says about him because he is united to Christ, instead of interpreting Christ and the gospel in light of his particular struggle at that moment? That is what we want to probe and consider.

These truths about union with Christ cannot be comprehended in one study or at one time. I want to encourage us all to think on these things. As Christians, we need to continue to ponder this throughout our Christian lives, continuing to ask questions about our lives and how we are connected to Jesus. How is your life or my life reflecting Jesus? How are we viewing our lives? Do we see our lives in union with Christ? Or do we see our lives through our struggles with work and marriage and children and relationships? This is an important avenue of growth, and there are some good resources for further study.[4] One that I would immediately suggest is by Sinclair Ferguson titled *In Christ Alone: Living the Gospel Centered Life*.[5] Let us not back away from rich and deep truths as Christians, but let us embrace them and seek to wrestle with them for the rest of our lives. We will see much spiritual growth if we do that.

But for now let us examine how Paul deals with his life in relation to this church in Thessalonica. In 1 Thessalonians 2 Paul is defending his ministry in the face of attacks. There are several ways to approach a passage like this. The most common way is to examine it in terms of the ministry, and Paul does provide a lot of insight concerning the ministry. We find here a good example of pastoral ministry.

- Pastors should not lose hope in ministry because it is not in vain (v. 1).
- Pastors should be bold to preach even in the face of suffering (v. 2).
- Pastors should have a pure motive in ministry, not attempting to deceive (v. 3).
- Pastors should not seek to please men but the Lord, who knows their hearts (v. 4).
- Pastors should be gentle, like a mother taking care of her children (v. 7).
- Pastors should work hard in service of others (v. 10).
- Pastors should exhort, like a father with his children (vv. 11, 12).

But we cannot stop with that reading of the passage. It does not go far enough because it doesn't get us to Jesus. It doesn't actually connect Paul's ministry to the gospel. And we have seen from all these other passages that Paul lives his life in such a way that he is always conscious of Jesus and reflecting Jesus. When Paul says in Colossians 3:3 that we have died and our life is hidden with Christ in God, Paul is explaining one of his most fundamental perspectives on the Christian life, and he is trying to draw us into that life.

Let's consider this passage in Thessalonians in light of Paul's union with Christ and how that shapes what he writes and how he ministers and how he lives. When Paul comes to write 1 Thessalonians 2, he doesn't leave behind his theology. In other words, when he speaks these words about his ministry, he is not leaving behind his identity in connection to Jesus, his union with Christ. His participation in the life of Christ is undergirding his ministerial outlook. Paul is consistently conscious of living in Christ, and we would be wise to consider how his union with Christ is shaping his ministry. When Paul comes to write this passage under the inspiration of the Holy Spirit, his choice of words and his choice of what he writes is being governed by his union with Christ.

In chapter 2 Paul tells the story of his ministry in Thessalonica. At this point he has been gone for several weeks, perhaps a few months. Remember that he had to be rushed out quickly, in the middle of the night, because of persecution. As Paul looked back on his time with these Christians, and as he started writing to this church under the inspiration of the Holy Spirit, the story that he chose to tell would be a story that not only speaks of him but also speaks of Christ.

We can see this in terms of a personal testimony. In some church traditions testimonies are very popular. Sometimes a whole service will be dedicated to sharing your testimony, and everyone is expected to stand up and share something about their lives and what Jesus has done. A testimony is a story of your life in shortened form. You are going to hit the highlights of what God has done for you and what honors him. But sometimes when we share our stories, it becomes much more about us than about God. We fall into the trap of talking about this event in my life or this work of service or that situation. Sometimes at the end we will add, "But it was all to the glory of God." But that type of testimony is not living out the reality of a union with Christ. It is not telling the story in a way that honors Christ at every level and reflects what Christ has done for us.

When we tell our story, our testimony, we should consciously be asking this question: is this the way Christ would tell my story? We should pause and consider how Christ would tell the story of our life, and we should tell our story in a way that highlights Christ and his gospel. Every time Paul tells his story, he has a reason for telling it the way he does, and the central reason why Paul tells his story the way he does is because of his union with Christ.

We can confirm this interpretation in 1:6, where Paul says, "You became imitators of us and of the Lord." Paul is not simply setting himself out as an example to be followed. Paul is living in such a way that he can point to his life and say, "I imitated Jesus. Jesus was working in me and through me when I came to Thessalonica, and my ministry was the ministry of Jesus to you." Let's work our way through 1 Thessalonians 2:1–12 and see the pastoral issues in light of Paul's union with Christ.

PAUL'S MINISTRY WAS NOT IN VAIN

Paul writes, "For you yourselves know, brothers, that our coming to you was not in vain" (v. 1). We first notice that in spite of Paul's suffering, his ministry was not in vain. I struggle with ministry when I face trials and difficulties, and I wonder if my work is producing fruit. I am tempted to think it might all be in vain. Why does Paul think his ministry was not in vain? Because he is united to Christ, and the great example of suffering that was not in vain is the work of Christ on the cross. The death of Jesus upon the cross was not fruitless. That work accomplished God's purpose. What is Paul doing here? Paul is not interpreting his suffering as if it were some judgment from God. He is interpreting his suffering as if it is part of his life in Christ. That means his ministry was not in vain. God is working out the cross in Paul's life, and this suffering will not be fruitless. It is part of the ministry of the gospel.

The other (incorrect) way to see this is to interpret the gospel in light of our struggle. If he had thought this way, Paul would have said, "The gospel has failed. I am suffering, I am struggling, and the ministry didn't work." Paul would thus be looking at his life and ministry in terms of his own struggle. He would not be looking at his struggle in terms of the gospel.

So Paul is interpreting his sufferings not as if they are judgments from God, but as if they are part of his life in Christ, and thus his ministry is not in vain.

PAUL WAS BOLD TO SPEAK THE GOSPEL

Paul continues in verse 2, "We had boldness in our God to declare to you the gospel of God in the midst of much conflict." In spite of the conflict, Paul was bold to speak the gospel, and that boldness was "*in our God.*" Think back to Jesus again. Jesus had to face an amazing amount of conflict in his ministry. Throughout the Gospels, religious leaders were in conflict with him. They tried to shut him up, to intimidate him. Jesus did not back down. He did not cower before them. Why? Remember Paul's little phrase, "boldness in our God." Jesus was bold as he finished his mission, trusting in his Heavenly Father. Jesus was the Son of God sent from Heaven to reveal the Father to us. Paul lived out the boldness of Jesus by seeing himself as part of the life of Christ. Paul's boldness came from God, and he was bold because he approached God through Jesus. Paul didn't have boldness because he thought everyone liked him or he was a great communicator but because of his confidence in God. It was an extension of Paul's union with Christ coming to bear on his ministry.

PAUL WAS APPROVED BY GOD

Paul let his approval come from God, not from the culture around him. Notice verse 4: "Just as we have been approved by God to be entrusted with the gospel, so we speak, not to please man, but to please God who tests our hearts." That is another way in which Paul lived out his union with Christ.

Paul looked at his life as being crucified with Christ and hidden with Christ in God. These were not just rhetorical phrases for Paul. He believed them! This was the reality of his life. Since his life was hidden with Christ in God, he was approved by God. Paul had been approved on the basis of Jesus, not on the basis of how well his ministry went or on the basis of how much people liked him. His approval came from God and from Christ, and if he was approved by God, that was all he needed to move forward in difficult ministry. That was precisely why he did not seek the approval of men. Such approval did not matter to Paul. He had the approval of Heaven. He did not need the approval of Rome or Jerusalem.

Watch the way this works out. Paul was approved by God because he was united to Christ, and that changed the way he lived. He didn't come to Thessalonica to fill a need of approval from men. His not having to seek the approval of men completely changed his approach to ministry. First, Paul says in verse 5, "We never came with words of flattery." He wasn't trying to gain their money like the traveling philosophers of that day. Second, he didn't come with "a pretext for greed." In other words, he wasn't using his ministry to hide his greed or his coveting. He didn't have to. He was approved by God, so he didn't have to live that way. Third, he didn't seek glory from men, "whether from you or from others" (v. 6), because he had the greatest glory anyone could have: he was hidden in Christ in Heaven. He had glory unspeakable. Fourth, he didn't make "demands" for financial support (although he could have as an apostle) because he rested in God's plan and approval for his particular situation. He decided to work to demonstrate to them an example (v. 9).

Do you see the connection? Because Paul is united to God's Son Jesus, because he is in God's Son, Paul looks at his life through his union with Christ. Did God approve of his Son Jesus? Yes! And if we are in him, he approves of us. God doesn't approve of us because of our life and greatness. He approves of us because he sees us through his Son. Since he was approved by God in Jesus, Paul's life was transformed, and his life ended up looking similar to the life of Jesus, who didn't come with flattering words, didn't come with greed, didn't seek glory from men, and didn't make demands upon people in terms of money.

Paul is describing himself in such a way that as we read chapter 2, we see the life of Jesus in Paul. Paul imitated Jesus, and the Thessalonians were to imitate Paul. But the apostle not only described what he did not do — he also described how he lived because of his union with Christ. Paul gives us some positive virtues. Because Paul was approved by God and didn't need the church's approval, he could give away his life for the sake of Jesus, and that is what he did. He lived a life among the Thessalonians the way Jesus lived among his disciples. We can identify six ways Paul reflected his union with Christ.

- Paul was *gentle*: "But we were gentle among you, like a nursing mother taking care of her own children" (v. 7). Because Paul was confident that they were united to Christ, he was patient and gentle, taking care of them like children. Again this goes back to Jesus. How many times did the disciples completely blow it, and Jesus gently moved them toward maturity. Because Paul saw himself connected to Jesus, he lived out that reality.
- Paul was *affectionate and giving*: "So, being affectionately desirous of you, we were ready to share with you not only the gospel of God but also our own selves, because you had become very dear to us" (v. 8). Paul's love for them was displayed in his giving of his life for them. Jesus didn't just come with words — he gave his life. He gave himself, and that is the definition of Christian love.
- He *labored and toiled* among them: "For you remember, brothers, our labor and toil: we worked night and day, that we might not be a burden to any of you . . . " (v. 9a).
- He *preached the gospel* to them: ". . . while we proclaimed to you the gospel of God" (v. 9b).
- His conduct was *Christlike*: "You are witnesses, and God also, how holy and righteous and blameless was our conduct toward you believers" (v. 10).
- He was like *a father* who exhorts his children: "For you know how, like a father with his children, we exhorted each one of you and encouraged you and charged you to walk in a manner worthy of God, who calls you into his own kingdom and glory" (vv. 11, 12).

All of these actions flow out of his identity with Jesus Christ, his union with Christ. We must see these connections and realize that Paul didn't just "gut it out." He didn't just "pull himself up by his bootstraps." Paul saw his obedience in light of his union with Christ, and we must see our lives in relation to Jesus Christ, letting our identities be shaped by our union with Christ and not by our struggles.

We need to see the importance of living our life as a Christian from the reality that we are united to Christ. First Thessalonians 2 is not just about Paul. He wrote these things to help the Thessalonians and us. He states it clearly in verse 14: "For you, brothers, became imitators of the churches of God in Christ Jesus that are in Judea." There it is again. They became imitators of the church "*in Christ Jesus*." They were imitating other churches that were living out their union with Christ as well.

Paul was helping them learn to interpret their lives in terms of what God said about them. He was helping them see their lives in terms of what God said about them because they were united with Christ. He was trying to make them stop interpreting the gospel in terms of their own lives and experiences and struggles. He was trying to get them to stop looking at the gospel in terms of everything going on around them and to look at it in terms of union with Christ.

As Christians, we are no longer just human beings created in the image of God. We are now persons who are hidden in Christ and are part of a new creation. We have been transformed by God, and the life we now live is not our own. The life we live now is the life of Christ being lived out in us. This is what Paul calls us to learn.

After understanding this message, if you told your story, your testimony, what would be different? What would you change? Would you tell it in a way that is consciously seeing the work of Jesus? Would you look for the areas where Jesus is conforming you to his image? Would you realize that your suffering is part of picking up your cross and following Jesus? We all must learn this. We must see this. We must embrace this.

It is part of the mystery of the Christian faith.

It is Christ in us, the hope of glory.

8

Preaching the Word
of Christ

1 Thessalonians 2:13

Several years ago I would have started a sermon on this verse with the question, what is preaching? I would have given several examples of preaching and argued for a particular method of preaching. But in our current situation the appropriate question would be, is preaching necessary? Preaching has fallen on hard times, and we can no longer assume that preaching is the main way in which God communicates to us and instructs us through his church. Preaching is being replaced by several different methods of communication.

In some traditions, singing completely takes the place of preaching. In those cases, singing accomplishes what preaching does because it either convicts people or encourages people. Drama has also gained popularity today. Instead of a minister preaching, some traditions will have a play with people acting out a story from Scripture. Another method that is challenging the traditional model of preaching is dialogue. The idea is to get the congregation involved in the sermon by active participation. We also have certain modes of technology, such as a PowerPoint presentation, replacing the preaching of a sermon.

To be sure, there is a time and place for each one of these, whether we are talking about a worship service or other avenues of ministry. Singing is important and crucial for worship, drama can be a useful ministry, dialogue should take place within the life of a church, and PowerPoint presentations can be used effectively. The question is not whether we can use these tools but whether these modes of communication can replace the traditional model of preaching the Word of God.

We are going to examine the central importance of preaching and how the church cannot do without it. By preaching I mean an authoritative proclamation of the Word of God and the acts of God by one called to be a minister. This is the traditional approach to preaching in the history of the church,[1] and there is a reason why the church has traditionally accepted this model of preaching. First Thessalonians 2:13 helps us understand why preaching is so crucial and important, and it sheds some light on why preaching should take priority in Christ's Church. We will consider the context of the passage, and then we will focus on the nature of preaching as it is found in verse 13.

At the beginning of chapter 2, Paul began to explain his ministry among the church in Thessalonica. He described how he lived and ministered among those people. Then in verse 13 he explained the response of the Thessalonians: "And we also thank God constantly for this, that when you received the word of God, which you heard from us, you accepted it not as the word of men but as what it really is, the word of God, which is at work in you believers." Notice that Paul says they received his word as "the word of God." This is an amazing response given that the city, for the most part, rebelled against this message. But Paul shows that the message was at work in the lives of believers in this way:

> For you, brothers, became imitators of the churches of God in Christ Jesus that are in Judea. For you suffered the same things from your own countrymen as they did from the Jews, who killed both the Lord Jesus and the prophets, and drove us out, and displease God and oppose all mankind by hindering us from speaking to the Gentiles that they might be saved — so as always to fill up the measure of their sins. But God's wrath has come upon them at last! (1 Thessalonians 2:14–16)

A process is described in these verses: 1) Paul preached God's Word; 2) they received the Word as God's Word; 3) they became imitators, suffering for the sake of the gospel.

With that context in mind, let us focus on verse 13. In this verse Paul provides for us the reason why people respond to the message of the gospel, and he provides a reason for the importance of preaching. There are three reasons why Paul seems to be describing the preaching of the Word. First, Paul stresses the *hearing* of the Word of God. He starts by giving thanks that they received the Word of God that they heard: "We also thank God constantly for this, that when you received the word of God, which you heard from us . . . " The emphasis in this verse is on the hearing of the Word of God. This would make sense because this church did not have a Bible as we do. What they knew about Christ came from hearing Paul, from hearing about Christ from the preaching of Paul. Although I do not want to diminish the reading of God's Word, this emphasis on hearing the Word is important.

Paul stresses hearing in this passage because he is highlighting something supernatural and unique that takes place when the gospel is preached.

Second, Paul explains that they *accepted* this message as God's Word: "not as the word of men, but as what it really is, the word of God." They did not simply think this message was Paul's opinion. They did not say that it was Paul's word. Their response was to accept Paul's message as the word of God, and Paul even says that they received it "as what it really is." It seems he is saying that the preaching of the gospel is called the word of God as well.

Third, they were not simply talking about Paul. What they heard did not come only from Paul: "You received the word of God, which you heard from us." Who is Paul talking about in this verse when us says "us"? He must be talking about Timothy and Silas. They accompanied him on this missionary journey, and they are listed in the greeting at the beginning of the letter. When Paul uses strong language to describe this message as "the word of God," he is not saying it was unique to him. We cannot simply say that Paul is talking about his own unique preaching because he includes Timothy and Silas. What makes this message unique is not Paul but the supernatural work that God does when his word is preached. When the Word of God is preached properly, it is as if that preaching is God's word. God is speaking through the preaching.

Fourth, the preaching that they heard from Paul and the other missionaries actually produced a work in the lives of believers. In other words, preaching produces fruit. It accomplishes the purpose that God intended. This is the message of Isaiah the prophet:

> For as the rain and the snow come down from heaven and do not return there but water the earth, making it bring forth and sprout, giving seed to the sower and bread to the eater, so shall my word be that goes out from my mouth; it shall not return to me empty, but it shall accomplish that which I purpose, and shall succeed in the thing for which I sent it. (Isaiah 55:10, 11)

Isaiah uses a powerful image regarding the way God's Word works by drawing on rain and growth. God's Word has the power to accomplish God's purpose. This is similar to Paul's message to the Thessalonians. Paul uses the word *energeo*, from which we get the word *energize*. God's Word energizes people and produces faith and repentance and obedience.

What can we conclude from this verse? When the Word of God is preached, it is as if God is speaking to the people. God speaks through his Word. I realize this is a strong statement, and it is open to abuse, but by describing preaching in this way, I am standing in a tradition that stretches back to the Reformation and the early church. Here is what John Calvin said:

"When a preacher who is duly called and appointed by God speaks, it is as if God himself were speaking through him. The Word of God is not distinguished from the word of the prophet. God wishes to be heard through the voice of his ministers."[2] Calvin states it more strongly than I did. When the minister speaks while preaching the Word properly, it is as if Christ speaks.

We might be tempted to think that John Calvin thought this up on his own, but it goes beyond Calvin. An early Reformed confession called the *Second Helvetic Confession* says, "The preaching of the Word of God is the Word of God." The reason the Reformed tradition says this about preaching is because of a passage like 1 Thessalonians 2:13. The Thessalonian believers accepted Paul's preaching not as the word of men, but as it really was, the word of God. One could say that this is a theology of preaching.[3]

Perhaps you are asking, how can you base this all on one passage? Are there other passages? Well, yes, there are other passages that indicate this truth, and I want us to examine two central ones — Romans 10 and John 10.[4] Here is the passage from Romans 10:

> How then will they call on him in whom they have not believed? And how are they to believe in him of whom they have never heard? And how are they to hear without someone preaching? And how are they to preach unless they are sent? As it is written, "How beautiful are the feet of those who preach the good news!" (Romans 10:14, 15)

In this passage Paul analyzes the process involved in calling upon the Lord's name. Paul's central point is that the salvation involved in calling upon the Lord's name is not something that can occur in a vacuum; it occurs only in a context created by the proclamation of the gospel on the part of those commissioned to proclaim it. All of this is summarized in verse 17: "Faith comes from hearing, and hearing through the word of Christ." Notice that Paul says we hear through "*the word of Christ*." This is where John Calvin gets the idea that the preacher is speaking the words of Christ.

To help see this, we need to examine a translation issue in Romans 10:14. The translators add some words in order to make sense of the passage. This is very typical, but in this case the addition obscures the actual meaning. Paul says in verse 14, "How then will they call on him in whom they have not believed? And how are they to believe *in* him *of* whom they have never heard? And how are they to hear without someone preaching?" The problem with the translation concerns the two prepositions "in" and "of." Those are not in the passage, and that leads John Murray to translate this passage literally this way: "How shall they believe him whom they have not heard?" Murray argues that we should not insert the prepositions. He goes on to say, "A striking feature of this clause is that Christ is represented as being heard in the gospel when proclaimed by the sent messengers. The implication is that Christ speaks in the gospel proclamation."[5] This helps clarify 1 Thessalonians 2:13. When the preacher preaches, Christ speaks through the Word. This is a supernatural work. This is something beyond us because it is a work of the Holy Spirit.

With all the abuses by ministers these days in the pulpit, any minister should teach these truths with fear and trembling, for this is not something that should lead to pride. Ministers are not called to use the pulpit as a place where they abuse and even the score with disgruntled members of the congregation. The minister is called to preach the gospel, and in so doing Christ speaks through the message. The key to preaching is whether or not you are hearing Christ's voice.

John 10 also gives us some insight into the meaning of 1 Thessalonians 2:13. John 10 is a passage about salvation, about Christ calling his sheep. Jesus says that the sheep hear the voice of the shepherd, and the shepherd calls the sheep by name and leads them (vv. 3, 4). They follow him because they know his voice. Jesus explains to the disciples that he is calling his sheep to him. But this does not stop with his own earthly ministry. Jesus explains in verse 16, "And I have other sheep that are not of this fold. I must bring them also, and they will listen to my voice. So there will be one flock, one shepherd."

This passage explains that as the gospel goes forth, others will hear the voice of Christ and will be brought into the fold. So let me ask a question: how do the sheep hear the voice of Christ? If Jesus is in Heaven, and we do not literally hear him as the apostles did that day, how do we hear his voice? How will these other sheep hear the voice of Jesus after he is gone? These "other sheep" would include us. How do we hear the voice of Jesus? We hear Christ's voice through preaching. John Piper calls this the great missionary text of the Bible, a text that has influenced the likes of David Brainerd, William Carey, David Livingstone, and Peter Cameron Scott.[6] They went to preach to pagans because they knew other sheep needed to hear the voice of Christ. That is what preaching is supposed to do.

Both of these passages, Romans 10 and John 10, shed light on what Paul is saying in 1 Thessalonians. Paul is saying that as the minister speaks, Christ is speaking, and it is the work of the Holy Spirit that makes this effective. This is why our hearts are warmed during the preaching. This is why after hearing the Word preached, we leave committed to following Christ. This is why we sometimes leave "energized," to use the expression Paul uses. This is why we who are Christ's sheep leave thinking we have heard his voice. We have.

We cannot do away with preaching because at such moments we hear Jesus in a way that we do not hear him with other modes of communication. Let us hold firm to the ministry of preaching because through that simple yet profound act we hear the voice of the Good Shepherd, we follow him, and he gives us everlasting life.

9

The Gospel and
Your Suffering

1 Thessalonians 2:14–16

Suffering is one of the most difficult aspects of life that we can face, and its difficulty is not diminished if we are Christians. When we suffer, or when someone else suffers, we are often at a loss as to what to do or how to handle it, but the Bible says a great deal about suffering, and it provides a proper understanding of suffering in the life of a believer. Paul's letters to the church in Thessalonica help us see suffering from God's perspective.

We can examine two basic types of suffering. One type of suffering could be called *redemptive*. By redemptive I mean that we are suffering for the purpose of our redemption and salvation — not so we can be forgiven, but so we can be conformed to the image of Christ. Because we are forgiven, we can see suffering through the gospel in a redemptive manner. God is using our suffering for a bigger purpose. For example, when we suffer as Christians, we need to remind ourselves that there is a reason behind our suffering. God has a purpose in our trials and afflictions. We need to remind ourselves of Romans 8:28: "God works all things together for good." This is the big-picture view of suffering as God works all of our suffering together for our good, to make us more like his Son, Jesus.

We can also state some more specific reasons why God allows us to suffer in this way. John Piper examined various passages of Scripture that speak of suffering and articulated five reasons why suffering takes place:[1]

1. Repentance: suffering is a call for us and others to turn from treasuring anything on earth above God.

2. Reliance: suffering is a call to trust God, not the life-sustaining props of the world.

3. Righteousness: suffering is the discipline of our loving heavenly Father so that we come to share his holiness.

4. Reward: suffering is working for us a great reward in heaven that will make up for every loss here a thousand-fold.

5. Reminder: suffering reminds us that God sent his Son into the world to suffer so that our suffering would not be God's condemnation but his purification.

Those are good examples of what I mean by redemptive suffering. God uses our suffering for the purpose of our redemption, our growth in holiness. Although this sees our sufferings as a struggle, this is the proper way to view suffering as a Christian.

The other way to view suffering is through the lens of condemnation or judgment. Sadly, this perspective is all too common among Christians, but Christians do not endure this type of suffering. This suffering does not have the goal of changing the person into the image of Christ. In this type of suffering, God's judgment and wrath are resting upon someone. The sad reality is that Christians often do not view suffering as God's work of redemption. Instead Christians are often tempted to view suffering as condemnation or judgment. We suffer, and we conclude that God is angry with us.

Paul's concern in 1 Thessalonians 2:14–16 is to help us see these two views of suffering. In this passage Paul explains both the view of suffering that is redemptive as well as the view of suffering that is judgmental. Paul helps us see as Christians that our suffering is for the purpose of salvation as God conforms us to the image of Christ. On the other hand, he also demonstrates that unbelievers are suffering under God's wrath and condemnation.

THE PATTERN OF SUFFERING

We need to get the context of verse 13 right in order to understand Paul's explanation of suffering. Paul is thankful that the Thessalonians accepted his message as it truly is, a word from God. Because they accepted the message as the word of God, God's Word was at work in them, and the specific way that God's Word was at work is this: they saw their suffering properly. The Word helped them see their suffering the way God sees it — redemptively. Paul was encouraging these Christians to view their suffering in light of the cross. God's Word taught them that their particular suffering was the same type of suffering that other churches were facing, so the Thessalonians were not alone in their suffering. That is why Paul could say that they "became imitators of [other] churches." Persecution was also happening to other churches, and those churches were persevering through their own suffering.

Paul, however, describes the Thessalonian believers' suffering as being more than just a pattern that he saw in other churches. Notice what Paul goes on to say: "who killed both the Lord Jesus and the prophets" (v. 15). Paul is explaining that the church in Thessalonica was part of the bigger pattern of the gospel, a pattern that includes not only other churches but also Jesus (v. 15) and the prophets (v. 15) and Paul (v. 15). So we have four different examples of this type of suffering: the suffering of the prophets, the suffering of Jesus, the suffering of Paul, and the suffering of various churches. Paul now included this church in Thessalonica in this gospel pattern of suffering. This was meant to encourage these Christians in Thessalonica, and us, too, as we see our suffering in light of this bigger picture. As Christians, we should look at our suffering and connect it to Jesus. That is how we view suffering through the eyes of faith. We must see our suffering in light of our union with Christ and the prophets and other churches and other people. Recognizing this pattern is crucial.

The specific type of suffering Paul is describing here is persecution. We suffer persecution because of our commitment to God and his Word. It is a type of suffering we go through because of our identity as Christians, but the general theology of suffering that Paul articulates here would be applicable to the suffering we face in various areas of life. Persecution should be seen in light of the suffering that Christians go through in all areas of their lives. In other words, persecution is one part of the suffering we face because of the curse. So it is legitimate to see not just persecution but all suffering and trials as part of our faith and growth, not as God's judgment on us for our sin. So steadfast hope in the face of suffering is a crucial component of the gospel no matter what kind of suffering we are experiencing as Christians.

GOD'S WRATH UPON UNBELIEVERS

What about the other type of suffering? Paul here not only explains redemptive suffering but also the suffering that takes place because of the wrath of God. This is terrible and dreadful, and we should not take it lightly. This type of suffering involves God's wrath and his condemnation. Paul describes two groups who were being persecuted in verse 14 as well as two groups who were the persecutors: "For you, brothers, became imitators of the churches of God in Christ Jesus that are in Judea. For you suffered the same things from your own countrymen as they did from the Jews." The similarity is that the Thessalonians were like the Judeans because both had been persecuted by their own countrymen — the Romans and the Jews. It didn't matter whether they were Jews or Gentiles, they all suffered "the same things." Then starting in verse 15 and moving into 16, Paul outlined several things that these Jews did.

They killed the Lord Jesus. They killed the prophets. They drove Paul out and persecuted him. They displeased God in this action. They opposed all mankind in this action. They hindered Paul from preaching

Now before we examine this, I need to make some preliminary comments. One scholar called verses 14–16 a "dreadful text" that contains a "passionate, generalizing, hateful diatribe against the Jews for having killed both the Lord Jesus and the prophets and for interfering with Paul's mission to the Gentiles."[2] This has led some scholars of a more liberal persuasion to argue that verses 14–16 form an interpolation, an inserted text not written by Paul but added later because it does not fit with the overall structure of the whole letter or Paul's theology.[3] Some of this concern by these scholars is due to the suffering of the Jewish people, especially in the Holocaust during World War II in Nazi Germany.

We want to affirm that the Holocaust was a terrible event, and what made it even more horrible was the use of the Bible to support these killings. Passages like this and others in the Bible (such as Matthew 23) that speak of the judgment of Jewish people because of the death of Jesus were ripped out of context and used to support the killing of a particular race, the Jewish people. This was not only a horrible event that should have never happened, but erroneous thinking used to justify it must be corrected. We must be clear as Christians on this matter: the Bible should never be used to justify killing any ethnic group, whether Jewish people or any other people group. We must correct this terrible mistake and clarify what these verses actually do mean.

Paul is not arguing against a race of people simply because of their race. This is not a racial or ethnic argument. He is arguing against them because of their denial of Jesus as the Messiah. He is saying that the Jewish people rejected their Messiah. The judgment that Paul describes in this verse is not a judgment that is in our hands or in the hands of any nation or state. Paul is not telling us to bring judgment against a particular people group. Paul is saying that judgment is in God's hands. He is the wise judge, and these judgments must be left up to God. Ultimately we will all be judged, and we need to be concerned about our own judgment, not that of other people. And that judgment will be the same for everyone, Jew and Gentile, because that judgment will take place on the basis of whether we accepted or rejected Jesus Christ.

We must realize that Paul is doing something in this particular passage that is very similar to what Jesus was doing in Matthew 23:29ff. Paul seems to be drawing from the language of Jesus Christ. In that passage the Lord Jesus was responding to the scribes and the Pharisees and pronounced seven woes. The particular language of that passage was even more severe and judgmental than Paul's. Jesus said, "Woe to you, scribes and Pharisees, hypocrites! For you build the tombs of the prophets and decorate the monuments of the righteous, saying, 'If we had lived in the days of our fathers, we would not have taken part with them in shedding the blood of the prophets'" (Matthew 23:29, 30). During the days of the prophets, the Jewish people rejected their message, and kings killed them. These Pharisees and scribes said they would not have done this, but according to verse 31, they were witnesses against themselves. Why would Jesus say they were witnessing against themselves? Because they were plotting to kill the Messiah, Jesus Christ.

Jesus continues with his condemnation of the Pharisees: "You serpents, you brood of vipers, how are you to escape being sentenced to hell? Therefore I send you prophets and wise men and scribes, some of whom you will kill and crucify, and some you will flog in your synagogues and persecute from town to town" (vv. 33, 34). Look closely at these words from Jesus. He says that this suffering is going to continue, and some people will be flogged in synagogues and persecuted from town to town. Wasn't this fulfilled in the life of Paul? Jesus looked back at what they had done and forward to what they were going to do.

Now we can understand what Jesus meant when he said to them, "Fill up, then, the measure of your fathers" (v. 32). This is the language that Paul used in 1 Thessalonians 2:16, and it has a long history in the Bible. This concept of "filling up sins" occurs in other places as well. Greg Beale says that "the concept of 'filling up sins' occurs elsewhere at significant redemptive-historical epochs to describe the opponents of God's plan to subdue earth with his truth by his redeemed people. God stated in each case that his enemies had to complete a certain amount of sin before they could be considered ripe for definitive judgment, which would always conclude a particular epoch and launch another."[4] It consistently appears when God is judging an old nation, an old way of doing things, and is moving into a new work.

For example, during the covenant ceremony of Genesis 15, God told Abram that his descendants would not emerge from Egypt until the sins of the Amorites were "complete" or filled up (v. 16). The image there is that the Amorites had a certain period of time to turn to God or else to fill up their sins and be judged. Daniel also spoke of a judgment that would come at the end of the age "when the transgressors have reached their limit," when their sins had been filled up (Daniel 8:23–25). This is a common Biblical expression and idea. The sins of the people will be "filled up," and then judgment comes. What Paul is saying in his letter is the same thing we read about in the Gospels and Acts concerning Israel, as well as other nations in the Old Testament. This is not a racial statement by Paul. This is a redemptive-historical statement. This is a statement concerning God's purpose and plan, which has now shifted from the nation of Israel to Jesus Christ, the true Israelite, and to those who trust him (his church).[5] As that shift takes place, there is a judgment on those who do not believe. The old is judged as the new comes.

We also know this is not a racial statement by Paul because he was a Jew. I find it odd that various Gentile scholars argue that Paul the Jew is a racist. Paul considered himself a Hebrew of Hebrews. He loved his countrymen, and as he said in Romans 9:3, "I could wish that I myself were accursed and cut off from Christ for the sake of my brothers, my kinsmen according to the flesh." But Paul freely admitted that there was a problem: his people had turned their back on their Messiah — Jesus Christ. By turning their back on the Messiah, they lost their only hope. Paul tells us that all they had to do was trust Jesus and they would move from the place of wrath to a place of grace. All they had to do was turn away from the temple as the place of God's dwelling and from the sacrifices as providing forgiveness and turn to Jesus as the embodiment of God and to the cross of Christ as providing forgiveness. And many of them did trust Jesus. But for those who rejected salvation in Christ, for those who continued to trust in the temple and its sacrifices, judgment was coming. That judgment came in A.D. 70 when God destroyed the temple through the hands of the Roman Empire. This was prophesied by Jesus in Matthew 24, and I think this is Paul's point in 1 Thessalonians 2:16 when he says, "But God's wrath has come upon them at last!" Because they rejected Christ's salvation, because they rejected God's plan, God's wrath was upon them. When you reject grace, the only thing left is wrath. "There is salvation in no one else, for there is no other name under heaven given among men by which we must be saved" — no name except that of Jesus Christ (Acts 4:12).

Finally, we know this was not a racial statement by Paul because he was not pronouncing judgment only on the Jews. In the context of the passage, Paul was also talking about the countrymen of the Thessalonians, their fellow Roman citizens. The comfort that the Thessalonians could draw from this was that just as God had judged the Jews, he would also judge the Romans. In fact, he will judge anyone who opposes his kingdom and his Messiah. Psalm 2 explains, "Why do the nations rage and the peoples plot in vain? The kings of the earth set themselves, and the rulers take counsel together, against the Lord and against his anointed, saying, 'Let us burst their bonds apart and cast away their cords from us.' He who sits in the heavens laughs; the Lord holds them in derision" (vv. 1–4). When the nations rise up against the Lord, he will "speak to them in his wrath, and terrify them in his fury, saying, 'As for me, I have set my King on Zion, my holy hill'" (Psalm 2:5, 6). It does not matter whether we are Jewish or Roman, European or African, Asian or American — if we reject God's offer through King Jesus, he will speak to us in his wrath. Only in Jesus can we find hope and forgiveness, grace and mercy, adoption and righteousness. If we turn away from Jesus, we turn right into God's wrath.

THE HOPE OF SALVATION

Let's not forget who is writing these words: Paul, the former Pharisee; Paul, one of the chief persecutors of the church in the book of Acts. Paul opposed God's plan and his salvation until he came face-to-face with Jesus, the one true Messiah, on the Damascus Road. When he met Jesus, he realized that Jesus was the true Messiah, and Paul had his heart changed by the Word who was made flesh, Jesus Christ. This man who once killed Christians — this man who once opposed God's plan with every ounce of energy that he had — this man who once lived with the wrath of God upon him — this man had met the grace of God in the person of Jesus Christ, and he was living in that grace and loving his fellow Christians and seeking to bring this good news to the world.

Paul now saw his suffering through his Savior, Jesus Christ. In fact, Paul saw everything in his life in relationship to Jesus. When he suffered, it was no longer as God's wrath but was part of God's redemptive work in his life. It was not God's judgment on him. That judgment passed from Paul to Jesus on the cross. Paul's suffering was no longer viewed as wrath but as grace, and that suffering was working an eternal weight of glory.

Is that true of you?

As a Christian, do you see your suffering as part of your redemption? Do you realize that it is through much suffering that we must enter the kingdom of God?

Do you view your suffering through the gospel, realizing that God is at work in your suffering not to destroy you but to save you?

Or are you still living your old life, viewing your suffering as a judgment of God? Do you still think he is out to get you?

If you, as a Christian, are still viewing your suffering as God's judgment, then you are not living by faith in his promise. God has promised you that there is *no condemnation* to those who are in Christ Jesus. You have moved from wrath to grace.

10

Living in Light of the Gospel

1 THESSALONIANS 2:17–3:13

Not long after establishing the church in Thessalonica, Paul ran into some difficulties. Luke tells us about these problems in Acts 17. People revolted against Paul's teaching, and they took some of the Christians into custody. The Christians in Thessalonica realized that Paul, Silas, and Timothy had to leave town in order to keep peace and to allow the church a measure of freedom. So the missionaries left in the middle of the night, an event Paul described as being "torn away" (1 Thessalonians 2:17) from that church. Paul went to Berea and then to Athens, but he was concerned that he had not finished the task of ministry in Thessalonica and that the young church was not prepared to face the trials and tribulations coming their way. First Thessalonians 2:17–3:13 gives us some background to all this.

According to Paul's words, he struggled deeply with leaving the Thessalonian church. After having to leave Berea in a similar way, Paul left Timothy and Silas behind in that city to encourage the church there. Eventually Paul sent word back to Berea, instructing Silas and Timothy to come to him in Athens.[1] Timothy rejoined Paul at Athens, but Paul could not bear it: "Therefore when we could bear it no longer, we were willing to be left behind at Athens alone, and we sent Timothy, our brother and God's coworker in the gospel of Christ, to establish and exhort you in your faith" (1 Thessalonians 3:1, 2). Paul's words reveal a deep love for the Thessalonian church.

Paul was expressing this great love for that congregation because they might be tempted to doubt his love due to the circumstances surrounding the gospel ministry in Thessalonica. So Paul wanted to go further than words. He wanted to demonstrate his love for them since he could not be present with them. But the question was, how? How could he demonstrate this love? Paul had been educated in the nature of the covenant in the Old Testament, and the church is based upon that covenant. Paul understood that the old covenant informs church life. It is the air that we breathe as Christians in the church. It is part of the relationship we have with each other in the life of the church. God's covenant is the basis of our relationship with him and with each other.

One example of the way the covenant works has to do with our relationship with each other. Paul understood what some would call the reciprocal nature of the Christian life. There is a giving and receiving in the covenant, in the Christian faith. It is the concept of loving one another, which is prominent in the New Testament. The covenant speaks to a mutual bond between God and his people. God grants us his grace, and we respond in praise and adoration and obedience. This relational dynamic is also evident in the life of Christians and, in the passage we are now considering, in Paul and these believers.[2]

You can see this mutual bond in Paul's letter. He called them his "hope or joy or crown of boasting," his "glory and joy" (1 Thessalonians 2:19, 20). Paul was grieved when he did not know how their faith was holding up, but he rejoiced when Timothy brought the good news of their faith and love (1 Thessalonians 3:6, 7). So Paul wrote, "For this reason, brothers, in all our distress and affliction we have been comforted about you through your faith" (1 Thessalonians 3:7). This is important language: Paul had been comforted through their faith. He was encouraged because they were "standing fast" (v. 8), and he wanted to return this back to them and "supply what is lacking" in their own faith (v. 10). That is a mutual relationship, a mutual reciprocity. Paul wanted to share with them, and he wanted them to share with him, and in that process both would be encouraged.

This whole section, 1 Thessalonians 2:17–3:13, describes the way we are called to love one another in the life of the church and to demonstrate the love of Christ to a lost and dying world. God has designed the church, his covenant people, to demonstrate Jesus Christ through mutual sharing and mutual giving with one another. This mutual giving and receiving is a life based on the gospel. In order to demonstrate this love, Paul did something that he could not do himself. Paul could not go, so he sent Timothy back to minister to them, to encourage them, and to strengthen them. Paul was not sending Timothy to strong-arm the church. Paul was not sending Timothy as a power play, forcing his authority upon them. Paul did not minister like that. Sending Timothy was an expression of Paul's deep love for this church and his desire to see them.

THE SACRIFICE OF SENDING TIMOTHY

Paul's sending of Timothy back to this church was a profound sacrifice. This was not simply a wise leader making plans for Timothy to minister in

Thessalonica. Paul was doing more than allowing Timothy to go back and minister to these Christians. Paul was communicating his love to this church in this action of sending Timothy because sending Timothy was a great sacrifice for the apostle. Notice what Paul says in 3:1: "Therefore when we could bear it no longer, we were willing to be left behind at Athens alone." Paul was willing to be left alone in Athens. Athens was one of the world's oldest cities, a center for the arts, learning, and philosophy, home to Plato's Academy and Aristotle's Lyceum, perhaps the birthplace of democracy, and a place that was hostile to the gospel. This city full of idolatry provoked Paul's spirit and led to his confrontation with the philosophers on Mars Hill. Paul was willing to be left alone in that great pagan city of Athens in order to send Timothy back to minister to the small church in Thessalonica.

Paul was willing to be left alone in a hostile environment — he was giving up a coworker in the gospel. These are the opposite sides of this sacrifice. Being alone is one thing, but losing a coworker for the gospel is another level to this act of love. Can you imagine the benefits of Paul and Timothy ministering together in Athens? Our initial reaction to situations like this is to maximize the place where we are ministering and to keep our coworkers with us. Maybe part of the motive is for the gospel, but we also want to preserve our own comfort. But Paul made the decision to send his coworker back to Thessalonica and to minister in Athens alone.

But there was more to this sacrifice. Paul was not just choosing to minister alone. Paul was not just giving up a coworker. Did you notice how he described Timothy in verse 2? He was giving up a "brother." I don't think Paul was simply using this term to describe Timothy as a brother in Christ. Paul's relationship with Timothy was deeper than that. The bond between them was more than coworkers for the gospel. Elsewhere Paul called Timothy "my true child in the faith" (1 Timothy 1:2), and this makes us realize the depth of Paul's sacrifice. No one else qualified to go to Thessalonica because no one else had the spirit and heart of Paul more than Timothy did. If Paul could not go, he would send his closest companion, his true child in the faith, Timothy.

That is the level of sacrifice that we must see in Paul's decision, but there is more. We need to put ourselves in Paul's shoes in order to see this sacrifice from another perspective. Let's think about what would have happened if Paul actually came back to visit the Thessalonians. If he were able to make his way back, there would be that mutual encouragement and love that we mentioned earlier. Yes, it would be a sacrifice to get there, but the result would be great joy. But Satan "hindered" Paul's trip (1 Thessalonians 2:18). We don't know the reasons, but Paul could not go there at that time. At that point Paul had a choice to make. Should he try some other plan, or should he just wait until he could visit the church in Thessalonica?

What choice would you make? I know how tempting it would have been for me to rationalize this. No one would have given another thought to the situation if Paul had decided not to send Timothy. In fact, they might never have known he even considered sending Timothy. Paul could have thought about the different dimensions of this decision and rationalized that he needed Timothy to stay with him in Athens. Paul had made it to that great city, the heart of Greek culture. Paul could have figured that he had a chance to impact these philosophers for the cause of Christ, and Timothy could have helped with that process. Perhaps together they could plant a church in Athens. Paul could have concluded that Timothy needed to stay in Athens and that he could not risk sending Timothy back to Thessalonica. If Paul would have worked through his situation in that way, no one would have thought any differently about his ministry. He did not have to send Timothy. Paul could have decided to wait for an opportunity when he could go. He could have chosen what was best for himself in that particular situation.

But that is not the way Paul lived. That is not the way Paul did ministry. Paul consistently chose what was best for others without regard for himself. Paul chose to give up a great source of joy and hope and consolation in order to provide it to the Thessalonians. This shows the depth of Paul's sacrifice. That helps us see the sending of Timothy on another level of Christian love. Paul could have made no greater sacrifice at that moment. As we see this and other situations when Paul made decisions like this, it appears that Paul's way of thinking was different from our way of thinking. It seems that Paul looked at what would be the greatest sacrifice he could make for these people in order to demonstrate how much he loved them. It seems that Paul's choice was based not on what would be best for him, but on what would be best for the church and what would demonstrate his love for them. So he chose to send Timothy. Even if he would have shown up himself, that would not have demonstrated the depth of his love in the same way that sending Timothy demonstrated. In sending Timothy, he was not just sending someone to encourage them, to give them a report about Paul, and to bring a report back to Paul. He was losing something. He was letting go of something. He was giving up the greatest asset he had in his ministry at that point.

Pause and consider the depth of love Paul was demonstrating in this decision, this sacrifice to send Timothy.[3] Paul seemed to be asking key questions: *What can I do to show them how deeply I love them? What is the greatest sacrifice I can make to demonstrate my love?* Paul looked across his ministry and his resources, chose to give up his own greatest blessing, his own coworker, his son in the faith, Timothy, and sent Timothy back to them and remained alone in Athens.

That is a way of life lived in light of the gospel.

This type of gospel-centered thinking was not unique to Paul's ministry in Thessalonica. In other words, this was not a one-time decision for

Paul but a pattern of ministry. This was a consistent and conscious way of life. Paul ministered to the church in Philippi in a similar way, and he was more explicit in that case than he is here: "I hope in the Lord Jesus to send Timothy to you soon, so that I too may be cheered by news of you. For I have no one like him, who will be genuinely concerned for your welfare. For they all seek their own interests, not those of Jesus Christ. But you know Timothy's proven worth, how as a son with a father he has served with me in the gospel" (Philippians 2:19–22). Notice Paul's words: "I have no one like him," and Timothy was like "a son" in the way he served Paul. Timothy was the embodiment of Paul, and that is precisely why the sacrifice was so great.

THE SIN OF POSSESSIVENESS

We do not think this way about life because it is our tendency to hold onto those people and those situations that bring us great joy and comfort. In the midst of a crisis we should make the decision that is best for the whole body, the whole church. Instead we make decisions that are bound up with our own good and our own benefit. We are a self-centered people thinking about our own privileges. We live in a world that tells us to think about ourselves and our own needs. We hold onto people and things that bring us joy, without considering what that would do for someone else, but that is not gospel-centered thinking. When we arrange situations to maximize our own joy, that is the opposite of gospel thinking.

When we do not live in line with the gospel, we behave in sinful patterns and in sinful ways with other people. We will give in to manipulation and will take advantage of situations when we do not see ourselves as free to let those things go that God wants us to release. The opposite of Paul's freedom and sacrifice is obsessiveness, manipulation, and control. We desire to control, so we manipulate people. We are obsessed with our own joy, so expressions of jealousy and pride and envy come out in our behavior. At the root of this type of behavior is a destructive form of possessiveness.[4]

Do not neglect the significance of this issue. These sins are bound up in our hearts, and the gospel is at work to break these patterns. Many marriages have been destroyed due to this form of possessiveness. Is it any wonder that Paul told us elsewhere, "Husbands, love your wives, as Christ loved the church and gave himself up for her" (Ephesians 5:25). Paul called husbands away from possessiveness and manipulation toward a life of sacrifice for their wives. Do you see how significant this matter of self-sacrifice becomes? The same could be said about children who have been emotionally damaged because of their parents' possessive tendencies. When the family falls apart and children become pawns in a domestic war, the root issue is that you have lost your joy in Christ and in each other; so you are holding on to whatever joy you can find, even if that means treating your child as a possession that belongs to you. On and on we could go, applying this to various areas of social relationships and corporate struggles related to jealousy, envy, and strife.

Over and against this picture of control and possessive manipulation stands the Apostle Paul. Paul gives up the comfort and joy he finds in Timothy for the benefit of the Thessalonian church. Paul's actions here are not just for ministers but for husbands and wives, for parents and children, for employers and employees.

The depth of Paul's sacrifice is in line with the gospel, and as we see this, we also realize how our lives do not measure up to the Apostle Paul's. That is what I saw in this story when I read it and heard someone else preach on it.[5] I am prone to maneuver myself into the best situation for my own benefit, my life, my family. That goes against the gospel logic of the Apostle Paul. We should embrace this type of self-denying, sacrificial love. G. K. Chesterton once remarked, "How much larger your life would be if your self could become smaller in it."[6] This is precisely what was motivating Paul, and it is a powerful testimony to the gospel. It should stir us to deny ourselves.

You probably run into the same struggle I run into when you choose to sacrifice and give something up for others. We often sacrifice with clenched fists, not open hands. In spite of knowing what to do, and even loving the idea of this type of sacrifice, when we do it, it just doesn't seem to bring joy, and we cannot do it freely. But this is where Paul is helpful. Paul not only sacrifices, but he finds comfort and joy in Timothy's work. It seems that he is even finding comfort and joy from giving Timothy to someone else; so he rejoices in this sacrifice as Timothy becomes an expression of Paul's own love.

THE SOURCE OF A SACRIFICIAL LIFE

If you struggle to live a sacrificial life, perhaps you are asking the same question I asked: How did Paul live this way? Where did he get the power to live sacrificially? If we can understand how Paul lived this way, perhaps we can learn how to live this way too. Paul's behavior was not natural. We know from Scripture what is fleshly and natural — sin, pride, idolatry, strife, jealousy, fits of anger, rivalries, dissensions, divisions, and envy, to mention a few. A sacrificial life was not natural to Paul's personality. Neither was this merely devotion to a principle — that type of devotion produces no joy. We can see the source of Paul's love in his concluding words of 1 Thessalonians 3:

> Now may our God and Father himself, and our Lord Jesus, direct our way
> to you, and may the Lord make you increase and abound in love for one
> another and for all, as we do for you, so that he may establish your hearts

blameless in holiness before our God and Father, at the coming of our Lord Jesus with all his saints. (vv. 11–13)

It was the Lord who was causing Paul to increase and abound in love for these Christians. It was the work of Jesus Christ that provided for Paul the motive and the power to live a sacrificial life.

Paul's sacrifice was rooted in the sacrifice of God the Father and God the Son: "For God so loved the world, that he gave his only Son, that whoever believes in him should not perish but have eternal life" (John 3:16). Paul's sacrifice was not made in a void; it was not just a principle or ideal. Paul's sacrifice for the Thessalonian church was rooted in the gospel and flowed from the gospel because his sacrificial life was rooted in the sacrifice of God the Father who sent his only begotten Son for us. Paul was motivated by the love of God that sent forth his own Son.

Paul's sacrifice for that church not only demonstrated his love for these Christians but also demonstrates God's love for these Christians. Have you ever doubted the love of God? All of us have at some point. Look to his sacrifice — he sent his Son. What greater sacrifice could there be? He could have given no greater gift than his Son (Romans 8:32). What great love is this! What greater sacrifice could there be?

If the Thessalonian church ever doubted Paul's love, they only needed to look to his sacrifice. Paul sent his son in the faith, Timothy. What greater sacrifice could Paul make? Could there have been a greater gift than sending Timothy? And as Paul lived this way, he was demonstrating the love of God to that church.

That is what we are called to do. We are called to live sacrificially for our wives, for our children, for our families, for our churches, for our neighbors in order to demonstrate the love of God to them. When we choose to sacrifice our own joy or comfort for someone else, we are living in light of the gospel, and that is the polar opposite of the way a natural man or woman lives. We thus witness to the great depth of love we have in Jesus Christ.

For Paul, the gospel caused him to change his approach to ministry and to other people. He demonstrated the love of God in his life, and God calls us to live this way too. He calls us to imitate Paul as Paul imitated Jesus Christ.

That is the way God's love is manifested in this world.

11

Become What You Already Are in Christ

1 THESSALONIANS 4:1–8

How are we to gauge what is right and what is wrong? Perhaps we determine what is right and what is wrong on the basis of our upbringing and our family traditions. Perhaps we determine what is right and wrong on the basis of our modern culture and its influences — television, radio, movies, books, and any other means of communication that we currently have. But as a Christian, our starting point should be the Word of God. What does the Word of God say about a particular situation?

The question of right and wrong is often described as a question dealing with ethics. The word *ethics* means a custom or usage or practice prescribed by law. In the New Testament, the concept of ethics refers to a manner of life or a pattern of conduct within the Christian faith that produces goodness, purity, and holiness.[1] This covers a way of life as well as areas of decision making. To put it in terms that Paul uses in 1 Thessalonians 4, we are called to "walk" in a manner that pleases God. Paul uses this metaphor of walking over thirty-two times in his letters to describe the Christian life.[2] We are on a journey, and as we travel along, we are called by God to walk a certain way, which means we are to live in a way that is consistent with the Word of God.

THE INDICATIVE AND THE IMPERATIVE

It is important for us to realize that when Paul gets to the point of addressing how we are called to "walk" as Christians, he has already provided a foundation for this particular way of life. Paul makes this connection explicit in

Ephesians when he prays that the church might "know what is the hope to which [God] has called you, what are the riches of his glorious inheritance in the saints, and what is the immeasurable greatness of his power toward us who believe" (1:18, 19). The emphasis in that passage is knowing what God has accomplished through Christ and in us because of Christ. That is the indicative. It is a statement of fact. When Paul gets to Ephesians chapter 4, he then "urges [the church] to walk in a manner worthy of the calling to which you have been called" (v. 1). That is the imperative. It is a command or an expressed obligation.

We must pause and consider this as we move into chapter 4 of 1 Thessalonians because this indicative-imperative structure is not only the basic structure of Pauline ethics[3] but also of Biblical ethics. Consider the pattern found in the Ten Commandments. If I were to ask you to recite them, you might start with the first commandment, but that is not the beginning. The Ten Commandments have a prologue that is God's statement to the Israelites (and to us): "I am the LORD your God, who brought you out of the land of Egypt, out of the house of slavery" (Exodus 20:2). This is the indicative. It is a statement of fact. It is a statement of what God had done. Only the Lord God could have brought them out of Egypt and out of slavery. That was the basis of their identity. The Lord then said, "You shall have no other gods before me" (v. 3). That is the imperative. It is a command. It is what God had called them to do. The indicative, the act of God, always precedes the imperative, the command of God. This is the basic gospel structure of the Bible.

One of the greatest struggles in the Christian life is a failure to understand this basic pattern regarding Biblical obedience. Since we do not understand what God has done, we are constantly struggling to obey. If we do not understand the indicative, the act of God, the cross of Jesus Christ, it is impossible for us to joyfully obey the imperatives, the commands of God. The gospel is so powerful that God has already transformed us. We have already been changed. As God's people, we have received all spiritual blessings in heavenly places in Christ (Ephesians 1:3), and we are seated with Christ in heavenly places (Ephesians 2:6). We have been called, regenerated, forgiven, and adopted. The Biblical ethic is that we are now called to live like that. In other words, we are called to become what we already are in Christ.[4]

WALK IN A MANNER THAT PLEASES GOD

Now we are at a place to understand Paul's call to a holy life. Paul has articulated believers' identity in the early sections of 1 Thessalonians; now he calls us to live a life that pleases God. So chapter 4 is a shift toward the area of Christian growth. Paul gets very specific about two areas — sexual immorality and brotherly love. He introduces us to the issue of a life that pleases God in verses 1, 2. This is a general introduction about how we should please God in everything. Then he gets specific with the first issue in verse 3 — sexual immorality. This goes on until verse 8. Then Paul picks up the second area of Christian growth in verse 9 — brotherly love. Paul's discussion of brotherly love runs until verse 12.

We have seen that this area of Christian moral conduct is described as a "walk," a way of life. In other passages of Scripture this is described as being the salt of the earth and the light of the world. Our way of life is a calling to reflect the holiness of God to the world around us: "You shall be holy, for I am holy" (1 Peter 1:16). The particular area of Christian conduct that Paul tackles here is as relevant to us as it was to the church in Thessalonica — sexual immorality. This is not a topic that we are comfortable discussing. In fact, in previous generations it was not considered proper to speak of these matters in public.[5]

We must, however, speak honestly about this matter because we live in a sexually obsessed culture. None of us can avoid this. If we watch television, we will see commercials and programs that explicitly promote sexual immorality. If we go to the movies, we will face the same problem. If we go to the mall, we will see stores and people who flaunt their sexuality. If we go to the grocery store, we will see magazines in the checkout line that openly address issues regarding sexuality, often with provocative photos. We cannot escape this because we live in a culture that is obsessed with sex and sexuality. In fact, we no longer have to leave our homes to see sexually provocative images because pornography can be accessed on the Internet.

This is a discouraging situation, but the world in which we find ourselves is not very different from the world in which Paul lived.[6] Paul and his fellow Christians faced these kinds of temptations and struggles too. They were bombarded with them, just as we are. In Paul's day, marriages in the Greek and Roman world were set up by family arrangements. Young men in their twenties and young ladies in their teens had barely met when they were married. Marriage was simply a legal arrangement for the exchanging of money and goods and the ability to have children.

This created an environment in the Greco-Roman world where most people didn't expect husbands to be committed to their marriages. Sexual misconduct and adultery were widespread. Prostitution was a business just like any other source of income. Innkeepers kept slave girls for the sexual entertainment of their customers, and adulterous activity was so widespread that Emperor August (63 B.C.–A.D. 14) established law codes to reform marital conduct. Living several centuries before Paul's time period, a man named Demosthenes explained the situation this way: "Mistresses we keep for our pleasure, concubines for our day to day physical well-being, and wives to bear us legitimate children."[7]

We are surprised that this is stated in such a matter-of-fact way, but many people in that culture saw this behavior as normal. In fact, some religious practices of the Greco-Roman world encouraged this type of behavior. Called cultic prostitution, temple prostitution, and religious prostitution, it is the practice of having sexual intercourse for a religious or sacred purpose. In Thessalonica, the cult of Cabiri of Samothrace sanctioned sexual relationships that would be considered sinful practices for Christians.[8] Converts to Christianity in Thessalonica would have come from some form of this background that encouraged such illicit sexual activity.

The struggles we face today are similar to the struggles that these early Christians faced. But note that Paul was not dealing with the evil in the culture. Paul's great concern was the conduct of the church. Remember what he told the church in Corinth:

> I wrote to you in my letter not to associate with sexually immoral people — not at all meaning the sexually immoral of this world, or the greedy and swindlers, or idolaters, since then you would need to go out of the world. But now I am writing to you not to associate with anyone who bears the name of brother if he is guilty of sexual immorality or greed, or is an idolater, reviler, drunkard, or swindler — not even to eat with such a one. (1 Corinthians 5:9–11)

Paul's concern was the church. He could not address how the world behaved. But as these Christians came out of a sexually immoral world, they had to understand how to walk in a manner that pleases God.

This topic is difficult to address for several reasons. First, the content itself is awkward. A conversation on sex and sexuality should be pointedly discussed in private. But as I said previously, there are elements of this issue that we must address openly, as Paul does.

Not only is the topic itself difficult, but a godly response to sex and sexuality is not a popular message. Paul is going to instruct us to discipline ourselves and to control our passions. This message is a radically different message than what we hear all around us in this world; it is not popular to talk about discipline and chastity. Of course, it wasn't popular then either, which is why Paul starts out by saying, "We ask and urge you in the Lord Jesus. . . . " Paul was both requesting and exhorting them toward proper conduct. But this is not just Paul's command or Paul's opinion about how they should conduct themselves. This is an urging "in the Lord Jesus." This becomes clear in verse 2: "For you know what instructions we gave you through the Lord Jesus," as well as in the concluding verse 8: "Therefore whoever disregards this [command], disregards not man but God, who gives his Holy Spirit to you."

This discipline, however, has two dimensions to it that we must see. Paul explained that they were already obeying in this matter but urged them to "do so more and more" (v. 1). Paul was getting across two aspects of the Christian life. On the one hand, he was reminding them of how they started the Christian life. They received the word of Jesus Christ and obeyed it. They turned their backs upon the world and its sexual immorality. That type of repentance is a crucial start. On the other hand, Paul was explaining that they must continue to obey Jesus and to persevere. Sometimes when we first believe the gospel, things seem to fall into place. Life makes sense because we are supposed to live this way. But as we continue in this walk, the path is often difficult to maintain in the face of all the obstacles. So Paul was urging them forward.

Do you see the progression? We should not move past this quickly. We received the word, and that is great; we have progressed in the faith, and that is crucial; but we must continue to grow. Why? Because the Christian life is not so much about how we start but how we finish. Where will we be in a year or two? What happens once we settle down into the long haul of the Christian life? When we get married and have children, will we still be faithful, or will the cares of the world draw us away? After a few years of marriage, will we still be committed to our spouse? Or will we be tempted to find excitement and pleasure somewhere else? Let us be committed to remaining steadfast in this journey and not view it as a sprint but as a marathon. We must press on in the faith and be a witness to a world that is obsessed with sexual immorality. We must demonstrate a different way.

SANCTIFICATION AND SEXUAL PURITY

Paul calls this new way of life "the will of God" and defines it as our "sanctification" (v. 3). The word "sanctification" is the noun *hagiasmos*, which is prominent in this section and occurs two more times in the following verses (4, 7). It can be translated as "holiness," and it conveys an important concept regarding the way of life for Christians. The root notion of this word is separation, expressing the idea that God's people should be set apart and separate from the world in their conduct. Weima says, "Holiness, therefore, is the boundary marker that separates God's people from all other nations."[9] Paul's instruction concerning holiness addresses a particular area: we should abstain from sexual immorality.

As Christians, our understanding of sex and sexuality makes us different and distinct from the world. The word for "sexual immorality" in verse 3 can "refer specifically to any illicit form of sexual intercourse or generally to any immoral sexual relationship."[10] The specific area of immoral activity is described in verses 4–7, but this section is one of the most difficult exegetical problems in the New Testament. The difficulty begins with verse 4: "that each one of you know how to control his own body in holiness and honor." There is a question about the translation of the word "body." It is the Greek word *skeuos*, which has a broad range of meaning. The ESV provides this marginal note: "Or '*how to take a wife to himself*;' Greek '*how to possess his own vessel*.'" The second note is the literal translation. The first note is an interpretation of the meaning of "vessel" as one's wife. So the question is, what does *skeuos* mean?[11]

I think the ESV got it right by translating the passage as knowing how to control our own body. Six other times Paul uses this word *skeuos* to mean "person" or "a person's body."[12] Paul told these Christians, living in a central city of the Roman Empire on a major road, a vital sea harbor, both of which bring business that caters to sexual immorality, to discipline their bodies in the area of sexuality. They should not live like the Gentiles who do not know God. Instead Paul instructs us to control our bodies with holiness and honor. Sexual immorality is wrong not because sexual activity is wrong in and of itself, but because we do not use it properly. God created sexuality, and he intends for us to know how we should use our bodies in the proper way. God designed sexual activity for a male and a female inside the covenant bonds of marriage, and in that context we should rejoice and be thankful in God's gift to us as husband and wife.

One of the great failures of the church in our generation is that we have constantly spoken about the negative issues and condemned sex outside of marriage, adultery, and homosexuality. Don't misunderstand my point — those are indeed wrong behaviors. Christians should not participate in such conduct. But the message here is not only negative. If all our children hear is no, they will not understand the proper role of sexual relationships. And if we do not teach them a proper understanding of sexual relationships, where will they learn it? We know the answer to that question. Our children learn about issues related to sexuality from television and commercials and movies. That is not healthy. We must not only state what is wrong, but we must explain what is right and glorious about sexuality in the way God created it.

Notice something very important about what Paul says regarding sexuality and lust. The "passion of lust" that is at the root of sexual immorality is based on the fact that Gentiles do not know God (v. 5). Paul tied sexual immorality to the Creator of the universe. In other words, if we know God, we will live differently because we will understand why God created the world the way he did, why he created male and female, and why he created sexual activity. We demonstrate the knowledge of God in our behavior regarding sexual activity. In his chapter "Sacred Sex" in the book *Growing in Christ*, J. I. Packer explains the problem:

> In the jungle of modern permissiveness the meaning and purpose of sex is missed, and its glory lost. Our benighted society urgently needs recalling to the noble and ennobling view of sex which Scripture implied and the

seventh commandment assumes: namely, that sex is for fully and permanently committed relationships which, by being the blend of affection, loyalty, and biology that they are, prepare us for and help us into that which is their archetype — "the happiness of being freely, voluntarily united" to God, men, and angels "in an ecstasy of love and delight compared with which the most rapturous love between a man and a woman on this earth is mere milk and water" (C. S. Lewis).[13]

We must understand and communicate to the next generation that sex is sacred and is in some mysterious way a picture of the love and delight of knowing God.

Let's make sure that as we explain this command, we understand not only the negative "thou shalt not . . . " but also the positive "thou shalt . . . " We must understand that God gave us this gift of sexuality for our enjoyment and as a picture of his love for us. In the midst of our defense of traditional marriage, let us also explain that our concerns are rooted in creation, redemption, and a knowledge of God. As Paul says in Ephesians 5, a husband and wife reflect Christ and his church. According to Paul, marriage is invested with a spiritual and redemptive significance. Indeed this is a great and glorious mystery.

We see that we are on track with this interpretation because Paul warns us against transgressing or wronging our brother in verse 6. Although some writers think Paul has shifted topics, I think he is consistently applying a Christian ethic to marriage. Paul views the relationships within marriage from the perspective of redemption. A believer's wife is not just his spouse but a fellow believer in Christ. If we are tempted toward adultery, we are not just offending another marriage — we are wronging a brother and sister in Christ.

For some reason Christians in our culture have lost their way regarding their walk and conduct. We are no longer committed to long-term relationships, we are not committed to the tough discipline it takes to make a marriage last, and we are not committed to behaving in a way that is radically different from the world.

In a study by the Barna Group that ran from January 2007 through January 2008 (based on interviews with a random sample of 5,017 adults, age eighteen and older), they concluded that born-again Christians were indistinguishable from the national average on the matter of divorce: "Among all born again Christians, which includes evangelicals, the divorce figure is 32 percent, which is statistically identical to the 33 percent figure among non-born again adults, the research group noted." George Barna, who directed the study, concludes, "There no longer seems to be much of a stigma attached to divorce; it is now seen as an unavoidable rite of passage."[14]

This is a problem for the church, and there are consequences to this type of behavior. We recognize the natural consequences — financial strain, diseases, sickness, getting caught, family trials. The spiritual consequences are even more devastating as we lose our witness not only to the world but also to our children. But Paul expressed something in this passage that we must take seriously: "the Lord is an avenger in all these things, as we told you beforehand and solemnly warned you" (v. 6). Paul referred to Jesus as "Lord" here and in 2 Thessalonians 1:7–12. He also attached a title to Jesus that is rooted in the Old Testament — the "avenger." This is the Old Testament idea that God is the avenger of evil that is done to others, and ultimately this avenging will take place when Jesus returns, as we see from 2 Thessalonians 1:7, 8. We should avoid this behavior not only because of the temporal consequences but also because of the heavenly consequences.

If we disregard these instructions, we are not disregarding Paul's opinions or my ideas. It is God who has called us to holiness. So Paul says in verse 8, "Whoever disregards this, disregards not man but God." God has called us to be different, to be holy. That means we are called to live a life of purity that goes against the cultural grain. We must fight this fight for the sake of our wife, for the sake of our children, and for the sake of the gospel. Paul, however, did not end his instructions without reminding us that we are not in this fight by ourselves. Notice the end of verse 8: "[God] gives his Holy Spirit to you."

God has called us (v. 7) and has given us the Holy Spirit to dwell within us (v. 8). This is why I started this study by reminding us of the indicative, the act of God. The gift of the Holy Spirit is God's work. He gives us the strength and holiness to please God and to serve him. It is the Spirit of God who is at work through our preaching, through our worship, through our prayers, through the sacraments of the Lord's Supper and baptism, through our families and our friends and our relationships. It is the Spirit of God who is at work in these common gifts of grace. And if we turn away from these means of grace and fall into this sexually saturated culture, we are disobeying God himself, and according to Paul, we are grieving the Holy Spirit, who indwells us (Ephesians 4:30).

No matter what has happened in our lives, no matter where we are now or where we came from, we already know this because we have the Spirit of God in us, and he is called the *Holy* Spirit. He will not allow us to remain in our sin. He will move us toward purity and maturity. He will not let us live in conformity to this world but will transform us into the likeness of Jesus Christ.

If we have stumbled and struggled, we must not give up. Jesus provides forgiveness through the Holy Spirit. We have all sinned and wronged others at some points in our lives. We have all been disobedient to God's command for purity. But we don't have to wait until Jesus returns to deal with it. We can deal with it now. We can confess our sins now. We can come to Jesus now, so that on that day, on the Day of Judgment, we will be safe. We can seek forgiveness now, so that when Jesus returns as the avenger, he will be working for us and not against us.

We must not lose heart. We must not forget what we are doing and why. We must not forget what kind of witness we are for our children, for our families, for our neighbors. And as we walk this life, we must remember that we are being transformed into a reality that we already possess. We must become what we already are in Christ.

12

The Fruit of the Gospel: Love

1 Thessalonians 4:9–12

Our Lord Jesus Christ, while he was ministering on this earth, explained to us how the world will know that we are Christians: "By this all people will know that you are my disciples, if you have love for one another" (John 13:35). He did not say that the world will know we are his disciples by our correct doctrine. He did not say that the world will know we are his disciples by the power of our words. He said that the world will know we are his disciples because of our love for one another.

Love is a powerful testimony to the reality of the Christian faith. In the third century Tertullian once reported that the Romans would say about the Christians, "See how they love one another."[1] Justin Martyr explained Christian love this way:

> We who used to value the acquisition of wealth and possessions more than anything else now bring what we have into a common fund and share it with anyone who needs it. We used to hate and destroy one another and refused to associate with people of another race or country. Now, because of Christ, we live together with such people and pray for our enemies.[2]

Christianity spread rapidly through the Roman world because of this love. We do not have records of missionary programs or evangelistic programs from that era. But we have examples of this type of love, and the world noticed, just as Jesus said they would.

In spite of the emphasis on love in the Scriptures, the Christian church is not known for love today. We are known for our divisions, our fights, our disagreements, our anger, our specific doctrines, but not for our love. And we must repent of this. We must get back to basic Christianity, to first things. We must regain our love for Jesus Christ, our love for one another, and our love for our neighbor. Love is at the heart of the Christian mission and our witness to the world because in our love for one another we reflect the love of Christ.

WALKING TO PLEASE THE LORD

In 1 Thessalonians 4:9–12, Paul is addressing this topic of love and the importance of it in the church, and he can help us regain a proper perspective regarding our love. Paul's words here concern practical Christianity. He is addressing what our lives should look like in light of the gospel: "Finally, then, brothers, we ask and urge you in the Lord Jesus, that as you received from us how you ought to walk and to please God, just as you are doing, that you do so more and more" (4:1). Paul is concerned about how we ought to walk and please God. We should live in a way that reflects our love for God and our love for each other.

Paul is picking up on a common terminology in Scripture by explaining that we should walk in a way that pleases the Lord. Psalm 1 describes this way of life. In fact, Psalm 1 describes the two ways of life, the way of the righteous and the way of the unrighteous. The psalmist says, "Blessed is the man who walks not in the counsel of the wicked, nor stands in the way of sinners, nor sits in the seat of scoffers; but his delight is in the law of the LORD, and on his law he meditates day and night." If we walk in the way of the Lord, if we live in a way that pleases the Lord, we will be "like a tree planted by streams of water that yields its fruit in its season, and its leaf does not wither." All that we do will prosper. The other path of life is the way of the wicked. The psalmist says, "The wicked are not so, but are like chaff that the wind drives away. Therefore the wicked will not stand in the judgment, nor sinners in the congregation of the righteous; for the LORD knows the way of the righteous, but the way of the wicked will perish."

Psalm 1 sets out the direction of the two courses that we can take in life — the course of righteousness, which is a life that pleases God and walks in a manner that is worthy of God, or the course that is wicked, which is a life that does not concern itself with God or care about what God says. Paul picks up on this imagery in chapter 4 of 1 Thessalonians by explaining what should be different for us as we live in a way that honors and pleases the Lord. The first thing that he points out in 1 Thessalonians 4 is to "abstain from sexual immorality." We are called to be pure and to relate to other people, both men and women, in a way that pleases God and honors the other person. The second area of life that Paul now addresses is brotherly love (vv. 9–12).

TWO DANGERS REGARDING BROTHERLY LOVE

As we examine this concept of brotherly love, there are two dangers we have to guard against in the Christian church. One danger is that we do not show love to each other. In other words, we are not looking for opportunities to love our fellow brothers and sisters. This could be simple acts of love like writing letters or making phone calls, or it can be more sacrificial acts of love like buying a meal or helping with issues in the home. We must be reminded to love one another, and we need to be open and honest about some of our struggles so we can fulfill this command.

The other danger to avoid regarding love is to show too much of it in the wrong way. That might sound surprising, but I think it is exactly what Paul is pointing out to us here. We can go too far with this sense of brotherly love and allow people to be irresponsible. In the name of love we excuse the behavior of other people. If someone loses a job, it is one thing to help them and get them back on their feet. But if that person seems to be living off the benevolent love the church has shown, then we have to shift gears from love to discipline. John Stott explains it this way: "True, it is an expression of love to support others who are in need; but it is also an expression of love to support ourselves, so as not to need to be supported by others."[3] We often do not consider that our own work is an expression of love to others because we do not need to be supported by them.

LOVE ONE ANOTHER: THREE COMMANDS

Paul now gets very practical about what brotherly love should look like. Paul told us to love one another and to live well with one another. Now he tells us what that looks like. Paul gives us three admonitions, three commands that we are called to obey, and then gives us two reasons why these commands are important. First, Paul commands us to live a quiet life (v. 11). Many translators have noted that this is something of an oxymoron. Gordon Fee explains that it could literally be translated, "strive hard to live quietly."[4] He also points out that the word "quiet" here does not carry the idea of "not speaking" or "being restful" but of not intruding into the lives of other people, especially brothers and sisters in the faith, and so becoming a burden to them. Paul is instructing us to live our lives in such a way as not to burden others, but he is also warning us not to draw attention to ourselves. We can see that in Acts 17. When Paul started this church, there was a great deal of attention drawn to these Christians because of a riot, and a well-known and possibly wealthy man named Jason was drawn out and taken into custody. Once he was released, the Christians had to sneak Paul and Silas out of the city by night.

Perhaps this ties into our passage. I imagine that Paul's detractors argued that he was being a coward by leaving in the middle of the night. Surely he should have been bold and should have gone into the middle of the city to preach Christ. Of course, Paul did this in other circumstances, but in Thessalonica he chose to leave quietly. This was a lesson for the Thessalonian believers, and they undoubtedly learned from that particular experience of the Apostle Paul. These Christians needed to be as cautious about how they lived as Paul was in his departure.

This also seems to be something that Paul addressed in other situations. A notable example is 1 Timothy 2:1–4. Paul urges us to pray "for all people, for kings and all who are in high positions, that we may lead a peaceful and quiet life, godly and dignified in every way" (vv. 1, 2). And the result in verse 4 seems to be that people will come to the faith. Peter describes the same situation for a marriage when he encourages wives to win their husbands "without a word" but by their conduct, which demonstrates "the imperishable beauty of a gentle and quiet spirit" (1 Peter 3:1–4). The point in both cases is that it is a Biblical notion for Christians to influence non-Christians by their quiet and humble life. In our culture sometimes Christians stir up problems for themselves because they do not know when to back away from an issue. We often say it's a sign of conviction to be bold in what we say, but such boldness can also be a sign of foolishness and can create bigger problems because we are not living a quiet and humble life before the Lord.

The second command Paul gives here is that we are to "mind your own affairs" (v. 11), or as the NIV puts it, "to mind your own business." These first two commands seem to be connected. We might say they are two sides of the same coin. Paul seems to clarify this command to do our own work in 1 Thessalonians 5:14: "And we urge you, brothers, admonish the idle." Some people in the Thessalonian church had become idle, which means they were not working with their hands. Instead of doing their own work, they were meddling in the affairs of other people. This continued to be a problem, for Paul explains in his second letter, "For even when we were with you, we would give you this command: If anyone is not willing to work, let him not eat" (3:10). The problem is "idleness" (2 Thessalonians 3:11), or perhaps a better translation would be that they are walking "disorderly." They are not "busy at work, but busybodies" (2 Thessalonians 3:11). What should such people do? Paul commands them "to do their work quietly and to earn their own living" (2 Thessalonians 3:12).

Now it seems that there are several problems taking place at one time in this situation. There is a problem with people not working. Since they do not work, they cannot earn a living, and this puts a strain on the life of the church. But their lack of work does not mean they are just sitting at home. Instead they are "busybodies." They are worrying about areas that are not their concern. Paul is talking about the kind of person who does not do his or her work but just hangs around while you are trying to do your work. So their not working creates a strain on the church both financially and relationally. Again this produces a situation that is not in line with the love that should be expressed within the community.

Paul's third command is to "work with your [own] hands" (1 Thessalonians 4:11). There are important connections here. Paul urges them to live a quiet life, which means they should mind their own business as well as work with their own hands. These commands in verse 11 are connected to a bigger problem in this church. There was something going on in the life of the church that was producing this situation. To be honest, we are not exactly sure what the cause was. There are several options. Some have said there was a shortage of work in the city. But the problem seems to be, as John Stott says, that the "idle are unwilling, not unable, to work."[5] Others argue that the church had accepted the Greek disdain for working with your hands, and what developed was a super-spiritual view of life that claimed Christians should be preaching and teaching and studying and evangelizing, not wasting their time working. Others point out that these Christians were confused over the second coming of Christ. Since they thought he would come back quickly, some quit their jobs, sold their homes, and waited for Jesus to return. But when he didn't come back, the church had to help these Christians get their lives back together.

One recently discovered possibility related to patron-client relationships within the church.[6] This is based on the idea that there were wealthy people in this church, according to Acts 17:4. Some women were apparently wealthy, and Jason was probably well-to-do since he had the room to house Paul, Silas, and Timothy. When some in the church are wealthy, it is often tempting to take advantage of them. Since they have money, we reason, surely they would not mind helping us out with our struggles. This is a real temptation lurking within the heart of men and women, and Paul is addressing this from a Christian perspective. If we approach others in that manner, we are not loving them. We are not living a quiet life, nor are we minding our own business and working with our hands. We are trying to put ourselves in a situation in order to benefit from the wealth of someone else.

Perhaps there was a combination of these issues, but whatever specific situation caused this problem, Paul's solution was the same: "aspire to live quietly, and to mind your own affairs, and to work with your hands" (v. 11). We want to avoid the temptation of never helping someone when they are in need, but we also want to avoid the problem of creating a needy situation. We all have different personalities and different perspectives on life. We are all different in various ways. So let me present brotherly love to you like this: if you are the kind of person who tends to be nosy and you want to know everything that is taking place in the church, this passage is telling you to mind your own business. On the other hand, if you are the kind of person who is very comfortable with your little world, if you do not want to bother others or others to bother you, then this passage is pushing you to move toward your brothers and sisters in a spirit of love. If you do not know what kind of person you are, ask a friend or ask your spouse. Or you could talk to a pastor or respected spiritual leader. However this manifests itself in our lives, this is precisely the way we are called to love one another.

WHAT IS THE RESULT?

Paul does not give us bare commands — he also provides reasons why we are supposed to live this way, and in this case he gives us two. First, Paul tells us that we are supposed to live this way so that we might "walk properly before outsiders" (v. 12a). This is an important reason for the way we are called to live. Paul worked with his own hands as a tentmaker, and some scholars now think that the way Paul did evangelism was through his work.[7] Weima explains:

> It is commonly assumed that Paul won converts by preaching in the marketplaces ("street corner" evangelism). Nevertheless, there is good evidence his missionary work took place in the workshop and the private home. We can picture the apostle in Thessalonica laboring in a local workshop, perhaps one owned by Jason (Acts 17:5). During the long hours at his workbench, cutting and sewing leather to make tents, Paul would have had opportunities to share the gospel with fellow workers, customers, and other citizens who were interested in this tentmaker-philosopher newly arrived in the city.[8]

We are called to live and work in that same manner so that non-Christians can see how we live and how we work. That is the primary means of drawing people to Christ. They can see the reality of the gospel in the way we live and work. This provides a missional thrust to the entirety of our lives.

The second reason Paul gives is in the last phrase of verse 12: "so that you may . . . be dependent on no one." Why does Paul give this command? I think there are two reasons. First, to be dependent upon someone else in the congregation is unloving. That has been Paul's point since verse 9, and he presses the conclusion upon us: it is a loving act to be self-sufficient in regard to our own work. But perhaps Paul has another reason in giving this command. As Christians we are called to be dependent upon the Lord to provide our daily bread, and if we get in a situation where we are dependent upon someone else, it could cause us to compromise some Christian convictions. This could compromise our walk before outsiders.

Here is Paul's point: if we live in a way that reflects brotherly love, it will be obvious to the people we come into contact with in our culture. We will not have to loudly proclaim our faith to outsiders, but they will see our lives. In the city of Thessalonica, everyone would have noticed the change of lives in these Christians. They didn't participate in religious ceremonies and sexual immorality in the pagan temples. They didn't cheat each other or strangers. They worked hard, they took care of each other, and they loved each other. If you want your faith to be evident to those around you, Paul says, live in this sacrificial way, a way that reflects the love of Jesus to other people.

A LIFE OF GROWTH AND SACRIFICE

As we conclude this section, let's remind ourselves of the big picture from Paul's point of view. Paul has been pressing a particular theme upon us since the beginning of chapter 4: "Finally, then, brothers, we ask and urge you in the Lord Jesus, that as you received from us how you ought to walk and to please God, just as you are doing, that you do so more and more." This theme is an emphasis on pleasing the Lord in our lives. Although Paul is addressing the specific areas of sexual immorality and brotherly love, those concerns fit within the broader framework of his two perspectives on the Christian life. The first is Christian growth. These Christians were walking in a way that pleased the Lord, and Paul urged them to "do so more and more." Paul called upon them not to be satisfied with their present state as Christians but to keep growing. The Christian life does not have a point at which we attain total maturity in this life. We do not stop growing as Christians. If we think we are doing what Paul describes in this passage, we must not stop. We must not grow weary in doing well but rather continue to follow the path that Jesus Christ has laid out for us.

The second area Paul highlights is the importance of a sacrificial life. This would be the Christian virtue of unselfishness. The Christian life is marked, to a great degree, by sacrificial living, and we need to hear that message over and over because we are inherently prone to be self-centered. This is demonstrated in Paul's opening words in 1 Thessalonians 4: "Finally, then, brothers, we ask and urge you in the Lord Jesus, that as you received from us how you ought to walk and to please God . . . " What's the goal here? Is the goal to please ourselves? No. Clearly we are called as Christians to please God. We should each consider these questions: Am I living a life that pleases God? Are my priorities in order? Or is my life consumed with myself and what I want? How am I using my gifts and abilities? Am I using them in the service of the Lord or in my own service? Am I living a God-centered life or a self-centered life?

Why is this so important? Why should we live this type of sacrificial life? Because we follow the One who sacrificed himself for us. We follow the One who gave up everything that he had in order to bring us to God. That's at the root of why we obey these things.

We should thank the Lord Jesus Christ that he did not decide to watch out for himself when he came to this world, but that he had the thought of our redemption, our forgiveness, our future on his mind when he went to the cross. May we imitate that kind of love to others.

13

The Second Advent of Christ

1 THESSALONIANS 4:13–5:11

Advent is the period of time that leads up to Christmas, and the season of Advent emphasizes our anticipation of the coming of the Lord. The English word *advent* is derived from the Latin *advenire*, "to come to." Often you will hear the first coming of Jesus Christ called the first advent, and the second coming of Jesus Christ the second advent.

In our culture Advent has been mostly forgotten. Although some Christian traditions continue to practice the season of Advent, others follow the culture and allow Advent to be swallowed up by the consumeristic notion of Christmas. The Christmas season seems to begin earlier and earlier each year, starting in November and even in October in many shopping centers. One of the problems with Christmas coming so early is that it plays into the notion of our culture being one big holiday. We live a life that allows us to get the things we need at any time. There is no waiting and saving. We have credit cards, and we can buy things at the spur of the moment. Instead of waiting in anticipation by saving, we can buy now and pay later. But that kind of mentality makes us worse Christians because one of the fundamental aspects of the Christian faith is patience and waiting. We are to wait patiently upon the Lord to act. He doesn't do things on our time schedule. We must wait for him to fulfill his promises. The struggle is that we rarely wait for anything, and that spirit and mentality has a direct bearing on our Christian lives.

This is the importance and significance of understanding the season of Advent. Advent emphasizes the hope we have in the coming of the Lord, and the Lord comes to us in several different ways. The Lord came to us in the Incarnation, when he was born of the Virgin Mary. The Lord also comes to us regularly in our own lives as Christians, but specifically on the Lord's Day as we gather to worship. Finally, the Lord will come to us at the end of this age when he will make all things new. The purpose of Advent is to remind us of Christ's first coming and to help us remember that he will keep his promise to come again to judge evil and wickedness in this world and to deliver his church.

Advent is not the same as Christmas, and the hymn "O Come, O Come, Emmanuel" is a good reminder of the themes of Advent. We sing,

> O come, Thou Rod of Jesse, free
> Thine own from Satan's tyranny;
> From depths of hell Thy people save,
> And give them victory o'er the grave.

Do you see the hope in those words, the eager anticipation that one day God will completely free us from Satan's tyranny? Or again:

> O come, Desire of nations, bind
> In one the hearts of all mankind;
> Bid Thou our sad divisions cease,
> And be Thyself our King of Peace.

We pray in this song that the King might come to end our divisions and bring peace. And then we cry out, "Rejoice! Rejoice! Emmanuel shall come to thee, O Israel." Emmanuel shall come again, and the season of Advent focuses upon that theme. In 1 Thessalonians 4:13–5:11 Paul explains the second advent of Christ, and he gives us hope in the face of our trials as we confidently wait for Christ to return.

As we examine the section of 1 Thessalonians that concerns the second advent of Christ, I want to provide a word of caution. Christians often go to extremes regarding this doctrine. It is a significant focus of the teaching and preaching in some churches. I grew up in an environment that stressed "biblical prophecy," especially when earthquakes and floods occurred. Every time something happened in the Middle East, more excitement would develop about the possibility of Christ coming very soon. We would have conferences with elaborate teaching on Russia and Iraq and Iran and how Christ would come back within the current generation.

This kind of teaching ironically produced both excitement and fear. There was a great deal of excitement and anticipation because this might be the one prophecy that is left to be fulfilled. But it also produced fear because it was based on the most recent news media report and the attempt to figure out what it meant for Christ's coming. Very little of the teaching started with the Scriptures. Instead it started with a report from the Middle East and worked back into Scripture.

During the first Gulf War, under the first President Bush, there was excitement about what was taking place. Many people in my church environment were saying that this was the beginning of the end. They were pointing to a book by John Walvoord titled *Armageddon, Oil and the Middle East Crisis*. This was in 1990. The description of that book says this:

> Never before in history has there been such a chain of events signaling the approach of Armageddon: war in the Middle East; nuclear technology in the hands of rogue states; instability in oil markets; terrorist attacks on U.S. soil; threats to wipe Israel "off the map"; and alliances between Russia and Middle Eastern nations. . . . These troubling world events confirm the forecasts made by Dr. John F. Walvoord, widely recognized as the "father of modern biblical prophecy." His predictions once seemed beyond the realm of possibility — until they began to happen. John Walvoord correctly predicted Israel's establishment as a nation. He foresaw that the Iron Curtain would fall. He warned us that oil would make the Middle East the center of world conflict.

As I looked into these claims, I discovered that this book was first released in 1974, around fifteen years before the first Gulf War! And fifteen or more years after that event, the book was revised again in 2007 to reflect the current crisis in the Middle East and was republished as *Armageddon, Oil, and Terror*.

I came out of that Christian environment, and after I moved away from those particular views about the second coming of Jesus Christ, I went to the other extreme and seldom considered the second coming. I was not making the connections between the second coming and my Christian life. I didn't understand the importance of the second coming and my life today as I face suffering and trials. The turning point in my own life came when I connected the second coming of Jesus to Advent and the hope and anticipation that surrounds that season. I realized that the second coming was not something that needed to be figured out by watching the nightly news report, but a cherished truth that provides comfort and encouragement for the faith.

Paul can help us understand the second coming in that way. This section of his letter provides an opportunity for us to see our Christian faith in light of the second coming of Christ. We want to see how it can strengthen our faith and encourage us in our journey as pilgrims in this life.

THE SECOND ADVENT OF CHRIST WILL HAPPEN

A study of the second advent of Christ provides information about the future. You can see this immediately in verse 13: "But we do not want you to be uninformed, brothers. . . . " Paul does not want us to be confused about the future. God is in control of history, and he is taking it to a specific goal. I start with this point because I do not want us to take this for granted. We know how this story will end. In the midst of our suffering and trials right now, we know what the future holds. Paul is specifically addressing the concern we have about those who had "fallen asleep," believers who have died physically. He does not want us to be confused concerning the death of our friends and loved ones. They are part of God's plan as well.

THE SECOND ADVENT OF CHRIST GIVES HOPE (4:13)

A study of the second advent of Christ also provides hope for the future. Paul says, "But we do not want you to be uninformed, brothers, about those who are asleep, that you may not grieve as others do who have no hope" (1 Thessalonians 4:13). This is an important statement that we often take for granted. Let's put ourselves in the first century with these Christians, living only twenty years or so after the death, resurrection, and ascension of Jesus Christ. Perhaps we think that we will see Jesus return. But then people start to die in our church. This is not how we expected the end to come, so Paul helps us: "that you may not grieve as others do who have no hope." Paul is saying two things in that statement. First, he is saying that it is right for a Christian to grieve, but out grief must be in the context of the hope of the gospel. In the midst of our grief, we should have hope as Christians.

What is the ground of that hope? Paul explains, "For since we believe that Jesus died and rose again, even so, through Jesus, God will bring with him those who have fallen asleep" (v. 14). The basis of our hope is that Christ died and rose again. Did you see how Paul connected the first advent to the second advent? Since Jesus died and rose again, and since those who believe upon Christ are in him, though they die, they will be raised again. The first advent (Christ's life, death, and resurrection) provides the basis for the hope of the second advent (when we will be raised from the dead).

THE SECOND ADVENT OF CHRIST BRINGS CLARITY (4:14–17)

A study of the second advent of Christ clarifies the events that will take place when Jesus returns. We see this in verses 14–17. Again, consider what it would have been like to be sitting in Thessalonica and hear these words: "For since we believe that Jesus died and rose again, even so, through Jesus, God will bring with him those who have fallen asleep" (v. 14). Imagine what it would be like to hear those words for the first time. Is it possible that Paul is saying that Christians who are currently dead will be raised from the dead and will come back with Jesus? Indeed he is, and he adds to it that we will join them in this resurrection: "For this we declare to you by a word from the Lord, that we who are alive, who are left until the coming of the Lord, will not precede those who have fallen asleep" (v. 15). What good news! The dead in Christ will rise first; then we will join them in the clouds.

What brings us clarity about the second advent is the sequence of events that Paul is describing. Christians will die in this life before Jesus returns. Believers who have died will come back with Jesus in the second coming. When the Lord returns, he will raise the dead first. Then those alive will ascend to the Lord. After that is accomplished, we will always be with Christ. This should provide confidence in the future because we know what will take place.

THE SECOND ADVENT OF CHRIST PROVIDES COMFORT (4:18)

A study of the second advent of Christ also provides comfort. The word translated "encourage" in verse 18 is the word for "exhort," and that has led some to translate it as "comfort" in this particular passage since we are dealing with the grief we face when loved ones die.[1] This is the reason Paul explains these events. He does not want us to be uninformed because he wants us to be comforted. His words are meant to strengthen our faith and provide hope, and hope is the basis of encouragement. We all struggle with our faith, with obedience and assurance. But we forget that we have been so influenced by the gospel that we live with a constant sense of hope.

The pagans in Paul's time had no way to comfort each other in the face of death because they had no hope. Their sense of hopelessness is reflected in this statement by Theocritus: "Hopes are for the living; the dead have no hope."[2] Or consider a second-century letter written by an Egyptian lady named Irene to a grieving couple as they faced the death of their son. After explaining they have done everything they can in those circumstances, she concludes her letter this way: "But nevertheless, against such things one can do nothing. Therefore, comfort one another. Farewell."[3] She ends with the same words as Paul — comfort one another — but it is an empty comfort. It is not grounded on hope. Only the gospel provides comfort for the living because the dead have hope in the coming of Jesus Christ. That is the practical and pastoral benefit of the second advent when we see it in light of the gospel.

THE SECOND ADVENT OF CHRIST PRODUCES DILIGENCE (5:1–7)

Studying the second advent also produces diligence. This seems to be Paul's point as we turn to chapter 5. Paul describes the second coming of Christ by using two images — the sudden labor pains of a pregnant woman and a thief. Both of these are illustrations of moments when we are surprised or caught off guard. Although a pregnant woman knows labor is coming, the actual labor pains are a surprise. The thief is also trying to catch you by surprise. Paul's point is that we are not in darkness about the second coming. We know it is coming, but we do not need to know the specific times and seasons. "So then let us not sleep, as others do, but let us keep awake and be sober" (5:6). This is the opposite of unbelievers, who are asleep and are not paying careful attention to their lives. So a study of the second coming should produce a life of diligence.

THE SECOND ADVENT OF CHRIST BRINGS SALVATION (5:8–10)

The second advent of Christ will bring us the hope of salvation, not wrath. Paul describes the Christian's life as having the breastplate of faith and love and the helmet of salvation (v. 8). By these descriptions, Paul prepares us for the life of faith as well as for the revelation of Jesus. On that day when Jesus returns, we will not receive the wrath of God. When everyone is judged by Jesus Christ, we will not be destined for the wrath of God. Instead Christ has granted us salvation, and that salvation has happened because Christ died for us. So the second coming of Jesus clarifies our understanding of salvation and the hope we will have when we stand before Christ.

THE SECOND ADVENT OF CHRIST PROVIDES ENCOURAGEMENT (5:11)

Finally, the study of the second advent of Christ will bring encouragement and will build us up in the faith. Paul uses the same verb *parakaleo* here as he used in 1 Thessalonians 4:18 ("encourage"). Whereas Paul was emphasizing consolation and comfort in the face of death in chapter 4, here he is emphasizing encouragement because some are fainthearted in anticipation of the second coming of Jesus.[4] In this context he is seeking to build up the Thessalonians.

Remember that the doctrine of the second advent of Christ is a doctrine that helps us live the Christian faith. Some of the crucial truths of the Christian faith are bound up with the second advent of Christ — comfort, hope, faith, the resurrection, encouragement. We are called to wait patiently for Jesus, and this is hard for us to do because we seldom have to wait for anything in our culture. But at the heart of the Christian faith is a patient waiting on God's promises. We pray,

> *O come, O come, Emmanuel,*
> *And ransom captive Israel,*
> *That mourns in lonely exile here*
> *Until the Son of God appear.*
> *Rejoice! Rejoice!*
> *Emmanuel shall come to thee, O Israel.*

As we study the second advent of Christ, let us be reminded of the need to cultivate a patient and enduring hope that looks beyond this world to the world to come.

14

Resurrection Hope in the Face of Death

1 THESSALONIANS 4:13–18

In *The Silver Chair*, C. S. Lewis tells the story of two children named Jill and Eustace, along with a funny little character named Puddleglum, who go through a great adventure to find Prince Rilian, the son of King Caspian. They discover that Prince Rilian is being held captive in the Underworld by a witch who can turn into a green serpent. After Prince Rilian is released and kills the green serpent, he leads the others through a series of tunnels in an attempt to reach the outside world and hopefully make it back to Narnia.

As they are traveling, they face the constant threat of death, and at one point Prince Rilian says, "Courage, friends. Whether we live or die Aslan will be our good lord."[1] As he encourages them each step along the journey, the focus is not on whether they live or die but on the irrefutable truth that Aslan is a loving lord. Whether they survive that journey or whether they die in the Underworld will not change the nature of Aslan: he cares about them.

Prince Rilian's statement made a lasting impression upon me. As I reflected on his words, I wondered if I could honestly say that about Jesus Christ. Can I say that whether I live or die, or whether a loved one lives or dies, Jesus Christ is and will be my good Lord? I think this is one of the crucial tests of faith in the Christian life. Will we believe that Jesus is a loving Lord no matter what trial we face?

One of my duties as a pastor is to teach and preach in such a way that my hearers are prepared for death.[2] We will all face death when friends and relatives die, and we will have to walk with them through that ordeal. But we will also face death ourselves, and we need to be prepared. When the trial of death occurs, we must not turn away from Jesus and the gospel, thinking that he has let us down. We need to believe that whether we live or die, Jesus is a good Lord.

In order to believe that Jesus is good in both life and death, we have to understand what the Bible says about the reality of death and the hope of the resurrection. We do not need to avoid this difficult topic as Christians because we can confidently face death with the power of the gospel. Too frequently the church has allowed itself to be caught up in attempts by our culture to ignore pain and suffering and death. We have become experts at distracting ourselves from the fact that we will die. One way we see this is the very modern notion of a funeral as a "celebration of life." The service for the dead in Christ has moved from the pain of death and the hope of resurrection to a celebration of this life,[3] often minimizing the fact that our hope is not in death but in the resurrection. Although Christians can be thankful that those who are dead in Christ are no longer suffering, we must nevertheless realize that death is not the final destination: we await the hope of the resurrection and the reality of a new creation.

The church once believed that what was most relevant about its ministry in this regard was the process of preparing for death and proclaiming the resurrection. That is why funerals were once called "witnesses to the resurrection." Death is a reminder of sin and weakness, and we cannot avoid the pain and suffering connected to it. Those who do not believe in Jesus seek various ways of escaping grief and putting off the fact that one day they will die. But Christians can look death in the face and believe there is hope. We can be confident that death will not have the last word. The basis of our hope is that Jesus is a good Lord, that in his first coming he destroyed the power of death, and that in his second coming he will put an end to death and dying and will bring about resurrection.

In 1 Thessalonians 4:13–18 Paul's concern was precisely this issue — hope in the face of death. He was very pastoral because this church was confused on the matter of death, and they needed to understand the doctrine properly so that hope would inform their life and their understanding of the future. When Paul planted this church, he left the Thessalonians with a great deal of hope, not only in the midst of their suffering but also in regard to their future. But at some point the Thessalonians moved from hope to despair.[4] They were grieving about those who had died, and that sadness was perhaps causing them to question whether or not the gospel is good and Jesus is a good Lord.

Paul sought to inform them about this confusion regarding those who have "fallen asleep" (1 Thessalonians 4:14), which is terminology for someone who had died. Paul was addressing confusion over the matter of death in the life of this church. We don't know if these deaths were from natural causes or from persecution, but however they died, there was confusion about the future. Paul sought to clarify these issues and to provide hope in the midst of despair.

We are going to examine the nature of this resurrection hope and how this hope should shape our lives so we can believe that whether we live or die, Jesus is a loving Lord. We are going to see that the Christian gospel provides hope both for the living and for the dead, which was contrary to the pagan notion stated by Theocritus: "Hopes are for the living; the dead have no hope."[5] This gospel hope is rooted in a proper understanding of Jesus' first coming — his life, death, and resurrection — as well as his future second coming. This hope allows us to face whatever trials come our way.

CHRISTIAN HOPE DOES NOT IGNORE THE GRIEF

We should begin with this observation: Christian hope does not ignore the pain and grief. These are a normal part of life, and the hope that we have as Christians does not ignore pain but redeems it. Two central notions are bound up in the command of verse 13 that we need to realize as Christians. First, grief is part of life. God created humans with the capacity for relationships. So when we lose a relationship to death, there will be intense grief. We must not allow the pagan philosophy of Stoicism to sneak into the Christian faith by denying our emotions. Christians need to acknowledge the struggle of grief because it reflects the reality of loss in this sinful world. This also means, contrary to popular opinion in Christian circles, that death is not a celebration. Death is not the way it is supposed to be. Since Adam's sin, death is a judgment by God.

Second, although we must realize that grief will be part of the struggle of this life in the face of death, we must also grieve with confident hope. That is why Paul explains that we should "not grieve as others do who have no hope" (v. 13). Paul does not forbid us to grieve. On the contrary, he acknowledges the grief and tells us to grieve with hope. John Calvin says, "[Paul] does not, however, forbid us altogether to mourn, but requires moderation in our mourning."[6] Our Christian hope transforms the pain and grief to the point that we realize that death does not have the final word. This is why Chrysostom says, "Weep, then, at the death of a dear one as if you were bidding farewell to one setting out on a journey."[7]

CHRISTIAN HOPE IS GROUNDED IN CHRIST'S DEATH AND RESURRECTION

The second observation is that our hope in the resurrection is based on our connection to Christ's death and resurrection. Paul explains in verse 14, "For since we believe that Jesus died and rose again, even so, through Jesus, God will bring with him those who have fallen asleep." Paul notes a parallel between the death and resurrection of Christ and the death and resurrection of those who believe in Christ. The first part of the parallel is that "Jesus died," and Christians "have fallen asleep." The second part of the parallel is that "Jesus . . . rose again," and God "will bring [those who] . . . believe" with Jesus when he comes. We can structure the verse as follows to make the point:

| Jesus died | Christians who have fallen asleep |
| Jesus rose again | God will bring with Jesus the dead in Christ |

Paul is setting up this parallel to point out how powerful our union with Christ truly is. If Jesus died and rose again, that will also happen to Christians who believe in Christ. Robert Cara explains:

> When we make the logical connections between "Jesus died and rose up" and "God will bring those who slept through Jesus with him," it becomes clear that the latter expression actually makes two points: in the first place, those who are sleeping will be raised; and secondly, those who are currently sleeping will be fully brought in the presence of Christ ("him") at the Second Coming. Therefore, Paul's antidote to the grief of the Thessalonians is to remind them that believing in the reality of the death and resurrection of Christ also includes believing, on the grounds of their union with Christ, in the reality that dead Christians will not only be raised but will be bodily present with Christ at the Second Coming.[8]

Our resurrection from the dead is absolutely true because Jesus Christ was raised from the dead, and we are united to him.

This central doctrine of union with Christ is not unique to Paul's first letter to the Thessalonians; it is a doctrine that permeates all of Paul's letters. The doctrine of union with Christ was first realized by Paul on the road to Damascus when he met the resurrected Lord Jesus Christ, who said to Paul, "I am Jesus, whom you are persecuting" (Acts 9:5). Paul was persecuting the Christians, but the union between Christ and his people is so real that Jesus said Paul was persecuting him.[9] Believers are so united to Christ that their own life is his, and his life is theirs. This includes not only forgiveness but also resurrection. Paul articulates this in other verses as well:

- And God raised the Lord and will also raise us up by his power. (1 Corinthians 6:14)
- But in fact Christ has been raised from the dead, the firstfruits of those who have fallen asleep. For as by a man came death, by a man has come also the resurrection of the dead. (1 Corinthians 15:20, 21)

• . . . knowing that he who raised the Lord Jesus will raise us also with Jesus and bring us with you into his presence. (2 Corinthians 4:14)

Our hope is that we are united in Christ. When Christ died, we died. Christ was raised, so we will also be raised from the dead. Our hope is focused on Christ's death and resurrection.

CHRISTIAN HOPE IS FOCUSED UPON CHRIST'S PRESENCE

The third observation is that our hope is focused upon the very coming, or to be more precise, presence of Christ. We see this in verse 15: "For this we declare to you by a word from the Lord, that we who are alive, who are left until the coming of the Lord, will not precede those who have fallen asleep." The word "coming" is the Greek word *parousia*, which can mean "coming" but can also mean "appearance" or "presence." All three convey the meaning, but when we think of the coming of the Lord, we should not primarily think about his appearance. Instead we should think of the presence of the Lord. That is what Paul is getting across here. When Jesus appears, he will be present with us in a way that he is not now. He is Immanuel, God with us, and when he returns, he will fulfill the covenant promise that he will be a God to us and we will be his people. Greg Beale explains, "What has been traditionally understood as the second coming of Christ is best conceived as a revelation of his formerly hidden, heavenly 'presence.'"[10]

Although the root meaning of *parousia* is Christ's presence, the term itself has taken on a more technical meaning that signifies the second coming of Christ and everything connected to that event. When we talk about the *parousia* of Jesus, we are referring to his second coming. This also makes sense in terms of the way it is used in Greek and Roman literature outside of the Bible. *Parousia* designates the arrival of a dignitary. For example, when Caesar came to a city, his arrival would be described as the *parousia* of Caesar, or in Latin the advent (from *adventus*) of Caesar. In Corinth archaeologists found "advent coins" commemorating Nero's visit to Corinth with the inscription *Adventus Augusti Corinthi*, which means "the Advent of Caesar Augustus in Corinth."[11] This coin was made during Paul's lifetime, so Paul was not creating a word here. He was using something his contemporary audience would know in order to describe the coming of Jesus Christ. The coming of the Lord will be similar to the coming of Caesar (or another dignitary) to the city of Thessalonica. And when Jesus comes, we will be in his presence.

There is a very obvious statement here that we take for granted. Imagine for a moment that we are Christians living in the first century, and we have no knowledge of this event. Paul explains to us that those who are alive when Jesus returns will not precede those who are dead. Instead the dead in Christ will be raised first. This is a profound and significant truth that we cannot take for granted. Paul indicates that those who are alive at the coming of Jesus do not have an advantage over those who are dead. Because we live two thousand years after this was written, we take our knowledge for granted. But the hope we have for those who have died, that they will be present with Jesus on that day, comes from this verse.

CHRISTIAN HOPE IS CONSISTENT IN LIFE OR DEATH

The fourth point is that our hope does not change whether we are dead or alive. This might be a surprise, but part of Paul's broader point here is that the living and the dead have the same hope — the resurrection. Those who die are living with Jesus Christ in what we often call Heaven. As far as we can tell from the Bible, Heaven is a dimension of reality that is invisible to us right now. When Christ returns, "The old world reality will be ripped away, and the dimension of the new, eternal reality will appear along with Christ's 'presence.'"[12] In their current state, the dead in Christ are spirits waiting to be reunited with their bodies at the resurrection. Christian theologians call this "the intermediate state," the state of the dead between death and resurrection. Anthony Hoekema provides a good summary of the Christian tradition on the intermediate state: "Since the time of Augustine Christian theologians have taught that between death and resurrection the souls of men enjoy rest or suffer affliction while waiting either for the completion of their salvation or the consummation of their damnation."[13]

What is often confusing and misleading for Christians is that we see so much hope in death that we think this intermediate state is a final destination, but it is a temporary destination. This "state" is not the new heaven and the new earth described in Revelation 21. Let's make the distinction between the intermediate state that we often call Heaven, the place where believers go when they die, and the eternal state, the new heaven and the new earth, where we will all receive glorified bodies after the resurrection.

Some have wondered if Paul thought he would be alive at the advent of Jesus because of his language: "we who are alive" (v. 15).[14] This perspective is not necessary because Paul is using what we often call a plural "we," just as I am using in this book. Paul is speaking in terms of a collective identity regarding everyone in the community. We can see another example of this in 1 Thessalonians 5:10: ". . . that whether we are awake or asleep we might live with him." Notice that Paul uses the plural "we" with the idea of whether we are alive or dead. Paul is not dead while he is writing this, but he is anticipating what will one day happen. Robert Cara explains, "Paul is using 'we' to mean whoever is alive at the Second Coming. He is unsure whether or not he himself will be among them, as his use of the expression 'thief in the night' (5:2) implies."[15]

Nevertheless, Paul's point here is that whether we are alive or dead when Jesus comes back, Jesus will bring with him a completely new reality bound up in the resurrection. In verses 16–18 Paul provides a sequence of events: 1) the Lord himself will descend from Heaven, 2) the dead in Christ will rise first, 3) we who are alive will be caught up together with them in the clouds, 4) and so we will always be with the Lord. The point of this sequence is to help us see that the dead in Christ will not miss out on the resurrection hope; in fact, they are eagerly anticipating it.

Our hope as Christians is not eclipsed by death. We believe in the resurrection of our body because Jesus Christ was raised from the dead. Death does not determine our fate, and it is not the determining factor in regard to the goodness of Jesus Christ. He has overcome death. So whether we live or die, Jesus is our good Lord.

15

What about the Rapture?

1 Thessalonians 4:16–18

When we deal with the second coming of Jesus Christ in 1 Thessalonians 4, it is necessary to pause and consider what some Christians call "the rapture." In order to examine this, it is necessary, at least on some level, to distinguish between different views about the future and about Christ's second coming. There are three main views about the coming of Christ: premillennialism, amillennialism, and postmillennialism.[1] Of course, the common root word in each term is *millennium*, which we get from the Latin word meaning "thousand." Everyone is trying to figure out when Jesus Christ will come back in relation to his thousand-year reign on earth.

Premillennialists believe that Jesus will come back *before* the thousand-year reign described in Revelation 20. Once Jesus returns he will usher in the Millennium. Amillennialists believe that the thousand-year reign is a symbolic number pointing toward Christ's reign from Heaven *now*. So the church age is the Millennium, and when Christ returns, he will bring about the new heaven and the new earth. Postmillennialists believe Jesus Christ will come back *after* the thousand-year reign. They also see that period of time as a symbolic number pointing toward a future day when the gospel will bring about an age of peace and prosperity on this earth before Jesus returns. There are different variations of these views, but those are essentially the main perspectives.

One of the unique views associated with this passage in 1 Thessalonians 4 is a version of the premillennial view called dispensationalism.[2] Most evangelicals are familiar with this view even if they don't know the term, especially if they grew up under the influence of the *Scofield Study Bible*. Since 1995, this view has been popularized in the fictional novels of the Left Behind series, written by Tim LaHaye and Jerry Jenkins. Sixteen volumes of the main Left Behind series are available, forty books in the Left Behind: The Kids series, as well as movies, video games, music CDs, and other resources. Many evangelical Christians hold the views presented in these books. The series is called Left Behind because it is a warning that if you do not trust Christ and follow him, you might be "left behind" when he returns to take his saints home in a secret rapture.

DESCRIPTION OF THE RAPTURE

At the heart of the view is this notion of a secret rapture. Seven years before the second coming of Jesus Christ occurs, a secret rapture will occur when Jesus takes Christians out of this world. They will just disappear. Perhaps you have seen videos showing clothing left behind, cars without drivers, planes without pilots, and massive catastrophes as the world tries to figure out where all these people went. This sets the stage for a seven-year period of tribulation when trials and sufferings get worse and worse. According to this view, that seven-year tribulation period is described in Revelation 4–19, with chapter 20 being the beginning of the Millennium when Christ actually returns.

What makes this view unique is that the rapture is not really the second coming. According to this particular view, the events described in 1 Thessalonians 4:16, 17 are not describing the second coming of Christ but this secret rapture. So we are going to examine this concept of a rapture in light of this passage. When I first studied this in detail, I was surprised that this view of the rapture was based on this passage. In fact, I was surprised to discover that the word *rapture* was not in the Bible, although just because a word is not in the Bible does not mean it isn't Biblical. The concept of a "rapture" comes from the word "caught up" in verse 17: "Then we who are alive, who are left, will be caught up together with them in the clouds to meet the Lord in the air." That is the Greek word *harpazo*, which means "to seize, catch up, snatch away." The word *rapture* is an English word derived from the Latin term *rapio*, which is the translation of "caught up" in verse 17 in the Vulgate translation.[3]

To be fair to dispensationalists, they argue that other passages describe the details of the second coming of Jesus, in Daniel and Revelation and Ezekiel. They also construct a theology of a pretribulational rapture from other passages, but then they argue that this passage, 1 Thessalonians 4:17, is *the* description of that event. For the other dominant views of Christ's second coming, there is no distinction regarding the timing of this event. The rapture takes place during the time of Christ's second coming. But in this particular view called dispensationalism, the event described in 1 Thessalonians 4:16, 17 is a unique event that is called "the rapture," and it is different from the event described in Matthew 24:29–31 or any other passage that describes the second coming.

Because of this view and its popularity, we are going to look closely at this passage, but I want us to be careful how much we put into verses 16, 17. Let's not load it up with elements that might not actually be in the passage; this passage cannot bear the weight of a pretribulational rapture that some writers place on it.[4] Gordon Fee provides a helpful caution when he notes that verse 17 in particular has "unfortunately . . . been the source of a great deal of eschatological speculation that is quite unrelated to Paul's own interests." When Paul speaks of the living who are left (v. 16), it has "nothing to do with anyone's being 'left behind'; rather, it simply describes the living from the perspective of those who have died, who are, after all, the primary reason for the passage at all."[5] Let's unpack the images that Paul uses to describe the return of Christ and keep Paul's concern to provide comfort and encouragement in the forefront of our interpretation.

FIRST IMAGE: THE SOUNDS

The first image to note involves the sounds associated with this event. Paul says in verse 16, "For the Lord himself will descend from heaven with a cry of command, with the voice of an archangel, and with the sound of the trumpet of God." Three images are associated with these sounds: a cry of command, the voice of an archangel, and the trumpet of God. Some argue that these terms all describe the same sound,[6] but I think they might be separate descriptions, as do other commentators such as Robert Cara: "Christ's shouting a command to the dead Christians; an additional general announcement of the Second Coming by an archangel; and a general trumpet blast related to the Second Coming."[7]

This also reads like a very public event, and that has always been a hang-up for me in seeing this passage as describing a secret rapture. In fact, the terms used to describe the noise are intentional by Paul. He seems to be making the point that this event is as public as the events in the Old Testament were when God sounded the trumpet for his people. In Psalm 98, the trumpets and the sound of a horn remind the people of God to make a joyful noise before the King as he comes to judge the earth (vv. 6–9). Other Old Testament passages describe the sound of a trumpet to proclaim the presence of the Lord as the Lord comes to battle his enemies and save his people. The trumpet is part of the military images in the Old Testament, such as in Zechariah 9:14: "Then the Lord will appear over them, and his arrow will go forth like lightning; the Lord God will sound the trumpet and will march forth in the whirlwinds of the south." The trumpet declares battle and judgment, and Joel in particular ties the sounds of the trumpet to the great and terrible Day of the Lord: "Blow a trumpet in Zion; sound an alarm on my holy mountain! Let all the inhabitants of the land tremble, for the day of the Lord is coming; it is near" (Joel 2:1). So the sounds imply a public event, and the specific use of the trumpet connects this description in 1 Thessalonians 4:16 with "the day of the Lord" in 1 Thessalonians 5:2.

Gordon Fee observes that Paul pulls together a "collage of items, from Scripture and Jewish apocalyptic on the one hand, and from the 'coming' of kings/emperors on the other."[8] Two more significant passages seem to be behind Paul's words. First, Paul is connecting the second coming to Psalm 47:5, which Fee translates, "Ascended God with a shout, the Lord with the 'voice' of a trumpet." Psalm 47:5 is the passage that speaks of Yahweh's enthronement at the temple in Jerusalem; thus Paul is tying that passage to the enthronement of Christ. Second, Paul is alluding to the theophany of Yahweh in Exodus 19:16: "On the morning of the third day there were thunders and lightnings and a thick cloud on the mountain and a very loud trumpet blast, so that all the people in the camp trembled." Notice that this is described with both a loud trumpet blast and a thick cloud, which connects us to the next image.

SECOND IMAGE: THE CLOUDS

Again, we have to see the Old Testament background for the image of the clouds. In the Old Testament, God's presence was demonstrated by the "glory cloud." We just saw this with the theophany of Yahweh in Exodus 19:16, which tied together the trumpet and the clouds. But there are also other significant passages that demonstrate the meaning of Paul's use of clouds.

- Exodus 16:10 describes God's glory appearing in the cloud: "And as soon as Aaron spoke to the whole congregation of the people of Israel, they looked toward the wilderness, and behold, the glory of the Lord appeared in the cloud."
- Psalm 104:3, 4 uses cloud imagery to describe the coming of the Lord on his chariot: "He lays the beams of his chambers on the waters; he makes the clouds his chariot; he rides on the wings of the wind; he makes his messengers winds, his ministers a flaming fire."
- Daniel 7:13 describes the coming of the Son of Man on the clouds of heaven: "I saw in the night visions, and behold, with the clouds of heaven there came one like a son of man, and he came to the Ancient of Days and was presented before him."

All this language in the Old Testament goes back to the glory cloud of the Lord with the children of Israel and other examples of God's presence being signified by clouds or smoke (such as Genesis 15). When we tie the trumpet blast and the cloud together, we get a picture of the coming of Jesus that is similar to the great comings of the Lord in the Old Testament, an event that will bring about the end.

Paul's use of the image of meeting Jesus in the clouds (1 Thessalonians 4:17) could be talking about literal, physical clouds, but based on these passages from the Old Testament, Paul is probably talking about the presence of the Lord on the day of his coming, and he uses cloud imagery to help us see that we will be enveloped into the presence of the Lord, just as the glory cloud came over the temple. This is precisely how the Old Testament helps us understand the New Testament. The more we understand about the Old Testament, the deeper our understanding of the New Testament will be. The more we know the images found in the Bible, the more exciting it is to read the Scriptures. When we read the language here in 1 Thessalonians 4, we should think about the temple and the cloud coming over the temple, and we should realize that when Jesus comes, it will be the fulfillment of God's glory cloud, God's presence coming to his people.

THIRD IMAGE: MEETING THE LORD

The third image concerns our meeting with the Lord. Where do Christians go after they meet Christ in the air? What happens after we meet Jesus? The text doesn't explicitly say where we go. It doesn't say we go up or go down, but Paul may have clued us in with the word "meet" (*apantesis*, 4:17). In secular literature this word is a technical term used to refer to citizens of a city who go out to "meet" an approaching dignitary and then follow him into the city.[9] This is connected to the term *parousia*. This word was used to describe the appearance of Caesar in the city. If this word "meet" is the same word that is used when Caesar appears, then the citizens go out to "meet" him and escort Caesar back into the city. Paul could be giving us an image of what Jesus will do when he returns. Jesus will appear and gather his saints in the air, and they will come back with him to the earth.

To be sure, Christians disagree on passages like this, and those who think there is a rapture followed by a seven-year tribulation period will not agree with this interpretation. But I think this fits well with what Paul is saying about the *parousia* of Jesus. When Christ appears, we will greet him as the King and then come back with him to the earth. This is consistent with the way the word is used in other passages of the New Testament. In Acts 28:15, when Paul is coming to Rome, Luke says, "And the brothers there, when they heard about us, came as far as the Forum of Appius and Three Taverns to meet [*apantesis*] us." After meeting Paul, the brothers escorted him back into Rome. If this is the intended metaphor, then this is the image we have: "as Christ comes towards earth (the city), but before he reaches it, his people come out to greet him as they meet in the air. Then Christ leads the procession to earth (into the city) with the people."[10]

FOURTH IMAGE: FOREVER WITH THE LORD

The fourth image that Paul gives us is one of permanence, and this is a healthy reminder to us of what really matters in this discussion. Whether I was right or wrong about meeting the Lord in the air and coming back with him to the earth, I would not want our geographical location to be the concern here. It is not our geographical location that matters. Paul's interest is not whether we are in Heaven or on earth. His overriding concern is that we will be with the Lord forever. This is the ultimate fulfillment of the covenantal language: God will be our God, and we will be his people.

Too often location becomes a primary concern when believers discuss these eschatological points. We have debates about the plot of land in Palestine and whether the Jewish people will inherit that land in the future. We have discussions about the nature of the earth — whether it will be completely burned or whether it will be renewed. Those discussions sometimes help us clarify issues that are addressed in Scripture, but we cannot lose sight of the focus: we will be with Jesus forever. Even Abraham realized, when he received the promise of land, that his hope was not an earthly city but a heavenly city, a place where God dwells (Hebrews 11:8–16). No matter what our eschatological arguments are concerning the details of this event, let us not lose sight of the fact that our ultimate desire is to be with Jesus Christ, our Lord and our God.

> "Behold, the dwelling place of God is with man. He will dwell with them, and they will be his people, and God himself will be with them as their God. He will wipe away every tear from their eyes, and death shall be no more, neither shall there be mourning, nor crying, nor pain anymore, for the former things have passed away." And he who was seated on the throne said, "Behold, I am making all things new." Also he said, "Write this down, for these words are trustworthy and true." (Revelation 21:3–5)

16

The Day of the Lord

1 THESSALONIANS 5:1–2

In our study of Christ's second coming, we must pause and consider an important phrase that Paul uses in this passage. "The day of the Lord" is an expression used throughout Scripture that refers to God's judgment and the defeat of his adversaries, as well as the salvation of his people. Because of its use in Scripture, we need to understand the Old Testament background before we can understand it in our New Testament passage; so we must examine the concept of "the day of the Lord" from a biblical-theological perspective. This approach is different from a topical study because we will be tracing this idea as it developed in the history of God's work of redemption. When we come back to 1 Thessalonians 5, we will have this Old Testament background in place so we can properly understand what Paul is teaching us.

Meredith Kline points out that the concept of the Day of the Lord begins in Genesis 3:8. We might find this strange because popular translations read that God came walking in the garden "in the cool of the day." Kline points out that this misses the element of judgment in that passage. The Lord was not casually walking up to have a conversation with Adam and Eve. He was coming in judgment because of their sin. Kline points out several features of this passage that clue us in to this judgment. First, the word for "sound" in the passage is the same word used to describe the voice or sound of God, which is a terrifying experience. It was the sound Israel heard that day at Sinai, which included lightnings and thunders, when the mountain burned with fire and the whole mountain quaked (Exodus 19:16–18). After Kline surveys these various passages, he explains:

> Whether it is the sound of the advancing Glory or the sound of the Lord's speaking from the midst of the Glory, the *qol yhwh* is characteristically

loud, arrestingly loud. It is likened to the crescendo of ocean and storm, the rumbling roar of earthquake. It is the noise of war, the trumpeting of signal horns and the din of battle. It is the thunder of the storm-chariot of the warrior-Lord, coming in judgments that convulse creation and confound the kings of the nations.[1]

God was coming in judgment on Adam and Eve, and that was why Adam and Eve hid.

Second, the phrase translated "in the cool of the day" is a translation of an obscure phrase, and Kline believes it is misleading. After examining several parallels in Scripture, Kline translates Genesis 3:8 this way: "They heard the sound of Yahweh God traversing the garden as the Spirit of the day." The sound of God indicated to Adam and Eve that God was coming in judgment. This indicates that the coming of the Spirit on that day was a foreshadowing of the coming of the Lord on the day of judgment. The conclusion is that Genesis 3:8 is what Kline calls a "primal *parousia*," the beginning of what Scripture later calls "the day of the Lord."[2]

Kline's argument is very convincing, and if he is right, we have a pattern established in Genesis 3:8 regarding the day of the Lord, a day when God comes in judgment that can result in condemnation or salvation. But the expression "day of the Lord" receives the most detail from the prophets. Isaiah describes the day of the Lord as a day when the Lord comes to judge a nation in history. In Isaiah 13 the prophet receives an oracle concerning Babylon. He hears the sound of tumult and an uproar of kingdoms as nations gather together. The Lord of hosts is coming for a battle, so Isaiah says:

> Wail, for the day of the LORD is near; as destruction from the Almighty it will come! Therefore all hands will be feeble, and every human heart will melt. They will be dismayed: pangs and agony will seize them; they will be in anguish like a woman in labor. They will look aghast at one another; their faces will be aflame. Behold, the day of the LORD comes, cruel, with wrath and fierce anger, to make the land a desolation and to destroy its sinners from it. For the stars of the heavens and their constellations will not give their light; the sun will be dark at its rising, and the moon will not shed its light. (Isaiah 13:6–10)

In this case, the day of the Lord is a day when God comes to judge Babylon. But notice the description: "the stars of the heavens and their constellations will not give their light." That sounds like the end of the whole world. And again Isaiah says that "the sun will be dark" and "the moon will not shed its light." When "the day of the LORD" comes, it is a day of judgment that will foreshadow the end-times judgment.

We see this also with the prophet Jeremiah. He received a word from the Lord concerning Egypt and the army of Pharaoh Neco, king of Egypt. Jeremiah explained that God will put Egypt to shame and judge the nation: "That day is the day of the Lord GOD of hosts, a day of vengeance, to avenge himself on his foes" (Jeremiah 46:10). The coming judgment upon Egypt is described as the day of the Lord. Ezekiel speaks of the day of the Lord as well when the word of the Lord comes to him: "Son of man, prophesy, and say, Thus says the Lord GOD: Wail, 'Alas for the day!' For the day is near, the day of the LORD is near; it will be a day of clouds, a time of doom for the nations. A sword shall come upon Egypt, and anguish shall be in Cush, when the slain fall in Egypt, and her wealth is carried away, and her foundations are torn down" (Ezekiel 30:2–4). We see several themes in these passages that are common with Genesis 3:8 — loud sounds, the coming of God, and the use of "the day."

Let's consider what God is revealing in the Bible. The day of the Lord can be an event in the Old Testament like the judgment of Babylon or the judgment of Egypt. But we also know from our passage in 1 Thessalonians 5 that the day of the Lord is a day of great judgment coming on the whole world. We can understand both of these truths as the way God designed history. Judgments in history foreshadow future judgments. The way it is described in Jeremiah is that the sky gets dark and everything seems to be coming apart. That judgment on Egypt, as bad as it is, is a foreshadowing of the judgment God will bring on the great day of the Lord when he judges the whole world. Each historical event is a foreshadowing of what is to come.

Another way to look at this is through our own personal lives. When we go through difficult trials and tribulations, those events produce one of two responses. We either grow in thankfulness to the Lord, or we become bitter and angry. If we experience a tragic event or a trial, we will either trust God to see us through the trial and grow, or if we turn away from God in unbelief, we get bitter and frustrated and angry at God.

The trials we face now, however, are nothing compared with the judgment at the end. But God in his grace allows these trials to function as fire that refines us as Christians, and we are called to trust the Lord and obey and grow through the process. "Count it all joy, my brothers, when you meet trials of various kinds, for you know that the testing of your faith produces steadfastness. And let steadfastness have its full effect, that you may be perfect and complete, lacking in nothing" (James 1:2–4). All of our trials should cause us to be thankful to the Lord God that we will not have to suffer through his fiery judgment on the great day of the Lord because we know Christ. So the day of the Lord functions in both of those ways. Events in history are called "the day of the Lord" because they foreshadow the future great day of the Lord.

Zephaniah helps us see these connections. In his prophecy of the day of the Lord, we see some similarities with Paul's language in 1 Thessalonians.

> The great day of the Lord is near, near and hastening fast; the sound of the
> day of the Lord is bitter; the mighty man cries aloud there. A day of wrath
> is that day, a day of distress and anguish, a day of ruin and devastation, a
> day of darkness and gloom, a day of clouds and thick darkness, a day of
> trumpet blast and battle cry against the fortified cities and against the lofty
> battlements. (Zephaniah 1:14–16)

Here Zephaniah describes the day of the Lord as a day of destruction
and darkness and judgment, but did you notice any other connections with
Paul? Zephaniah also mentions that it is "a day of clouds" and "a day of
trumpet blast and battle cry." Remember what Paul said in 1 Thessalonians
4: the coming of Christ is a day of clouds and a day of trumpets and the cry
of commands. These similarities help point us beyond the historical event
to the final event, the great day of the Lord.

The prophet Joel demonstrates this clearly. His whole prophecy is a
reminder of the judgment of God. The children of Israel have not lived
faithfully, and God will judge them. Joel begins by describing an invasion of
locusts, and then we come to the passage about the day of the Lord:

> Put on sackcloth and lament, O priests; wail, O ministers of the altar. Go in,
> pass the night in sackcloth, O ministers of my God! Because grain offering
> and drink offering are withheld from the house of your God. Consecrate
> a fast; call a solemn assembly. Gather the elders and all the inhabitants of
> the land to the house of the Lord your God, and cry out to the Lord. Alas
> for the day! For the day of the Lord is near, and as destruction from the
> Almighty it comes. Is not the food cut off before our eyes, joy and gladness
> from the house of our God? (Joel 1:13–16)

Joel tells us that priests and ministers were called to repentance because
Israel had been so wicked that the Lord was coming to judge them. They
must repent because the day of the Lord is near.

Here is an example in which the day of the Lord was coming upon
Israel at that point in their history, but this experience has similarities to
the great day of the Lord. One of the central images in the book of Joel is a
terrible locust plague that affected every area of life — food, animals, and
economics. But this locust plague was not an end within itself. Instead it was
a metaphor for the day of the Lord. As bad as the locust plague was, the day
of the Lord will be far worse! Notice how Joel described this coming day:

> Blow a trumpet in Zion; sound an alarm on my holy mountain! Let all
> the inhabitants of the land tremble, for the day of the Lord is coming;
> it is near, a day of darkness and gloom, a day of clouds and thick dark-
> ness! Like blackness there is spread upon the mountains a great and pow-

erful people; their like has never been before, nor will be again after them through the years of all generations. Fire devours before them, and behind them a flame burns. The land is like the garden of Eden before them, but behind them a desolate wilderness, and nothing escapes them. (Joel 2:1–3)

Here we have an image of the blowing of a trumpet and a call to repent because the day of the Lord is coming. It is described as a day of darkness and gloom, a day of clouds and thick darkness. This should sound familiar. It is the same imagery reflected in 1 Thessalonians 4:16, 17. Again, Joel uses more imagery that is picked up in the New Testament — earthquakes, the sun and the moon darkened, the stars withdrawing, the Lord uttering his voice. Who can endure the day of the Lord? (Joel 2:10, 11)

As the prophecy unfolds, in spite of this terrible day of judgment there is an element of hope. If you repent, you will escape that great day of the Lord. Notice what the Lord says immediately after this picture of judgment:

"Yet even now," declares the LORD, "return to me with all your heart, with fasting, with weeping, and with mourning; and rend your hearts and not your garments." Return to the LORD your God, for he is gracious and merciful, slow to anger, and abounding in steadfast love; and he relents over disaster. Who knows whether he will not turn and relent, and leave a blessing behind him, a grain offering and a drink offering for the LORD your God? (Joel 2:12–14)

In the middle of the coming day of the Lord, there is hope. In the middle of judgment and devastation, the people are called to return to the Lord and to seek his mercy and grace.

As we turn to the New Testament, we find the fulfillment of Joel's prophecy in Acts 2 on the Day of Pentecost. On that day, as Jesus was pouring out his Spirit upon the church, Peter proclaimed, "this is what was uttered through the prophet Joel," and he then quoted Joel 2:28–32:

And in the last days it shall be, God declares, that I will pour out my Spirit on all flesh, and your sons and your daughters shall prophesy, and your young men shall see visions, and your old men shall dream dreams; even on my male servants and female servants in those days I will pour out my Spirit, and they shall prophesy. And I will show wonders in the heavens above and signs on the earth below, blood, and fire, and vapor of smoke; the sun shall be turned to darkness and the moon to blood, before the day of the Lord comes, the great and magnificent day. And it shall come to pass that everyone who calls upon the name of the Lord shall be saved. (Acts 2:17–21)

There is something very important bound up in this prophecy. At each day of the Lord event, we can see both the threat of judgment and the hope of salvation. The day of the Lord is a day of judgment on those who do not believe, but salvation for those who do believe. Meredith Kline pointed this out with the Genesis 3:8 passage and the "*parousia*-presence" of the Lord. The day of the Lord involves judgment on God's enemies and salvation for God's people.[3]

The New Testament provides for us the first stage of the fulfillment of the day of the Lord. Malachi had prophesied, "'Behold, I will send you Elijah the prophet before the great and awesome day of the LORD comes.' And he will turn the hearts of fathers to their children and the hearts of children to their fathers, lest I come and strike the land with a decree of utter destruction" (Malachi 4:5, 6). When was this event fulfilled? It was fulfilled in the coming of Jesus. The opening of the Gospel of Mark indicates this:

> The beginning of the gospel of Jesus Christ, the Son of God. As it is written in Isaiah the prophet, "Behold, I send my messenger before your face, who will prepare your way, the voice of one crying in the wilderness: 'Prepare the way of the Lord, make his paths straight.'" (Mark 1:1–3)

The day of the Lord comes in the work of Jesus Christ. But when? Do we see a day of judgment and salvation? Where, in the life of Jesus Christ, can we see the great and terrible day of the Lord? The cross is that day of the Lord. On the cross Jesus takes our judgment and provides our salvation. For those who look to Christ, there is salvation. For those who turn away from the cross, there is judgment.[4]

This all unfolds as we come back to 1 Thessalonians. What we have seen is the background of this phrase. The day of the Lord will be a day of judgment and fire, a remaking of the heavens and the earth, but those who believe will be saved. That is why Paul says in 1 Thessalonians 5:9, "God has not destined us for wrath, but to obtain salvation through our Lord Jesus Christ." When the final and great day of the Lord comes, we will not receive wrath if we are children of God. According to Paul, we are in the light regarding that day, and we have the breastplate of faith and love, and we have the helmet of salvation (v. 8). We have been found in Christ and forgiven. We do not have to fear that day, for it is the day of our salvation.

But we must not be caught unawares when he comes. We must live diligently, with faith and repentance in anticipation of the coming of the Lord. The Lord comes to us on the Lord's Day, the day of worship, and we draw near to him in confession and receive forgiveness. The Lord comes to us through the week, and he draws us near to him. The Lord comes to us as we face death, in order to see us through that valley.

The reason we call this message good news is because on that great day, on the day of the Lord, on that day of wrath and fire and judgment, there is hope, there is salvation. If we believe on Christ, he will see us safely through that day.

If you have not yet come to Christ, don't turn away from this warning. Trust Christ now. Confess your sins now. Receive forgiveness now.

17

Concerning Times and Seasons

1 THESSALONIANS 5:1–11

For many years John Stott was the pastor of All Souls Church (Anglican) in London and a well-known evangelical leader across the world. In his commentary on 1 and 2 Thessalonians, he observes that two distinct problems have always fascinated human minds. He writes, "The first relates to what happens after death. Where are our loved ones, and shall we see them again? The second relates to what will happen at the end of the world. Is there going to be a day of reckoning, and if so, how can we prepare for it? The first is the problem of bereavement, and concerns others who have died. The second is the problem of judgment, and concerns us as well."[1]

That is a helpful summary of 1 Thessalonians 4:13–5:11. In chapter 4 Paul answered the first question by explaining that those who have died in the Lord are with the Lord, and they will be part of the great day of resurrection. If you trust in Christ, you have hope in the face of death. But as we turn to chapter 5, Paul shifts to a slightly different focus, although he continues with the same theme of Christ's coming. Now his point concerns those who are alive when Jesus returns. Paul tells us what to expect on that day of reckoning and how we should prepare for it.

It is clear from 1 Thessalonians 5:1–11 that Paul had taught these Christians something about these truths when he was with them. Paul writes, "Now concerning the times and the seasons, brothers, you have no need to have anything written to you. For you yourselves are fully aware that the day of the Lord will come like a thief in the night" (vv. 1, 2). These Christians in Thessalonica had already been taught some aspects of the coming judgment. Paul says that they were "aware" that Jesus will come like a thief in the night. It is not hard to imagine that Paul would have taught these Christians the Old Testament background of the day of the Lord, explaining that Zephaniah warned us that the day of the Lord will come with wrath (Zephaniah 1:14–16), and Joel describes it as "the great and awesome day of the LORD" (Joel 2:31), though at the same time providing hope in the midst of that judgment for those who repent and turn to God (see Joel 2:12–14).[2]

THE PROBLEM OF "TIMES AND SEASONS"

As we think about this coming day, this day of reckoning, we want to be ready. So how do we prepare for that day? It seems that the Thessalonian Christians had a solution for that day of reckoning — they wanted to know a date! It seems that one of the questions that Timothy brought back from this church was a question about when the day of the Lord will take place. "Now concerning the times and the seasons, brothers, you have no need to have anything written to you" (v. 1). Why didn't they need something written to them about times and seasons? Paul says in verse 2, "For you yourselves are fully aware that the day of the Lord will come like a thief in the night." In other words, the reason not to write about the times and the seasons is that we simply do not know when they will happen.

In spite of not knowing, it has been tempting for the church to try to fig-ure out the times and seasons; this is not just the error of the Thessalonians. This is the same thing that the apostles asked Jesus in Matthew 24:3 and at the beginning of Acts (1:6). After being told by Jesus and Paul that we do not need to worry about times and seasons, we might think that is enough. Surely we would not keep trying to figure out when Jesus is coming back . . . right? And yet we continue to guess at the dates and to struggle with this. We reason that if we just knew the date, we would be ready! So we continue to set dates for the coming of Christ.

In 1988 I was in middle school, and I distinctly remember standing on a hill outside our school talking to several other students about the return of Christ. A former NASA engineer named Edgar C. Whisenant had writ-ten a book titled *88 Reasons Why the Rapture Will Be in 1988*,[3] which predicted that Jesus would return to rapture his church during the Jewish holiday of Rosh Hashanah on September 11–13, 1988. Many evangelicals took Whisenant's predictions seriously, and by some estimates his book sold over four million copies. The Trinity Broadcasting Network (TBN) actually interrupted their regular programs in order to help Christians prepare for the rapture.[4] When it did not happen, Whisenant shifted the date to October 3. When that date failed, he told *Christianity Today*, "The evidence is all over the place that it is going to be in a few weeks anyway."[5] When the rapture did not occur, Whisenant continued to predict a date in 1989, 1993, and 1994.

Oddly enough, this has been very tempting for Christians throughout church history. In *The Last Days Are Here Again: A History of the End Times*, Richard Kyle documents that end-times prediction and speculation has been a repeating temptation throughout church history.[6] Every time there is conflict in the Middle East, every time there is a conflict over oil, every time a significant leader arises on the world scene, "end-times experts" come out to predict that this is the moment Jesus will return. I even discovered a website called The Rapture Index.[7] Here is a description of the purpose of that website:

> The Rapture Index has two functions: one is to factor together a number of related end time components into a cohesive indicator, and the other is to standardize those components to eliminate the wide variance that currently exists with prophecy reporting.
>
> The Rapture Index is by no means meant to predict the rapture, however, the index is designed to measure the type of activity that could act as a precursor to the rapture.
>
> You could say the Rapture Index is a Dow Jones Industrial Average of end time activity, but I think it would be better if you viewed it as prophetic speedometer. The higher the number, the faster we're moving towards the occurrence of pre-tribulation rapture.
>
> Rapture Index of 100 and Below: Slow prophetic activity
> Rapture Index of 100 to 130:   Moderate prophetic activity
> Rapture Index of 130 to 160:   Heavy prophetic activity
> Rapture Index above 160:   Fasten your seat belts

The chart documents various reports of false Christs, the occult, unemployment, inflation, interest rates, the economy, ecumenical ventures, globalism, Israel, Russia, Persia (Iran), volcanoes, earthquakes, plagues, and on and on we could go.

PAUL'S SOLUTION #1: BE READY

Paul's words in 1 Thessalonians 5 are a warning against such behavior. His short answer is that we simply cannot know the precise timing of the coming of Christ, so we should not speculate. In order to demonstrate this, Paul gives us two illustrations or metaphors about the coming of the Lord. First, the day of the Lord will come like "a thief in the night" (v. 2). The problem with a thief is that you do not know when he is coming. The thief does not tell you. You are taken by surprise, and that element of surprise is heightened if it occurs during the night.

Paul confirms this when he goes on to write in verse 3, "While people are saying, 'There is peace and security,' then sudden destruction will come upon them." We see two things taking place in this illustration. First is the language of "peace and security." Whenever talk of peace and security takes place in a country or across the world, some Christians get very nervous because it seems to be the beginning of the end. With the development of the United Nations and other peacekeeping organizations, many Christians believed that Jesus was coming back soon.

We need to question this attitude because peace and security are good things. We should be thankful for them. We should encourage attempts to make peace all across the world. But we must realize that the problem with this type of peace is that it is not rooted in the gospel. Paul's point here is that as Christians we cannot find true peace unless it comes through the gospel. We cannot rest our faith and our hope on a false peace. The immediate concern in this passage is the city of Thessalonica and the Roman Empire. Do you remember what happened in Acts 17:6–8? Some of the Christians were accused of turning the world upside down. That is not the language of peace. So the city leaders told these Christians to stop preaching the gospel and talking about their King, Jesus, because that would disrupt the peace and freedom in Thessalonica. "Caesar has brought peace and security, and you are turning the world upside down." But the Christians were saying no, their opponents didn't understand true peace and security. The peace of Rome, *Pax Romana*, is a false peace. We cannot bank our hope on peace that comes from the kingdoms of this world.

So the first illustration here is telling us not to find peace and security outside of the gospel, and this is a word of warning to us. Many Christians in the United States of America are deceived into thinking that they have peace and security because our country has a strong military and powerful resources, but they are deceived. Those things can be idols, and we dare not find our peace in the strength of a country or a kingdom because the kingdoms of this world are nothing before the Lord. Paul's point is that when people are calling for peace and security outside of the gospel, we can be confident that it will not last. Sudden destruction will come upon us if we bank our hope on the kingdoms of this world.

Paul's second illustration is also found in verse 3: "sudden destruction will come upon them as labor pains come upon a pregnant woman, and they will not escape." The point of this illustration is to emphasize the suddenness of Christ's coming. When labor pains happen, there is a certain degree of surprise, but a pregnant women knows she is pregnant. In other words, she knows that labor is coming — she is just not sure precisely when.

John Stott helpfully draws these two illustrations together by pointing out that although both are sudden, the thief is unexpected, but the labor is expected. He explains, "So, putting the two metaphors together, we may say that Christ's coming will be (1) sudden and unexpected (like a burglar in the night), and (2) sudden and unavoidable (like labor at the end of pregnancy).

In the first case there will be no warning, and in the second no escape."[8] An important point about both of these illustrations is that you can make preparations. You can have a plan for a thief, such as a safe and a burglar alarm, and you can have a plan for the pregnancy, such as having your bags packed and friends on call. And that leads to Paul's next point about how we should live.

PAUL'S SOLUTION #2: STAY ALERT

As we turn to verses 4–8, Paul provides another solution: we should stay alert.

> But you are not in darkness, brothers, for that day to surprise you like a thief. For you are all children of light, children of the day. We are not of the night or of the darkness. So then let us not sleep, as others do, but let us keep awake and be sober. For those who sleep, sleep at night, and those who get drunk, are drunk at night. But since we belong to the day, let us be sober, having put on the breastplate of faith and love, and for a helmet the hope of salvation.

Notice what he didn't say. He didn't say that one event will happen after another, then in thirty years Jesus will come back. That is not Paul's solution. His solution is not to guess dates but to stay alert.

This emphasis upon staying alert is evident in the imagery Paul uses — darkness and light, day and night, asleep and awake, drunk and sober. These images all emphasize alertness. In fact, the images of light rather than darkness are connected to the importance of being people who are alive in the age of the gospel. It seems that Paul is drawing from Isaiah with these images:

> Arise, shine, for your light has come, and the glory of the LORD has risen upon you. For behold, darkness shall cover the earth, and thick darkness the peoples; but the LORD will arise upon you, and his glory will be seen upon you. And nations shall come to your light, and kings to the brightness of your rising. Lift up your eyes all around, and see; they all gather together, they come to you; your sons shall come from afar, and your daughters shall be carried on the hip. (Isaiah 60:1–4)

Isaiah is contrasting two ages, two groups of people. Those who have received the glory of the Lord have received the light, and that light will penetrate the darkness of this world. If we lift up our eyes, we will see kings and nations coming to the light of the gospel.

I do not think that Paul's use of light and darkness is accidental in

1 Thessalonians 5. He is drawing on this prophetic tradition and tying it to the gospel. When Jesus was born, God used a star to guide the wise men to Jesus. That light is symbolic. The light has broken through the darkness of the old age, the darkness of Adam's sin. The light of the glory of God has broken upon the darkness, and we are living in the light. We are children of the day; a new day has dawned. We live with the knowledge that the light has broken forth on this world.

Paul brings his point to a conclusion in verses 6–8. With the knowledge that God has given us about the gospel, we have a responsibility to the world. Paul is dividing people into two groups — those who see the light and those who do not. Those who see the light need to live and reflect that reality: "So then let us not sleep, as others do, but let us keep awake and be sober" (1 Thessalonians 5:6). We must not ignore the coming of Jesus. We dare not pretend that it will never happen. Instead we must live with the expectation of seeing the fullness of the light. It doesn't matter if we are alive when Jesus actually comes back or not. That is not the point. The point is that we all, as Christians, must live with the knowledge that Jesus is coming.

Paul continues his image of a thief in verse 7: "For those who sleep, sleep at night, and those who get drunk, are drunk at night." Night, sleep, and drunkenness are at least three reasons why someone would be unprepared for a thief. In Paul's words, these images take on a spiritual dimension because these are examples of not being alert. As Christians, we are called to be alert, and Paul says that explicitly in verse 8: "But since we belong to the day, let us be sober, having put on the breastplate of faith and love, and for a helmet the hope of salvation." Paul has twice commanded us to be "sober" (vv. 6, 8). This means we are to be self-controlled and calm in spirit, especially as we await the return of Jesus Christ. The solution is not to know the day or the time, but to be prepared as a child of light for the day when the King breaks the light of the new heavens and the new earth upon this old creation.

Paul also explains that we have "put on the breastplate of faith and love, and for a helmet the hope of salvation." Paul uses the images of armor to highlight the crucial virtues of the Christian life — faith, hope, and love. But Paul is making an interesting statement here. Beale points out that Paul is making both a statement about our identity and our responsibility. He quotes from Gaventa, who renders the verse as follows: "Since we are children of the day, clothed with the breastplate of faith and love, and as a helmet the hope of salvation, let us be sober."[9] Beale then explains, "If the armor, indeed, is figurative for Christian virtues, then the question needs explicitly to be asked why Paul exhorts the readers to be self-controlled. The answer is that Paul is encouraging them to become what they already are in Christ and to grow even more in him."[10] We are called to live out of the reality of what Christ has done as we wait for the day of his return. Our hope is not based on the idea of figuring out the day. Our hope is based on the knowledge that he will return and that we are part of the children of the light who are prepared for that return.

KNOWING JESUS, NOT A DATE

Paul now concludes by helping us see the foundation of our hope. This is an important conclusion that should not be overlooked. When Jesus returns, it will be the great and terrible "day of the Lord." It will be a day of darkness and wrath. So what kind of hope will we have in that day? Paul reminds us of what God has done for us: "For God has not destined us for wrath, but to obtain salvation through our Lord Jesus Christ, who died for us so that whether we are awake or asleep we might live with him" (1 Thessalonians 5:9, 10). Do you see how this ties back to chapter 4? Paul has now reminded us that whether we are awake, which is what he has been talking about in chapter 5, or whether we are asleep, which is what he was talking about in chapter 4 regarding the death of Christians, our hope is the same — we will live with Jesus.

Paul does speak of God's wrath that will come with the day of the Lord; it is the wrath that God will unleash when Jesus returns. But on that day of judgment we have no need to fear. If we believe upon Christ, we have not been destined for that wrath. We have been destined for salvation because Jesus died for us. This good news gives us confidence and hope both now and for the future. Paul's main point is that as a child of the light and a child of the day, we are not destined for wrath. Christ died for us. Christ took the wrath of God upon himself on the cross, the darkness of sin and misery. He died for us so that we might live and so that we might live in the light.

We must not trust in the peace of our country. We must not trust in the power of our military.

Rather we must trust in Christ and find our peace and security in him.

Paul's concern is not that we know the times and seasons but that we know Jesus Christ.

18

A Gospel Community

1 THESSALONIANS 5:12–28

As we come to the end of Paul's first letter to the church in Thessalonica, Paul is concerned to leave these Christians with a picture of a gospel church. How should we conduct ourselves together, as Christians, in the community of the church? We could say that Paul has been doing this in the last few sections of his letter. In chapter 4 he describes a life that is pleasing to the Lord. Then he reminds us that we must see our trials and suffering from the perspective of the second coming of Jesus and the hope it provides. That hope provides the basis of our encouragement to one another in the community. These are examples of how we should live as Christians, but now Paul turns his attention particularly to life within the church.

John Stott called this section "Christian Community" or "How to Be a Gospel Church." The church is described as a family in the New Testament, and we are to treat each other as brothers and sisters. This concept of the family of God is an important theme for Paul in this section. At the very beginning of verse 12 Paul addresses these Christians as "brothers," and he continues that in verses 14, 25, 26, and 27. So this section is not just a lot of dos and don'ts, but this section is gospel life, the way brothers and sisters should live together in the church because they have been united to Christ. This is what life should look like because of the gospel. We have here something like family guidelines for the congregation, and Paul groups these guidelines under three sections regarding congregational responsibility: toward the pastor (vv. 12, 13), toward each other (vv. 14, 15), and toward worship (vv. 16–22).

THE CONGREGATION AND THE PASTOR

First, Paul addresses leaders in verses 12, 13. There has always been some tension in the church about its leadership. Sometimes in church history we see leaders placed in exalted positions that are not Biblical. At other times Christians want nothing to do with leadership within the church. These two extremes are always temptations for the church, but Paul wants us to understand that neither one is right. God has called and placed leaders within his church, pastors and elders to shepherd Christ's people; and Christ has delegated to these pastors the responsibility of oversight for his sheep.

Paul describes leaders in three ways. First, Christian leaders "labor among you." The ministry is a life of work. The word translated "labor" is the word for toil, a word used for farming in other passages. Ministers labor in the preaching and teaching of the Word, preparing sermons, visiting the sick, counseling, instructing, baptizing, marrying, and burying. It is mental and emotional labor. Other passages in the New Testament describe what this labor looks like in detail, but Paul's concern here is to stress the labor involved in pastoral ministry as hard work.

Christian leaders also have the responsibility to shepherd the people of God, which is Paul's point when he says they are "over you in the Lord." It is tempting to read this as a statement of control and power. Many leaders are tempted to lead that way. This charge, however, is not a charge of power. Gospel ministry must follow the pattern of Jesus Christ, who leads by serving. In the Gospels, Jesus taught that whoever wanted to be first in God's kingdom would be last, and at one point he told his disciples:

> You know that those who are considered rulers of the Gentiles lord it over them, and their great ones exercise authority over them. But it shall not be so among you. But whoever would be great among you must be your servant, and whoever would be first among you must be slave of all. For even the Son of Man came not to be served but to serve, and to give his life as a ransom for many. (Mark 10:42–45)

That is the call of the minister. To be great, the leader must serve. To be first, you must be the slave of all. Jesus himself did not come to be served but to serve us by giving his life as a ransom for us. Christian ministers are called to give their lives for the sheep and to lead by serving.

Finally, Christian leaders must admonish. This is a rather difficult part of the job, but it is essential. The Christian life is an ethical life. We believe the gospel and trust Christ, but we are called to live differently. Christian leaders are charged with the responsibility to instruct believers in the area of their conduct. This admonishment certainly happens when a minister preaches and warns the congregation against bad behavior and its consequences. In this letter Paul admonishes the disorderly or unruly (5:14), and he will do it again in his next letter to this church (2 Thessalonians 3:7–15). Pastors must be wise and cautious in how they admonish individuals because different people require different types of admonishment. We have to take into consideration the person who is sitting across from us. To admonish someone does not justify being harsh — there must be a concern for the person. Leon Morris explains, "while its tone is brotherly, it is big-brotherly."[1]

In some cases if the behavior does not change, the leaders of the church will have to take the next step beyond admonishment and possibly discipline someone in the congregation because of unrepentant sin. That seems to be the consequence of a continuing life of disorderliness. Paul says in his second letter, "If anyone does not obey what we say in this letter, take note of that person, and have nothing to do with him, that he may be ashamed" (2 Thessalonians 3:14).[2] Although this type of discipline is not popular, it has been part of the history of church ministry, and it is a crucial aspect of our growth and holiness. The neglect of this discipline diminishes the glory of the church, and as John L. Dagg once said, "It has been remarked, that when discipline leaves the church, Christ goes with it."[3] He said those words in the nineteenth century. How much more is the warning relevant for us today.

Paul now addresses the attitude of the congregation toward the leaders. Believers are not to exalt pastors or to despise them but are to offer respect and esteem to the minister because of the particular work he does. Even in the midst of disagreements and difficulties, there should be a combination of respect and affection, and if this is the attitude within the congregation, we will see the result that Paul describes in verse 13: "Be at peace among yourselves." Do you see what Paul is doing? How many times have churches and pastors gone head-to-head, and the result is devastation and sin and destruction to the body of Christ. That is not reflecting the gospel. If we believe the gospel and we believe Christ has forgiven us, we should be able to work through our difficulties with respect for one another. Pride destroys peace, but the gospel brings peace and well-being.

THE CONGREGATION AND ACTS OF LOVE

Paul now turns his attention to the church as a whole by addressing believers' responsibility toward each other in the church in verses 14, 15. One reason we know that Paul is shifting to the whole congregation is his use of "brothers" (v. 14). This charge is to the whole family of God, not just to the leadership of the church. These are the responsibilities that we have to one another, and this is a helpful corrective to a view that places too much responsibility at the feet of the pastor. Paul did give instructions regarding the role of the pastor, but now he is helping us see that it takes the whole body working together to bring true peace.

Paul describes three groups of people who need to be loved. First he says, "admonish the idle." The word "idle" here is not the best translation. The word does not mean "lazy," which is what we think of when we hear "idle." Greg Beale suggests that the word be translated as "disorderly" or "disruptive,"[4] and Gordon Fee suggests that the word be translated as "unruly."[5] This gets across the meaning that Paul intends. These Christians were out of order. Paul called them "busybodies" in his second letter (2 Thessalonians 3:11), and he encouraged them to "do their work quietly and to earn their own living" (2 Thessalonians 3:12). Such Christians disrupt the peace of the church, and they must be warned, not only for their own benefit but for the benefit of the whole body.

Paul also urges us to "encourage the fainthearted." Beale says that the word "fainthearted" literally means "the small of soul" or "the discouraged."[6] There were two primary reasons someone could be discouraged in Thessalonica. We know from the background of this church and from Paul's words that these Christians faced persecution. They could quickly become discouraged in their faith. But another reason they might be discouraged is because of death. Death is a disrupting of peace, and Paul has just explained to this church in chapter 4 that they should not grieve as those who have no hope in the face of death. The Christians in Thessalonica were anxious about their dead loved ones. Will they be saved? Paul answered that question and told them to encourage one another with his words (4:18). Now Paul is reminding us that in our gospel community, we need the encouragement of our brothers and sisters as we face these difficulties and trials. In our church we not only need to rejoice with those who rejoice, but we need to weep with those who weep.

Finally Paul urges us to "help the weak." We could understand the word "weak" here in a spiritual way and argue that Paul is telling us to help those who are weak in their faith, but it seems that Paul just addressed that concern with the phrase "encourage the fainthearted." If we back up and look at our three categories of ministry here, perhaps we can gain some insight into what Paul is saying. "Admonish the idle/disorderly" concerns those who are not living the way they should as Christians, the spiritually disobedient. "Encourage the fainthearted" concerns those who are struggling spiritually with discouragement. "Help the weak" then is the category of those Christians who have physical needs.[7] Perhaps the weakness is sickness or some economic difficulty. Instead of seeing this as a spiritual category of ministry, perhaps we should see this as a physical category of ministry, the area of service that would be provided by deacons in a church. We must be aware of the physical needs of those in our congregation and seek to help meet their needs.

Paul has two concluding remarks that draw this section to a close, and these two concluding remarks are connected to one another as we minister to each other. Paul concludes by telling us, "Be patient with them all." As we seek to minister to different types of Christians, those disobedient, those struggling spiritually, and those struggling physically, we need to be patient and minister to them in their own situations. We should not minister to them in the way we would want someone to minister to us. Instead we must consider each individual person and his or her struggles. Do you know what this really is? It is loving your neighbor. This is what loving your neighbor looks like — ministering to brothers or sisters where they are in their circumstances — and that requires patience. But Paul doesn't stop with the command to be patient. He adds, "See that no one repays anyone evil for evil, but always seek to do good to one another and to everyone" (v. 15). Why did Paul put this here? What does it have to do with ministry in the church?

Have you ever tried to minister to someone and your service was not appreciated or accepted? What temptation rises up in you at that moment? Vengeance. "I took all that time to serve you and this is what I get?"

When we minister to others, sometimes they return evil for good. There could be any number of reasons. Perhaps a brother or sister is having a hard time with a physical problem, and anger is what we receive back for our attempt at love. We must not be tempted to pay a brother or sister back with an evil response. When our service is not accepted, we must not be tempted to pay people back but rather seek to do good to them in the midst of their pain. We must seek to be Christ to that person, for we too have rejected the ministry of Christ at various points in our lives. We should not be surprised when others reject our service and love but instead take it as part of our growth in the faith and see it as part of keeping the peace of the church.[8]

THE CONGREGATION AND WORSHIP

Paul has addressed the relationship of the congregation to its leaders and the congregation individually to one another. Now he turns his attention toward the congregation corporately gathered in worship (vv. 16–22). At first sight this does not look like a passage on worship — it looks like a list of responsibilities toward God. Abraham Malherbe, one of the commentators on Thessalonians, even titled this section "Responsibilities to Oneself,"[9] and that prompted Gordon Fee to respond by saying that Malherbe seems to be reflecting Western individualism more than Paul.[10] I think Gordon Fee is right, and I too was pushing too much of my Western individualism into this text when I first started reading it. Fee provided some of the reasons why I now think that Paul is talking about the corporate life of worship in this section and not our individual life toward God.[11] Although we can certainly apply these insights to our individual lives, there are several reasons for seeing this passage as addressing the corporate life of the church.

First, all the verbs here are plural. So it seems that Paul is describing a collective and public act, not individual and private Christian duties. Depending on our geographical location, we would say, "You all" or "You guys." Secondly, the prophecy in verse 20 is a public act, an act that edifies the body. Third, the holy kiss found in verse 26 was a public greeting in the early church. Finally, verse 27 encourages the reading of this letter to everyone who was present. What we see here is that rejoicing, praying, and thanksgiving are acts of the church in worship.[12] This section is also used by Ralph Martin, a scholar of worship in the early church, as an example of elements in a worship service. Martin even says that this section reads like headings in a church service.[13]

Paul begins with three commands: "Rejoice always, pray without ceasing, give thanks in all circumstances" (vv. 16–18). Paul's commands are probably shaped by the Psalter, and the three acts of joy, prayer, and thanksgiving should be themes in our worship of the Lord.[14] The note of praise is an important part of worship, and we should express that joy with singing and prayers and thanksgiving. When Paul tells us to "pray without ceasing," this should be a characteristic of worship too. If we look at this in an individualistic way, this is a difficult command and impossible to fulfill. But in corporate worship we are to season the whole service with prayer, and that type of attitude should carry us through the week. The same is true with giving thanks. As these Christians gathered for worship in Thessalonica, they were subject to threats by the city leaders, but Paul called them to be thankful nevertheless. This expression of thankfulness in our worship overflows to our daily life. The pattern here is from corporate worship to private life.

Paul now moves us toward the importance of God's Word. John Stott titled this section "Listen to the Word of God!"[15] Although that exact expression is not used here, it is the topic Paul covers in verses 19–22. Paul has now moved from our worship directed toward God (rejoice, pray, give thanks) to our worship directed toward building one another up in the Word. The main issue Paul addresses here is prophecy. Gordon Fee translates verses 19–21 this way: "Do not put out the Spirit's fire. Do not treat prophecies with contempt, but test them all; hold fast to what is good, reject whatever is harmful."[16]

Prophecy is a controversial matter, and one of the difficulties in dealing with prophecy concerns the various views of it.[17] Older Puritans called preaching prophecy, highlighting the aspect of communicating the Word of God.[18] This makes sense because the prophets in the Old Testament were not primarily foretellers of the future but were forthtelling the Word of God. So preaching plays a prophetic role in the life of the church. The traditional Reformed view on prophecy argues that it died out by the time the canon of Scripture was finished.[19] A more recent view argues that prophecy has changed since the Old Testament and continued on in the New Testament and even today. This view has been popularized by Wayne Grudem,[20] but it is part of a broader movement called the Third Wave.[21] This movement emphasizes the revelatory gifts of prophecy, tongues and interpretation, words of wisdom, and words of knowledge. Perhaps this is a gift that allows an individual to have some level of insight into life or various situations, but they would call this insight prophetic.

Whatever view one holds, we need to acknowledge a distinction between the prophecy in the New Testament that ends up being the inspired Word of God and whatever the Spirit does with us in the life of the church after that period of redemptive history.[22] We must maintain a high view of the Word of God and its role in the explanation of nonrepeatable redemptive-historical acts of God.[23] One way to deal with this problem is to limit the word *prophecy* to those who were prophets in the New Testament and connected to the written Word of God. Then we could call our gifts and ministries "prophetic" to make a distinction.

As we examine our particular passage, we need to start with a basic distinction that is rooted in the text in 1 Thessalonians 5:20, 21 and in other passages of Scripture. We know that a certain type of prophecy becomes the Word of God. Prophets speak, and those words become Scripture. We also know there is a type of prophecy that has to be tested and compared with the Word of God. That is what Paul is teaching here. There is a distinction between a standard authority that is unchangeable (the Word of God) and something that must be tested (in this passage, prophecy).

If we are talking about our brothers and sisters from the charismatic tradition, we must acknowledge that Paul here commands that we test prophecy. The notion of prophets and prophecies in that tradition cannot go forth without being challenged. Those ministers and Christians must ensure that their words are in submission to the Word of God, and those words need to be tested and proved by God's Word. The traditions that do not submit to God's Word as the final authority are not following Paul's commands.

For those of us who are not part of the charismatic tradition, we too make statements about the Christian faith that have to be tested against the Word of God, and if they do not measure up to the Scriptures, that could be harmful to our faith. We should take the words of counsel that friends provide and test those words through Scripture. Godly advice and counsel must be tested through God's Word. It does not matter whether we are talking about sermons or counsel about life or friends at work who say, "God told me to tell you . . ." All of it must be tested by God's Word.

Now we can make a little more sense out of the final statements here. Remember, Fee translated them as "hold fast to what is good, reject whatever is harmful."[24] If we receive counsel that is good and is in line with Scripture, we should "hold fast" to it. If the counsel is harmful and not in line with Scripture, we should reject it. This is crucial in regard to preaching. The preaching and teaching from the pulpit must be scriptural. This becomes very clear in Paul's second letter. In 2 Thessalonians 2:1, 2 he writes to these Christians about the coming of the Lord, and he says, "We ask you, brothers, not to be quickly shaken in mind or alarmed, either by a spirit or a spoken word, or a letter seeming to be from us, to the effect that the day of the Lord has come." They had received a prophecy or something similar that said the day of the Lord had come. That was a harmful word. So Paul rejected it and provided the proper explanation of the day of the Lord.

GOD WILL DO IT

We have examined Paul's explanation of church life by looking at the life of the congregation in regard to its leadership, its love, and its worship, but we have also come to the end of our study on 1 Thessalonians and have reached Paul's concluding words. Throughout this letter Paul has addressed concerns regarding our doctrine and our life, what we believe and how we live. We have covered practical areas in the life of the church, and Paul has given us several commands about a life of faith that grows and trusts the Lord, a life of love that serves those in the church, and a life of hope that is confident in the future and knows that this life of faith, love, and hope is not an accident. The life of the church is formed by God in the context of the gospel. Faith, love, and hope are possible because of God's promise: "Now may the God of peace himself sanctify you completely, and may your whole spirit and soul and body be kept blameless at the coming of our Lord Jesus Christ" (1 Thessalonians 5:23).

Whatever God calls us to do, in terms of being obedient or loving one another, in terms of our relationships, our business practice, or sexual purity, all those commands that are included under what it means to live a life that pleases God (1 Thessalonians 4:1) must first of all be rooted in the gospel. If we do not grasp that, our whole life will be one of frustration. Paul came into Thessalonica with the message of the gospel, and he did not have the time to stay there and teach them all he intended; but Paul had confidence in God. God would continue the work and transform these Christians, and God has promised he will continue that work in our lives as well. When Paul wants to encourage us, he ties everything back to the gospel and explains, "He [God] who calls you is faithful; he will surely do it" (1 Thessalonians 5:24).

Let us be confident that God will keep his promises. God is faithful, and he will finish what he started.

19

The Right Perspective on Suffering

2 THESSALONIANS 1:1–5

Have you ever experienced a situation where the light came on and something suddenly made sense? Those experiences often produce a drastically different perspective on life. The famous American theologian Jonathan Edwards had an experience like this regarding the sovereignty of God. In his "Personal Narrative," Edwards describes his own experience this way:

> From my childhood up, my mind had been full of objections against the doctrine of God's sovereignty. . . . It used to appear like a horrible doctrine to me. But I remember the time very well, when I seemed to be convinced, and fully satisfied, as to this sovereignty of God. . . .
>
> But never could I give an account, how, or by what means, I was thus convinced, not in the least imagining at the time, nor a long time after, that there was any extraordinary influence of God's spirit in it; but only that now I saw further, and my reason apprehended the justice and reasonableness of it. However, my mind rested in it; and it put an end to all those cavils and objections.
>
> And there has been a wonderful alteration in my mind, in respect to God's sovereignty, from that day to this; so that I scarce ever have found so much as the rising of an objection against it, in the most absolute sense. . . . I have often since had not only a conviction but a delightful conviction. The doctrine has very often appeared exceeding pleasant, bright, and sweet. Absolute sovereignty is what I love to ascribe to God. But my first conviction was not so.[1]

He describes this change as an alteration in his mind. Edwards had a new perspective on God's sovereignty that made it now appear pleasant and sweet to him. This new view of the sovereignty of God allowed Jonathan Edwards to live with a different perspective on life.

This is precisely the kind of change we sometimes undergo in the Christian faith, a transformation that happens many times over the course of our spiritual journey. Perhaps you have had an experience similar to that of Jonathan Edwards concerning the sovereignty of God, and you have been able to find peace. I have had that type of experience not only with the sovereignty of God but also with a whole host of other Christian truths such as the doctrines of justification and union with Christ, to mention only two.

We should view Paul's letters to the Thessalonians as a pastoral attempt to change their (and our) perspective regarding several aspects of the Christian faith. For example, we can take the opening of the second letter as an attempt by Paul to help us gain the right perspective: "Paul, Silvanus, and Timothy, to the church of the Thessalonians in God our Father and the Lord Jesus Christ: Grace to you and peace from God our Father and the Lord Jesus Christ" (1:1, 2). The first change of perspective from this greeting is the very fact that Paul is writing them. Imagine the joy they would have had in hearing from Paul and in Paul's identifying them as "the church" in Thessalonica. They were the people who had been called out by God. They were God's outpost in Thessalonica.

Also notice that Paul is shaping their identity. These Christians in Thessalonica were "in God our Father and the Lord Jesus Christ." Is our perspective on the Christian life that we are hidden in God and that we participate in the love of the Godhead — the Father, Son, and Holy Spirit? This is how Paul viewed not only the Thessalonian Christians but also all Christians who have come after them, including us. This is the great doctrine of union with Christ. We have died, and "[our] life is hidden with Christ in God" (Colossians 3:3). If we let that perspective sink into our "spiritual bones," it will change the way we live.

Finally, Paul is encouraging us in this greeting to gain the right perspective on what God has done for us. Not only does he describe us as a church and as being hidden in the Father and the Son, but he says this is possible through the grace and peace of God. God's own action, God's own initiative, is undergirding our status before him. It is God's grace that has made us part of the church, and it is God's grace that has placed us in him. This is God's grace at work, bringing us peace.

FAITH, LOVE, AND HOPE

After the initial letter opening and greeting, Paul continues to refine our perspective on the Christian life, and he does so regarding the area of thanksgiving. This section is often called the "Thanksgiving Section." You can see this immediately in verses 3, 4: "We ought always to give thanks to God for you, brothers, as is right, because your faith is growing abundantly, and the love of every one of you for one another is increasing. Therefore we ourselves boast about you in the churches of God for your steadfastness and faith in all your persecutions and in the afflictions that you are enduring." Paul is giving thanks to God for three areas in the lives of these Christians: growing faith, increasing love, and steadfast hope.

When Paul speaks of growing *faith*, one of the things that he certainly means is our growth in the knowledge of God. Consider what Jesus said in John 17:3: "And this is eternal life, that they know you the only true God, and Jesus Christ whom you have sent." We should not quickly dismiss the fact that eternal life is knowledge of the one true God. This type of knowledge has a depth to it that does not just involve cognitive content in your head. This type of knowledge involves what we often call both the head and the heart.

After tying faith to our knowledge of God, it makes sense that Paul would now be thankful about their *love* for one another. Their faith in God was being evidenced by their love for each other in the life of the church. Jesus tells us that the Law and the Prophets depend upon two commandments: "You shall love the Lord your God with all your heart and with all your soul and with all your mind. This is the great and first commandment. And a second is like it: You shall love your neighbor as yourself" (Matthew 22:37–39). This love expressed in the church in Thessalonica was a sacrificial love. These Christians had faced terrible trials, and some were even thrown into prison. So sometimes love means leaving the confines of our homes to visit a brother or sister in jail. This love for one another has a practical aspect concerning areas we might have to face and a willingness to sacrifice for each other (see Hebrews 10:32–35).

Paul is also thankful for their steadfast *hope*. The word "steadfastness" (v. 4) means endurance or perseverance, and it is the same word Paul used in 1 Thessalonians 1:3. Although the word *hope* is not used in verses 3, 4, "The mention of faith, love, and endurance is in the same general order as in 1 Thessalonians 1:3, where the third element is expanded to 'endurance inspired by hope.' Therefore, 'hope' likely is implied in 'endurance' here, so that Paul's triad of faith, love and hope also commences this epistle."[2] In order to face the trials and sufferings that they were going through in Thessalonica, hope was a crucial element of their ability to persevere, and this last virtue turns our attention to trials and suffering.

THE DIFFICULTY OF TRIALS

Paul told this church that he was so thankful for them that he was boasting about them in the presence of other Christians, and Paul was boasting because these Thessalonians were being faithful in the face of persecutions and afflictions. Paul was boasting that in the face of persecutions from the unbelieving world and the general afflictions that result from the fall, these Christians in Thessalonica had the proper perspective on suffering and so suffered with hope. This is a crucial part of Paul's point in this opening section of 2 Thessalonians because it will help us get a proper perspective on suffering.

Let's consider the way we suffer as Christians. One of the best paradigms to explain the importance of perseverance in the face of trials is Jesus' parable of the sower and the seed in Matthew 13:1–9. Jesus described a sower who sows seed in four types of soil or ground. Three of the areas where the seed lands produce no fruit — the walking path, the rocky ground, and the thorns. Only one area produces fruit because it is good soil. Then Jesus explained the parable to his disciples:

> When anyone hears the word of the kingdom and does not understand it, the evil one comes and snatches away what has been sown in his heart. This is what was sown along the path. As for what was sown on rocky ground, this is the one who hears the word and immediately receives it with joy, yet he has no root in himself, but endures for a while, and when tribulation or persecution arises on account of the word, immediately he falls away. As for what was sown among thorns, this is the one who hears the word, but the cares of the world and the deceitfulness of riches choke the word, and it proves unfruitful. As for what was sown on good soil, this is the one who hears the word and understands it. He indeed bears fruit and yields, in one case a hundredfold, in another sixty, and in another thirty. (Matthew 13:19–23)

Please take note of the second and third explanations — the seed that falls on the rocky ground and the seed that falls among the thorns. Jesus gave us two reasons why the seed does not produce fruit there — trials (tribulation and persecution) and temptations (the cares of the world and the deceitfulness of riches). These trials and temptations can draw us away from the gospel of Jesus Christ and his church. Many have started the Christian life with blazing speed, wanting to teach and serve, but eventually drifted away from the church or completely turned away because of these issues.

GOD'S RIGHTEOUS JUDGMENT

Paul focuses on the area where Christians are often tempted to give up — the area of suffering. If we are going to guard our hearts against the temptation to turn away from Jesus when we suffer, we must have the right perspective on suffering and trials. Let's be honest. We are often tempted to see suffering as a negative situation or even as a judgment from God for our failure or sin. When we see suffering in that light, we are not looking at it through the gospel. Paul is going to help us get the right perspective on suffering: "This is evidence of the righteous judgment of God, that you may be considered worthy of the kingdom of God, for which you are also suffering" (v. 5).

We need to wrestle with Paul's words in this verse. What is the "judgment" that Paul is referring to, and what "evidence" should this be for us? As is the case with any complicated verse like this, there are different views. Some commentators think the language in verse 5 alludes to a future judgment that is further described in verses 6–12. That is certainly a possible way to read this, but Paul seems to be describing something more than the future judgment. Paul's description here reads like a present judgment of God.

Before we examine the passage in detail, we need to consider what the term *judgment* means. What do we think of when we hear that word? I would guess that we all predominantly think of something negative. Maybe we think of a particular experience when we hear the word *judgment*, perhaps a moment when someone was unfair to us and judged us harshly. Maybe we think about bad experiences with someone's negative judgment of our life or situation. Whatever our particular ideas about judgment, we tend to look at it negatively.

I want us to move beyond that perspective to a proper understanding of judgment. Consider what a judge actually does. He passes judgment. What is the result of that judgment? Sometimes it is a guilty verdict, and the person being judged is sent to jail. That is certainly negative, but is judgment always negative? Not at all. Sometimes the judge will pass a verdict of not guilty. That judgment is positive and righteous and releasing. The judgment of God is similar because his judgment has both aspects to it. God's judgment can be righteous and just and releasing and freeing, or God's judgment can be condemning and painful and ultimately full of wrath.

The rest of chapter 1, verses 6–12, describes what God's judgment will be like when Jesus returns to inflict "vengeance on those who do not know God and on those who do not obey the gospel of our Lord Jesus" (v. 8). On that day, "they will suffer the punishment of eternal destruction, away from the presence of the Lord and from the glory of his might" (v. 9). That is a negative judgment. That is God's judgment of vengeance and wrath. But verse 10 says that on the day he renders that judgment, he will be "glorified in his saints." That judgment will have two aspects to it — a positive aspect called salvation and a negative aspect called condemnation.

Let's go back to verse 5. Paul is thankful for their growing faith in God, their increasing love toward one another, and their steadfast hope in the face of trials. He then explains that their steadfast faithfulness during persecutions and afflictions is "evidence of the righteous judgment of God." In other words, their current suffering is evidence that God has judged rightly and they are indeed his people.

That is the exact opposite of what we think when we are suffering. Our immediate reaction to suffering and trials is that God is angry with us, that God is paying us back for something. When we go through trials, the various hardships and pains of this life, we are immediately inclined to think that God is angry. But that is the wrong perspective. Paul wants us to think differently. If we continue to trust God through our trials and afflictions, *that*, the perseverance of faith in trials, is evidence that God's judgment has been passed upon us and we are part of his kingdom.

When I first examined this verse, I did not think Paul was talking about the present moment. I thought Paul was summarizing the future judgment in verse 5 and expounding it in detail in verses 6–12. Now I am convinced that Paul is talking about a present experience of judgment in the life of a believer.[3] This present experience of judgment in the life of the believer will be consummated at the last day when Christ returns, but it seems that Paul is describing a judgment that is intruding into history. Perhaps we should describe the final judgment as having an *already* and a *not yet* aspect to it, in the same way that the kingdom of God has an *already* and a *not yet* aspect to it.[4] God's judgment has already started at the cross, but that judgment continues throughout history, and he will consummate it at the second coming. The key point, however, is the significance of a present judgment.

If Paul is saying that we have been judged by God and declared righteous, and our suffering is evidence of being worthy of God's kingdom, then that view should completely and drastically change our perspective of suffering. In the midst of our trials we should have a different perspective. Instead of throwing in the towel and giving up, we can continue to trust the Lord. In the midst of our trials, we need to grow in faith, love each other, and remain steadfast in hope. In order for that to happen, we have to believe that God is for us.

We can we see an example of this kind of faith, love, and hope in the life of these Thessalonian Christians. They were steadfast and faithful in the face of suffering. People they knew were attacking them for the gospel. The world they knew was coming apart. In the face of those trials, they continued to trust Jesus. That steadfast perseverance was evidence of the righteous judgment of God on those Christians. God called them; God granted them grace. Their faith was growing, their love was increasing, and in the midst of trials they remained steadfast and faithful. That was evidence that they were worthy of the kingdom.

This is true of us, too. God called us. God granted us grace. Our faith is growing, our love is increasing, and in the midst of trials we remain steadfast and faithful. That is evidence that we are worthy of the kingdom. Judgment has been passed, and we have been declared righteous. This judgment, although it will be fully realized at the second coming, is bound up in history. Whatever we face this week or next month or next year, we can face it with the confidence that God knows what he is doing. In the midst of the suffering, God is demonstrating that we are worthy of his kingdom.

If we actually believe that, our perspective on sufferings and trials will change. Instead of viewing them as signs of God's anger, we can look at them as evidence of God's grace, demonstrating that we are worthy of the kingdom. Look again at the phrase in verse 5: "This is evidence of the righteous judgment of God, that you may be considered worthy of the kingdom of God, for which you are also suffering." The key to the verse is what "this" actually refers to. I am taking "this" to mean that we are steadfast and faithful in the face of persecution and trial and suffering. This suffering, these trials is making us worthy of the kingdom.[5] To read this as a future judgment does not make good sense of the passage.[6]

This interpretation fits with other passages where Paul demonstrates this teaching. He reminds the church in Philippi that their suffering is a clear sign of destruction regarding those who persecute them, but that their suffering is a sign of their own salvation (Philippians 1:28). Paul and Barnabas also tell us that we must enter the kingdom of God "through many tribulations" (Acts 14:22). This also comports well with James, who explains, "Count it all joy, my brothers, when you meet trials of various kinds, for you know that the testing of your faith produces steadfastness. And let steadfastness have its full effect, that you may be perfect and complete, lacking in nothing" (James 1:2–4). Or consider the great hymn "How Firm a Foundation," which says:

When through fiery trials thy pathways shall lie,
My grace, all-sufficient, shall be thy supply;
The flame shall not hurt thee; I only design
Thy dross to consume, and thy gold to refine.

God has designed suffering to work for us and not against us. He has designed it to change us, to consume our dross and refine our gold. He will supply his all-sufficient grace through the fiery trials of life, and those trials are actually evidence that God is for us and not against us.

I think this is profoundly important for our Christian life. If we view our suffering as part of being in the kingdom of God, if we see our afflictions as part of a just process, then we will see trials as part of the work of God in our lives. Our trials are a judgment, but that judgment is not negative. God is not angry with us. His judgment is good, and he has justified us, declaring us righteous and forgiven, demonstrating that we are worthy of his kingdom.

If we view suffering that way, then we view suffering through the lens of the gospel because God poured out his wrath upon Jesus Christ on the cross. All our sins were nailed to the cross. Not part of them — all of them.

All God's wrath was poured out upon Christ on the cross. Not part of it — all of it. So whatever suffering we are experiencing now, whatever valley we are walking through, whatever affliction is wearing us down, those things are not God's wrath.

The only way Paul can make a statement like the one he does in verse 5 is because Jesus died on the cross for our condemnation. When we suffer by faith, trusting God, then we can be confident that God is on our side, that he loves us, and that he knows what he is doing beyond our ability to see. It is all because of the gospel. The gospel should drastically transform our view of suffering.

These Christians in Thessalonica got it. Their perspective on suffering was corrected by the cross. They were pressing on and picking up their cross to follow Jesus. In those actions, they were being counted worthy of the kingdom.

Do we see this? As we pass through the waters, God will be with us. The rivers will not overwhelm us. When we walk through the fire, we will not be burned, and the flames of life will not consume us (Isaiah 43:2). If we see that, we are viewing our lives through the gospel.

20

Eternal Destinies

2 Thessalonians 1:6–12

Do not fear those who kill the body but cannot kill the soul. Rather fear him who can destroy both soul and body in hell."

These words were not spoken by Augustine or Calvin or Edwards.[1] These words were spoken by the Lord Jesus Christ in Matthew 10:28, and these words reflect the staggering reality of an eternal destination. Jesus is warning us not to fear those who can kill us in this life, but to fear the one who can destroy body and soul by casting us into the eternal judgment of hell.

This does not match the picture of Jesus that many people have. The common picture of Jesus is meek and mild, nice and kind, loving and compassionate. Jesus is all that, but he is not only that. If you have that picture of Jesus, what do you do with Jesus' words, "Do not fear those who kill the body but cannot kill the soul. Rather fear him who can destroy both soul and body in hell"? Or to get to the point of our text, what do you do with the image that Paul gives us of Jesus in 2 Thessalonians 1, where he describes Jesus as one who will return "in flaming fire, inflicting vengeance on those who do not know God and on those who do not obey the gospel of our Lord Jesus" (v. 8)? This picture of Jesus should strike fear in our hearts.

The words of our Lord Jesus and of the Apostle Paul reflect the reality of what Christians have called Hell, a place of eternal punishment. Of all the witnesses in the Bible to this doctrine of eternal punishment, Jesus is often the most clear and most forthcoming in his statements. According to the Scriptures, there are only two destinies — Heaven or Hell. That is the way we traditionally speak of it, and our destination is directly connected to Jesus.

The topic of eternal destinies is sober and important, not only because of 2 Thessalonians 1 but because of the consistent witness of Jesus. Let's start by simply asking the question, why did Jesus come? One of the most memorized verses in the Bible is John 3:16, which tells us that Jesus came so that we "should not perish but have eternal life." This everlasting life comes to those who believe, those who have faith in Jesus Christ. There is a danger of not believing in Jesus and perishing. And John goes on to tell us:

> For God did not send his Son into the world to condemn the world, but in order that the world might be saved through him. Whoever believes in him is not condemned, but whoever does not believe is condemned already, because he has not believed in the name of the only Son of God. (John 3:17, 18)

If we do not believe, we are condemned, the wrath of God will remain on us, and we will perish in our sins.

One of the central reasons Jesus came into the world is for our salvation — so we will not perish but have everlasting life. And one of the central burdens of Jesus and his ministry is to remind us that this world is not the final destination. There is another world, another kingdom, new heavens and a new earth that Jesus is making for those who are his people, and if we are not trusting Jesus and looking for that city whose builder and maker is God, then that will not be our destination. Since this is a central burden of Jesus Christ, it must also be a central burden of the church. As Revelation 22 says, when the kingdom of God comes in its fullness, there will be one of two destinations: we will either dwell in God's glory and God's fellowship, or we will be cast outside the kingdom.

Sinclair Ferguson once preached a series of messages on "Universalism and the Reality of Eternal Punishment" at the Bethlehem Conference for Pastors in 1990. Ferguson's sermons are a sober reminder that this life is not our final destination. He pointed out that in the Gospel of Matthew Jesus takes up this great theme of the Old Testament regarding two ways and two destinations. We see this in a central passage like Psalm 1, which describes the way of the wicked and the way of the righteous.

This pattern starts at the beginning of the Bible. After the fall, God cursed the serpent by saying, "I will put enmity between you and the woman, and between your offspring and her offspring; he shall bruise your head, and you shall bruise his heel" (Genesis 3:15). There are two courses in life: you are either the seed of the serpent or the seed of the woman. And it didn't take long to see the evidence of this in the life of Eve's sons, Cain and Abel. Cain chose the way of the serpent and killed his brother Abel, the seed of the woman. Jesus took up this great Old Testament theme in Matthew and explains it through parables:

- The parable of wheat and tares explains for us that one day Jesus will judge everyone, and the righteous will inherit the kingdom of God, while the wicked will be delivered to that place where there will be weeping and gnashing of teeth (Matthew 13:24–30).
- The parable of the net describes the kingdom of Heaven as being like a net thrown into the sea. There are bad fish and good fish, and the bad fish are cast away. This is like the wicked who will be thrown into the fiery furnace (Matthew 13:47–50).
- The parable of the wise and foolish virgins describes five wise virgins and five foolish virgins. The foolish virgins did not keep oil in their lamps, but the wise virgins did. When the bridegroom came, the wise virgins were ready and went with him to the marriage feast. The foolish virgins were shut out of the feast (Matthew 25:1–13).
- The parable of the sheep and the goats describes the judgment as a time when Jesus will gather the nations and will separate them from one another as a shepherd separates the sheep from the goats. The sheep will inherit the kingdom, but the goats will be cursed to forever suffer the eternal fire prepared for the devil and his angels (Matthew 25:31–46).

These parables demonstrate the two ways and the two destinations, and traditionally we describe these two destinations as Heaven and Hell. We usually use these terms to describe the destination of mankind after death, which is temporary because the Bible also explains that when Jesus returns, he will judge everyone. At the second coming of Jesus Christ, we will either be brought into his eternal kingdom because we have trusted him, or we will be cast into the utter darkness of eternal damnation because we have rejected him. That destination will not be temporary. That destination will be eternal.

In 2 Thessalonians 1, Paul takes up this topic of eternal destinations and addresses the issue of the righteous judgment of God. Paul has indicated to us that in our present world we will face suffering and trials for our faith. As we face those trials and sufferings with a growing faith, an increasing love, and a steadfast hope, Paul explains in verse 5 that this is evidence that we are part of the kingdom of God. Paul then unpacks that statement from verse 5 in verses 6–10.

How is it that we are accepted right now by God, yet still suffer? What will happen to those who oppose our faith and who oppose the church? What will happen to those who are persecuting the church and oppose God's kingdom? Paul explains this in verses 6–10 by describing what will happen when Jesus returns, demonstrating that there will be a future judgment for which we must be prepared. I want to ask and answer three questions in order to focus our attention on this passage. Each question focuses upon the future and addresses the when, the who, and the what: When will this judgment take place? Who will be judged? What will happen at this judgment?

WHEN WILL THIS JUDGMENT TAKE PLACE?

Paul indicates that this final judgment will take place when Jesus returns from Heaven. Verse 7 says, ". . . to grant relief to you who are afflicted as well as to us, when the Lord Jesus is revealed from heaven with his mighty angels." Relief will be granted to us "when the Lord Jesus is revealed from heaven." This is what we call the second coming of Jesus Christ. Paul has already indicated that this judgment has started in some way. In 1 Thessalonians 2:16 Paul indicates that God's wrath has already come upon those who opposed the church, and in 2 Thessalonians 1:5 Paul explains that we see evidence of the righteous judgment of God in our own lives when we are suffering. So we must see the judgment of Jesus Christ as having an *already* aspect to it in our present lives and a *not yet* aspect to it that awaits the future.

We also see this in John 3 where John writes, "Whoever believes in him is not condemned, but whoever does not believe is condemned already, because he has not believed in the name of the only Son of God" (v. 18). There is a condemnation already resting on those who do not believe. Paul says something similar in Romans 1:18: "The wrath of God is being revealed from heaven against all the godlessness and wickedness of men who suppress the truth by their wickedness" (NIV, which catches the present, continuous mode of the verb). There is a twofold aspect to this judgment. Just as Jesus accomplished our salvation on the cross but will finish it when he returns, there is judgment resting on those who do not believe, and that judgment will be fully realized when Jesus returns.

WHO WILL BE JUDGED?

As we discussed earlier, we are prone to see judgment as a completely negative term, but it does not have to be negative. Judgment can be a positive term. A judge can render a not guilty verdict or a guilty verdict. So both those who believe in Jesus and those who do not believe in Jesus will be judged, and Paul has already indicated in verse 5 that those who believe in Jesus, those who have a growing faith, an increasing love, and a steadfast hope, have already been judged and found worthy of the kingdom. But in these verses Paul is describing a judgment that is wholly negative. It is a future judgment on those who have rejected Jesus, and in this future judgment there will be a certain amount of punishment inflicted.

Paul describes two groups that will be judged and punished. The first group is mentioned in verse 6: "since indeed God considers it just to repay with affliction those who afflict you." At this future judgment, those who have afflicted the church will be repaid with affliction by God. This might be rooted in the Old Testament concept of *lex talionis* ("an eye for an eye, a tooth for a tooth," Exodus 21:24, etc.).[2] We see this also in Revelation 22:12, 13, when Jesus himself says, "Behold, I am coming soon, bringing my recompense with me, to repay everyone for what he has done. I am the Alpha and the Omega, the first and the last, the beginning and the end." When Jesus comes back, he will pay back what is due to people. This is also part of Paul's point in Romans 12 when he tells us not to repay evil for evil (v. 17) and not to avenge ourselves (v. 19) because we are to "leave it to the wrath of God, for it is written, "'Vengeance is mine, I will repay, says the Lord.'" This judgment and affliction is coming. However men and women have treated or afflicted other people, that will be the judgment given back to them.

The second group that will be judged is described in verse 8: "those who do not know God and . . . those who do not obey the gospel of our Lord Jesus." Paul is not only talking about those who have afflicted the church but also about those people who do not know God and have not obeyed the gospel. In other words, judgment and punishment will not only come to those who have actively rejected and persecuted the church, but judgment and punishment will come on those who have not believed and have not obeyed the gospel.

There is no concept here of what some have called fire insurance. Some people pray a prayer simply because they do not want to go to Hell. Walter Marshall saw this problem and attempted to address it back in the 1600s. He explained that our faith in Christ must not be "constrained for the fear of damnation, without any hearty love and desire towards the enjoyment of him . . . this love must be to every part of Christ's salvation; to holiness as well as forgiveness of sins. We must desire earnestly, that God would *create in us a clean heart and right spirit,* as well as *hide his face from our sins* (Psalm 51:9, 10); not like many, that care for nothing in Christ but only deliverance from hell."[3] We cannot say that we believe in Christ and never participate in his church. If we prayed a prayer in order to avoid Hell, and there is no other sense of love in our life toward Christ and his church, we have not believed and obeyed the gospel. We must demonstrate a growing faith, increasing love, and steadfast hope. Remember, there are only two groups of people — the wicked and the righteous, the good fish and the bad fish, the sheep and the goats, those who are prepared and those who are not prepared. To be counted among the righteous on that day is to be participating in the church now.

Perhaps we see this message in the Scriptures and are concerned for our own souls. That should be the case if we are Christians because Christians are naturally concerned about their souls. If this message concerns us, we should make sure we understand what we are describing — perseverance. We are not talking about how often we fall or how often we struggle. We are talking about perseverance. Will you still be following Jesus in ten years or twenty years or however long it takes for God to finish his work in you and call you home? We cannot just say a prayer. There is more to the Christian life than a short prayer at the beginning. Our faith must grow, our love must increase, and our hope must remain steadfast. When Paul says that Jesus will inflict vengeance on "those who do not know God and on those who do not obey the gospel of our Lord Jesus Christ," he is not making a distinction here. Those who do not know God are those who do not obey the Lord Jesus Christ. No matter what we might confess with our mouths, if our life does not line up with our confession, we could be deceiving ourselves. Let us be among those who believe on Christ, increase in our love, and remain steadfast in our hope. Those who trust in Christ and follow him will be safe on the day of judgment, but those who do not believe God and do not obey the gospel will receive the vengeance of Jesus Christ on that day of judgment.

WHAT WILL HAPPEN AT THIS JUDGMENT?

Our final question concerns the content of this judgment: what will happen on that day when Jesus returns? What will this judgment look like? To answer this, we turn to Paul's description of this judgment, a description that is unlike any other description that Paul gives of Jesus Christ. In fact, I think this description of Jesus is unrivaled until we get to the book of Revelation. Notice the description of Jesus Christ in these verses: "when the Lord Jesus is revealed from heaven with his mighty angels . . . " (v. 7). When you read this verse, do not think of the little, cute, plump angels you see in a gift store. These angels in verse 7 are warriors, and Paul describes them in verse 8 as coming "in flaming fire" for the purpose of "inflicting vengeance." This is military language. This is the King coming with his army. Those who have believed and obeyed the gospel are safe, but those who are not will suffer the full fury of this King, Jesus Christ.

This King did not come in fury and wrath during his first visit to this world. At that time he came with humility and love and grace. He came to ransom his people from the enemy. He died on the cross for rebels. The first coming was a rescue mission, but this second coming will be a war. There will be nothing to hold back King Jesus. He will come with the full force of the heavenly army that will be under his command, and Paul says that he will inflict vengeance "on those who do not know God and on those who do not obey the gospel of our Lord Jesus" (v. 8).

In verse 9 Paul describes the punishment and vengeance in more detail: "They will suffer the punishment of eternal destruction." This topic has become a controversial issue in the church during our time. Some wonder whether Paul is talking about eternal and everlasting judgment or whether he is talking about the destruction and annihilation of unbelievers. Some evangelicals have recently argued that the New Testament is not talking about an eternal and everlasting judgment but about annihilation when the writers refer to the final judgment.[4] John Stott is representative of this view when he makes this comment on our passage:

> Do these words throw any light on the debate between biblical Christians about the nature of hell? That the final state of those who reject God and Christ will be awful and eternal is not in dispute. But the question whether their exclusion-destruction means conscious torment or ultimate annihilation cannot be settled by an appeal to this verse and its vocabulary, since the apostle does not here clearly allude to either.[5]

Aside from Stott's particular belief about everlasting punishment, he does not think that this particular verse helps in the debate. We are, therefore, left with a general statement about the awful and eternal nature of punishment, not the particular issue of whether it is everlasting or not.

This language in this verse, however, is more clear than Stott allows. Both Greg Beale and Gene Green provide some detailed analysis of this passage in light of the Old Testament and the Jewish literature, but I. Howard Marshall provides a concise summary:

> In favour of everlasting punishment it can be argued: (1). Jesus believed in it, and Paul will have shared his outlook (Matt. 5:29–30; 12:32; 18:8–9; 25:41, 46; Lk. 16:23–25); (2). Jewish teaching of the time accepted the fact of eternal punishment (1QS 2:15; 5:13; *Pss. Sol.* 2:35; 15:11; 4 Macc. 10:15); (3). In the present context the reference to separation from the Lord is of little significance if those punished are not conscious of their separation.[6]

If we take into consideration the broader teaching of the New Testament, as well as Jewish literature, we can conclude that Paul is being consistent in this passage and is describing an eternal, conscious, everlasting punishment. This view is also supported by the fact that "in flaming fire, inflicting vengeance" is a quote from Isaiah 66:15, which is the only place in the Old Testament with this combination of terms. This is important because a few verses later is the description of those who have been judged: "their worm shall not die, their fire shall not be quenched" (Isaiah 66:24), which is a reference to unending punishment.[7]

Although various terms are used to describe this type of punishment, usually the most common term is Hell. Wayne Grudem defines Hell as follows: "Hell is a place of eternal conscious punishment for the wicked."[8] This is the consistent teaching of Christians in church history.[9] Paul's explanation of this punishment for those who reject Jesus is terrifying. At the end of verse 9 he describes them as being cast "away from the presence of the Lord and from the glory of his might." Those who suffer this punishment will not behold the glory of the Lord. They will see his fury and wrath, and they will receive his vengeance. There will be no grace on that day. There will be no joy on that day. There will be no marveling at the Lord. On that day those who do not believe will be cast away from the only source of grace and eternal joy — Jesus Christ.

Any good thing that we enjoy in this life, anything that brings us pleasure, ultimately comes from the hand of God. The description Paul gives of this eternal punishment implies that those joys will be taken away because those judged will be cast away from the source of all joy and pleasure. The Psalms describe God as providing joy unspeakable. Psalm 16 says that at God's right hand are pleasures forevermore. The glory of Heaven is that we will have greater joy and satisfaction there than anything we ever had in this life. The terror of Hell is that sinners' worst days and worst moments of this life will not compare to what happens there when they are cast away from the presence of the Lord and the glory of his might.

WORTHY OF HIS CALLING

What I have been describing is the bad news, but we must understand the bad news before we can truly rejoice in the good news. R. C. Sproul explains this in his book titled *Saved from What?* We have to understand what we are saved from before we can appreciate the full joy of salvation. The good news is that we are saved from God's wrath, fury, and vengeance. We must believe upon Christ, and that changes how we will approach that final day. This terrible event for unbelievers will be a glorious event for those who believe. Notice what Paul says in verse 10: "when he comes on that day to be glorified in his saints, and to be marveled at among all who have believed, because our testimony to you was believed." We are talking about the same event, the second coming of Jesus Christ. That event should strike fear in the hearts of those who do not believe, but it should bring joy and glory for those who do believe.

Paul's hope and prayer is that we will be included in those who glorify Jesus in his second coming and will marvel at the work he does. It is for that purpose or to that end that Paul concludes this section by praying "that our God may make [us] worthy of his calling and may fulfill every resolve for good and every work of faith by his power" (v. 11). We must live in a manner that is worthy of God as we await the coming of Christ, so that the name of our Lord Jesus may be glorified.

Note the two little phrases in verse 12. Paul prays that "Jesus may be glorified in you, and you in him." Paul's prayer is not only that we will glorify Jesus in our lives and obedience, but that we will be glorified in Jesus. The grace of God will work in such a way as to make us participants in the life of Christ, and on that day when Jesus returns, we will be completely transformed into his image. The Bible calls that our glorification, and that was Paul's great goal in pastoral ministry. It is to that end that he focused his life. While we struggle through various trials in this life, the good news for us as Christians is this: we can know that God's righteous judgment has passed, and we do not have to fear this threat, and we await the day of our glorification when Jesus Christ returns. Our growing faith, increasing love, and steadfast hope demonstrate that we are part of the kingdom of God. We will marvel at how he judges and re-creates this world for us to dwell with him throughout eternity. That is the good news we have from Jesus Christ.

21

Jesus Will Not Come Until . . .

2 THESSALONIANS 2:1

Is the return of Jesus Christ imminent? In other words, could he return at any moment? Or will certain events happen before Jesus returns a second time? Your answer depends upon how you read certain passages of the Bible, and one of the central passages is 2 Thessalonians 2. As we examine that chapter, we are going to ask several questions: Is Paul talking about the return of Jesus Christ to receive his church? Must certain events take place before Christ comes to receive his church? If so, what are those events?

Let me start, however, with a word of caution. In discussing this matter and examining Paul's words, we will not agree upon a specific interpretation. In other words, you might think Paul is saying Jesus will return imminently. I might think that his return is not imminent. What we need to agree upon, however, is this: Jesus Christ will return. As long as we affirm with the Apostles' Creed that Jesus Christ will "return again to judge the living and the dead," we can disagree on exactly how that will take place. So our interpretation of this passage is not a matter that decides whether someone is a Christian. Christians have different views and perspectives about the second coming of Christ, and as long as we affirm that he will come, we should be open and honest about these various views.

I grew up in a church that would be described as dispensational in its view about the second coming of Jesus. *The Scofield Study Bible* and charts by Clarence Larkin[1] that provided detailed explanations of the end times influenced our view of the second coming. Hal Lindsey's book *The Late Great Planet Earth* was a popular book that was passed around the congregation. In this environment there was a lot of speculation about the precise time when Jesus would come back. Some of that speculation came to a climax in the 1990s during the first Gulf War. I remember talking to my mother about the possibility that Jesus could return any day because prophecy was being fulfilled in the Middle East. When the Left Behind books came out, some pastors suggested that these books were helpful guides for Christians regarding the end times, in spite of the fact that they were written from a fictional perspective.

I lived and breathed this version of dispensationalism as I was growing up. Teaching on the end times was always focused on what would happen with the nation of Israel. Some believed that the formation of national Israel in 1948 was a fulfillment of prophecy and that the generation that saw the formation of that nation-state would also see the second coming of Jesus (based on Matthew 24:32–34 and the lesson of the fig tree). That interpretation created a lot of excitement about the reality of seeing Christ come within a generation from 1948. So the next event would be the secret rapture. At that moment Jesus would rapture out his people and leave behind all those who have not trusted in him. Of course, that is the basis of the terminology *left behind*.

After this event things get complicated. Seven years of tribulation follow the rapture, and during this tribulation God will draw the nation of Israel back to himself. Those who believe upon Christ must go through great suffering, and sometime in the middle of this tribulation, the "great tribulation" begins, revealing the Antichrist. Israel and everyone else who opposes the Antichrist will almost be destroyed, but Jesus will come back at the right moment, the second coming (which is a different event from the rapture), and judge the whole world, set up his millennial kingdom in Jerusalem, and reign for a thousand years. At the end of the thousand-year reign, there will be another rebellion, and Jesus will finally bring an end to everything and usher in the new heavens and the new earth. That is why we needed charts.

This is a summary of a popular version of dispensationalism. To be fair, there are all kinds of versions of dispensationalism, and I cannot describe all of them. We simply need to know the major points and to specifically see that at the heart of this view is the idea of two different types of the Lord's coming. The first is called a rapture, and the second is called just that, the second coming of Jesus. The purpose for bringing this up is that our passage has a significant role to play in our view of these events. In fact, 2 Thessalonians 2 is the passage that forced me to rethink my position on the end times and ultimately change my view. To be specific, this passage caused me to examine whether there are two future events in which Jesus raptures his church and then later returns to this earth. What are the aspects of this passage that we need to evaluate?

First, observe what Paul is describing for us in verse 1: "Now concerning the coming of our Lord Jesus Christ and our being gathered together to him . . . " Paul was speaking to them about the time when Jesus will come back — "the coming of our Lord Jesus Christ." But Paul says clearly that this particular coming is "our being gathered together to him." This seems to be straightforward. This coming of Jesus is when Jesus comes back for his church. The description here is a gathering of the saints to Jesus.

Second, Paul was explaining this event because the Thessalonian believers were concerned: "We ask you, brothers, not to be quickly shaken in mind or alarmed, either by a spirit or a spoken word, or a letter seeming to be from us, to the effect that the day of the Lord has come" (vv. 1, 2). Paul had to explain the coming of the Lord and our being gathered together to Jesus because some of the Christians in Thessalonica were concerned that this event had already happened. They thought they had missed it. To use a phrase we use, they thought they had been left behind. So Paul approached this from a pastoral perspective. Paul was trying to calm their fears.

Perhaps we find it hard to believe that they thought Jesus had already returned, but we have to remember the period. First, this was written in the early stages of the Christian church, and the first written explanation of the coming of Jesus was in 1 Thessalonians. It takes time to wrap your mind around these truths. Second, Paul indicates in 2 Timothy that there was a movement in the early church that spiritualized the second coming.[2] Some seemed to be saying that the second coming of Jesus Christ was not going to be a literal event but a spiritual event in one's own life, perhaps when one becomes a Christian. Finally, these Christians could have thought that the second coming involved events that were not visible. Perhaps they thought that Jesus had started his second coming, but they could not see his work of remaking the world.

We might find that unusual, but in the late 1800s a pastor named Charles T. Russell taught that Christ would return invisibly in 1874 and make himself known to the world in 1914. Another leader in that movement, Judge J. F. Rutherford, explained that Russell was wrong in his calculations. Christ came back on October 1, 1914, but it was an invisible coming. In that invisible coming Christ exchanged an ordinary seat at the Father's right hand for the throne of his kingdom. Those were the beginnings of what we know as the Jehovah's Witnesses.[3] That is a rather recent event in church history, and the Jehovah's Witnesses themselves claim about seven million people as part of their religion — seven million people who claim to be Christians but find themselves in a tradition that is confused on this issue of the second coming of Jesus Christ.

It should not surprise us that these early Christians were struggling with this doctrine and that some of them thought they had been left behind. How did Paul help them? Notice his words in 2 Thessalonians 2:3: "Let no one deceive you in any way. For that day will not come, unless . . . " I find this a staggering claim. Paul is comforting these Christians by saying that Jesus will not return until several things happen. What I understand Paul to be saying is that this day, the day when Jesus will gather us together to himself, the day when Jesus comes back for his church, will not happen until other events take place. Paul was talking about the event when Jesus comes back for his church because he described it as the day when Jesus "gathers [us] together" in verse 1. This should make sense because they were worried about missing that day. It would not make sense if Paul were talking about a day when Jesus does not gather his church.

Paul comforts these Christians by explaining that they have not been left behind because two events must happen before Jesus returns. We see these two events described in verse 3: "the rebellion comes first, and the man of lawlessness is revealed." Paul first mentions a rebellion. A better translation would be "apostasy" since it is the Greek word *apostasia*. Greg Beale explains:

> Though the word *apostasia* can refer to a political or a religious crisis, the latter is the only use in the Greek Old Testament and the New Testament, and that is its meaning here. Such a meaning is apparent because of the immediate context of false teaching (2:1, 2, 9–12) and the clear allusions to Daniel's prediction of an end-time opponent who will bring about a large-scale compromise of faith among God's people. The apostasy will not occur primarily in the non-Christian world but rather within the covenant community.[4]

This apostasy is a rebellion, but it is a particular rebellion against the faith. The second event is the revelation of the man of lawlessness, also described as the son of destruction. The verses that follow go on to describe this man of lawlessness, but that is not our concern at this point.

The main point so far is this: Paul tells us that two things have to take place before Jesus comes back to gather his church. First, an apostasy must take place, a rebellion against the faith. Second, a revelation of the man of lawlessness must occur. In other words, Paul is saying to Christians who are worried that they have missed this day, "Don't worry, brothers and sisters. You have not missed the coming of Jesus Christ because the apostasy has not happened and the man of lawlessness has not been revealed." The precise nature of these two "signs" is not the point right now. The point is that these two things have to happen before Christians are gathered together to Jesus. Perhaps I can paraphrase Paul this way: "I know you have heard that Jesus has come and you missed it. Don't worry. Jesus will not come for you until two 'signs' take place first — rebellion and the man of lawlessness. Jesus will not come to gather you to himself until those two events take place."

I think that is the only way to read the passage and allow it to make sense of the comfort Paul is bringing to these Christians, but I do want to be fair to Christians who read this passage differently. Before I changed my view on this passage, I once thought Paul was saying something else. I once thought that the coming of Jesus to gather us together to him would happen first, and it was called the rapture. Then after Jesus took his people out, the man of lawlessness would be revealed. My last-days timeline went like this:

- rapture (gathering saints to Jesus)
- tribulation
- falling away
- man of lawlessness/Antichrist
- second coming/day of the Lord

You see, in that sequence of events I made a distinction between the rapture when Jesus will gather his saints to him and the Day of the Lord. I even thought it was in this passage. I read verse 1 as talking about the rapture and verse 2 as talking about the Day of the Lord, the final coming.[5]

Eventually, however, that reading of the text began to fall apart. I started struggling with it because that view did not help these Christians; it did not provide any comfort for them. Why? Because they were supposed to be gone when the two signs take place if you believe the rapture takes place before the apostasy and the man of lawlessness. What kind of comfort would it provide these Christians for these two signs to be after the point when Jesus takes out his church?

Perhaps a conversation on the text here would help clarify this. Let's try to imagine what a conversation would have sounded like between the Apostle Paul and these Christians in Thessalonica.

Thessalonians: How do we know that we have not missed the coming of the Lord and our gathering together with him?

Paul: Have you seen the two signs?

Thessalonians: What signs?

Paul: The great apostasy and the revelation of the man of lawlessness.

Thessalonians: No, we have not seen that.

Paul: Then you didn't miss it.

I think that kind of conversation is what is taking place here, but if we read the passage as I used to read it, making a distinction between the gathering in verse 1 and the day of Christ in verse 2, then the passage does not make sense. If we change the conversation slightly to reflect my previous view on this passage, this is how the conversation would look:

Thessalonians: How do we know that we have not missed the coming of the Lord and our gathering together with him?

Paul: Have you seen the two signs?

Thessalonians: What signs?

Paul: The great apostasy and the revelation of the man of lawlessness.

Thessalonians: Yes, it looks like those are the signs we are seeing right now.

Paul: Well, if you are here when the two signs happen, um . . . well . . . I think . . . I hate to tell you . . . but you actually did miss the coming of the Lord. Sorry, but Christians will be taken out before those two signs appear. You really were left behind, but hang in there . . . Jesus will come again after these signs have been revealed.

By reading it that way, the two signs provide no comfort, but that misses the point of Paul's passage. These two signs are to provide comfort in the midst of confusion for those who are waiting for the return of Jesus Christ.

GUARD YOURSELF

This might not be convincing to you, but it was helpful for me to think through how we should look at the end. However one views and interprets this passage, Paul is stressing that we must be on guard against two concerns — apostasy and lawlessness. There are times in the history of the church when Christians thought this was taking place and the end was near. Although we want to avoid speculating about the timing of Christ's return, we must be on guard against these two threats to our faith. The Christian church will always face moments when we look around and see these two temptations. In fact, Paul warned Timothy against these temptations in the first century. Timothy was to avoid lawlessness, and Paul describes that kind of behavior as "lovers of self, lovers of money, proud, arrogant, abusive, disobedient to their parents, ungrateful, unholy, heartless, unappeasable, slanderous, without self-control, brutal, not loving good, treacherous, reckless, swollen with conceit, lovers of pleasure rather than lovers of God, having the appearance of godliness, but denying its power. Avoid such people" (2 Timothy 3:2–5).

Paul was telling Timothy to be on guard against these people in his own time, the first century. We look around our culture and see this lawless behavior, and we look in our own hearts and see the temptation to engage in this type of sin. This is not something new. We must be on guard against lawlessness for our own sakes. As we give in to lawlessness, there is a temptation to turn away from the church and the faith.

The book of Hebrews is instructive here. We find constant warnings about not turning away from the faith. You know what the temptation is in Hebrews? It is not always open rebellion and what the Bible calls highhanded sin. It is drifting. With many people in the church who fall away, it is a slow drift. It just becomes easier not to read the Bible or not to pray. It becomes easier to stay at home on Sunday . . . and slowly we drift. The book of Hebrews warns us against this slow drift because it can produce a hard heart.

That is what Paul is talking about in our passage. The warning here is that at any moment there could be a rebellion or falling away from the faith, and there is no way to know at that moment if you are participating in a large-scale falling away from the faith that is setting up the second coming of Jesus Christ. That is the danger of lawlessness and apostasy.

Let us all be careful not to be so caught up in the details about how Jesus will come back that we forget about these warnings. Instead of spending so much time trying to figure out the rapture and the second coming and the great tribulation, let us focus our attention on Paul's point: you can always be tempted to turn away from the faith, and it starts with a slow drift that results in a destination that you never intended.

Do not be discouraged. No matter how difficult life becomes, and no matter how far you have drifted from where you were a year ago, do not forget that Jesus is a gracious Savior who is sitting on his throne in Heaven. Apostasy and lawlessness do not surprise him. He is in control, and he calls you back to your first love.

May God give you the faith and the grace to persevere until the end.

22

Rebellion and Hope

2 Thessalonians 2:1–12

William Ernest Henley wrote a well-known poem titled "Invictus."

Out of the night that covers me,
Black as the Pit from pole to pole,
I thank whatever gods may be
For my unconquerable soul.

In the fell clutch of circumstance
I have not winced nor cried aloud.
Under the bludgeonings of chance
My head is bloody, but unbowed.

Beyond this place of wrath and tears
Looms but the Horror of the shade,
And yet the menace of the years
Finds, and shall find, me unafraid.

It matters not how strait the gate,
How charged with punishments the scroll,
I am the master of my fate:
I am the captain of my soul.

This poem captures the essence of human rebellion. The last two lines are well-known and are powerful descriptions of the fall. We want to be the masters of our own fate. We want to be the captains of our own souls.

In 2 Thessalonians 2 Paul gives us a glimpse into the future and explains to us what to expect when Jesus comes back — and we should expect the kind of rebellion signified in Henley's "Invictus." This section originally begins with a problem in verses 1, 2. There was some confusion about when Jesus would come back. Evidently some of these Christians thought they had missed the return of Christ. Paul provides an answer for them by giving them two signs — apostasy and the revelation of the man of lawlessness. It is the explanation of these two signs that we are concerned with now, for after Paul tells us about these signs, he goes on to explain some details about them. It seems to me that at the center of Paul's concern is the issue of apostasy and lawlessness, and these two events are interconnected. This man of lawlessness is part of the reason why there is apostasy.

Before we get to the details of this passage, let's pause and consider the theme of apostasy and rebellion against God in the history of redemption.[1] What do apostasy and lawlessness look like in the Scriptures? Such rebellion began in the Garden of Eden, where we first see humans rebel against God, and this influence toward rebellion is empowered by Satan himself, who comes disguised as a serpent. Satan said to Eve in Genesis 3:4, 5, "You will not surely die. For God knows that when you eat of it your eyes will be opened, and you will be like God, knowing good and evil." That was the initial rebellion in this world. Adam and Eve ate of the fruit in an attempt to be like God. This is the center of human rebellion — the temptation to be like God, to be the masters of our own fate and the captains of our own souls.

This type of apostasy and rebellion established in the Garden of Eden by Adam and Eve continues through the rest of the Bible. This rebellion, however, gains some specific clarity when we get to the prophets. In the writings of Isaiah and Ezekiel we see this rebellious spirit among kings and emperors. Isaiah tells us that the king of Babylon would fall because of his pride and rebellion:

> You said in your heart, "I will ascend to heaven; above the stars of God I will set my throne on high; I will sit on the mount of assembly in the far reaches of the north; I will ascend above the heights of the clouds; I will make myself like the Most High." (Isaiah 14:13, 14)

The historical context here is the king of Babylon who would attempt to make himself like the Most High God, but within the Christian tradition we have also understood this passage to be referring to the fall of Satan. If indeed that is the case, which I think it is, then we are seeing a connection here back to the Garden of Eden and Satan's influence in this rebellion and sin, as well as a connection to the man of lawlessness in 2 Thessalonians 2 who is influenced by Satan. This rebellion is at the heart of sinful humanity.

In the book of Ezekiel, the ruler of Tyre called himself a god: "Son of man, say to the prince of Tyre, Thus says the Lord GOD: Because your heart is proud, and you have said, 'I am a god, I sit in the seat of the gods, in the heart of the seas,' yet you are but a man, and no god, though you make your heart like the heart of a god" (Ezekiel 28:2). This rebellion that opposes God and exalts a man in the place of God is seen repeatedly in the Scriptures, and it is a rebellion that will reach a climax at the end of time.

This type of rebellion is demonstrated again in the book of Daniel. Daniel explains the fall of King Nebuchadnezzar because of his pride and rebellion. That ruler looked at his own kingdom and attributed it all to his own glory and power, but God judged him and made him dwell with the beasts of the field until he realized that the Most High God reigns and God's dominion is everlasting and God's kingdom endures from generation to generation (Daniel 4:28–37).

Eventually Daniel goes on to describe this rebellion in chapters 8–12 as he describes the rebellion of a person who will exalt himself in the Holy of Holies. This person's rebellion is described as "the transgression that makes desolate" (Daniel 8:13) and "the wing of abominations" that makes desolate (Daniel 9:27). Daniel then provides this description: "And the king shall do as he wills. He shall exalt himself and magnify himself above every god, and shall speak astonishing things against the God of gods. He shall prosper till the indignation is accomplished; for what is decreed shall be done" (Daniel 11:36). This king will set himself up as God. Many think that these prophecies primarily reference an event around 169 B.C. During that time, the Syrian King Antiochus IV, known as Epiphanes, brought desecration upon the temple in Jerusalem. He entered the Holy of Holies, and he erected an altar to Zeus on the altar of burnt offering and sacrificed a pig on it. This was the event known as "the abomination that causes desolation," the desolating sacrilege, or the "Awful Horror."

Although there is a historical fulfillment during that period, Jesus picked up Daniel's language in Matthew 24 and described someone who would come and create abominations. In that passage Jesus provided a prophecy concerning the destruction of the temple. And now we see Paul picking up this same language in 2 Thessalonians 2. Notice that Paul describes this man of lawlessness as one "who opposes and exalts himself against every so-called god or object of worship, so that he takes his seat in the temple of God, proclaiming himself to be God" (v. 4). The description of this person is similar to what we read in Isaiah and Daniel as well as what we heard from Jesus.

What does this mean? There are many different views on this issue, but we will examine two or three primary views.[2] The most common view is that Paul is talking about a future, historical figure who will be revealed near the end of time, right before Jesus returns. Another view is that Paul could be talking about the prophecy given by Jesus in Matthew 24. Paul wrote his letter before A.D. 70, and his words here could apply to the destruction of

Jerusalem at that time instead of the event related to the second coming of Jesus Christ. Finally, Paul could be talking about a general movement and not a specific person who is yet to be revealed in the future.

I tend to think that the proper interpretation can be a combination of these various views. In our survey of Biblical passages related to rebellion, what we see is an interpretation and reapplication of this theme by the prophets (Ezekiel and Isaiah), then by Jesus, and now by Paul. So Paul's language can be interpreted as a movement of people who fit this description. This would correspond with the Apostle John who writes, "Children, it is the last hour, and as you have heard that antichrist is coming, so now many antichrists have come. Therefore we know that it is the last hour" (1 John 2:18). John explains that many antichrists have already come. Evidently John sees that those who turn away from Jesus and rebel against the Lord are antichrists. Notice what he goes on to say in verse 22: "Who is the liar but he who denies that Jesus is the Christ? This is the antichrist, he who denies the Father and the Son." So there is a way to understand these descriptions of the king of Babylon, the king of Tyre, King Nebuchadnezzar, and the person in Matthew 24 as descriptions of antichrists because they have exalted themselves above Christ and have denied the one true Messiah. This would also be true of Roman emperors living at the time of Paul when they tried to force the early Christians to call Caesar Lord instead of seeing Jesus Christ as the only Lord. Thus they would be antichrists.

Now the question is this, is a future antichrist still coming? I have wrestled with this position.[3] Sometimes I think Paul is describing a type of movement, and sometimes I think Paul is describing a future, historical person. John does say, however, in verse 18, "you have heard that antichrist is coming." I think that Paul and John are both talking about a future person who will be revealed who is described as the Antichrist and the man of lawlessness. I do not think it will be so clear that we will be able to pinpoint the fact that a certain person is the Antichrist, but I believe that this is referring to a historical person yet to be revealed.

THE ANTICHRIST

If there is a future, historical person who will be revealed as an antichrist, who is it? Church history is profitable here.[4] Let me give you some of the examples of those who have been designated as antichrists throughout church history. In the early church, various Roman emperors were considered the Antichrist. Eventually, however, the Roman emperor became a Christian and was not considered the Antichrist anymore because he confessed Jesus as the Christ. During the time that the Roman Empire was considered predominantly Christian, the Antichrist became those various kings and leaders outside the Roman Empire who attacked Rome.

That did not last long because Islam rose in power. So the Christians described Muhammad as the man of lawlessness. Christians believed that he had taken many Christian holy places and that his religion caused Christians to turn against Christ and commit apostasy. If you were a Christian living in the Middle East during that time, you would have thought the end was near. Islam and Muhammad were fulfilling the prophecies from Jesus and Paul. There was rebellion, apostasy, and a person who placed himself above Jesus Christ.

The advance of Islam was stopped by the kings of the Holy Roman Empire in the Middle Ages just in time for the controversy of the Protestant Reformation. During that time, many Christians called the pope the Antichrist because the Roman Catholic Church had become wicked. Many Christians in addition to the Reformers realized this problem. About five hundred years before the Protestant Reformation, some Franciscan monks called the pope the Antichrist. The pope and the Roman Catholic Church did not sit idly by while others were casting the name of Antichrist at them; the Roman Catholic leaders responded by calling Luther the man of lawlessness because of his rebellion against the Roman Catholic Church. Over the past hundred years, the most common attempt to identify the Antichrist has been connected to political leaders such as Napoleon, Hitler, Mussolini, Stalin, and many others.

Should we be guessing at the identification of the Antichrist? I don't think so. It's just not helpful. I think what we learn from this brief history is that we will always make wrong judgments about people regarding the "real" Antichrist. So what can we learn from this passage? I think we should draw from this the *characteristics* of the Antichrist. Many of these figures throughout church history have the characteristics of the Antichrist, and that seems to be John's point when he explains that many antichrists have already come. We might not know the specific identification of the Antichrist, but we can certainly say that this person is exhibiting certain characteristics connected to the Antichrist, and we should be on guard against these types of actions and behaviors, as well as against individuals who tempt us to turn away from Jesus Christ.

What can we say about this man of lawlessness, this antichrist? First, he will oppose God and exalt himself (v. 4). It is the same rebellion rooted in the Garden of Eden and the kings of the Old Testament, as well as in the fall of Satan himself. This man of lawlessness will claim worship for himself above Jesus Christ. There is a question in verse 4 as to what Paul means when the Antichrist "takes his seat in the temple of God."[5] Every time we come upon a phrase in this passage we could talk about four or five different views, but briefly some think Paul is talking about a literal temple that will be rebuilt before Jesus returns. Others think it is a figure of expression indicating a person who craves worship. I think the language of the temple of

God is describing the church. The other ten occurrences of the term "temple of God" in the New Testament are figurative and refer to Jesus Christ or his church.[6] Paul is arguing that this person, the Antichrist, will try to take center stage in the church and draw people away from Christ, and this matches both what Paul says about the apostasy and John's description of the Antichrist as someone who is part of the church but leaves as a false teacher.[7]

Second, the antichrist will be aligned with Satan (v. 9). Paul describes this person's coming as "the activity of Satan," and he will display "false signs and wonders." The point here is that Satan is the one behind this work. In verse 7 Paul says that "the mystery of lawlessness is already at work," which is similar to John's statement. The false teaching and rebellion is already happening, and that is a satanic influence. Satan wants to deceive us just as he deceived Adam and Eve: "Has God really said?"

Third, the antichrist will deceive those who refuse the truth (v. 10). At the root of lawlessness and apostasy and rebellion is a refusal to love the truth. This refusal to love the truth results in further deception. This is a warning to all of us. Our only hope when we face this type of deception is to be well-grounded in the gospel and in God's Word. We must love God's truth, the very Word of God, so we will not be deceived by the evil one. One of the areas we should be on guard against today is the idea that Christians will never have to face persecution. Some views of the future encourage Christians to think they will escape the future trials and struggles and persecutions. Pause for a moment and consider the significance of this issue. Let's say we believe that God will rescue us from persecution and suffering. Then things change, and we have to face severe persecution for our faith. Let's even assume, for the sake of the argument, that we end up going through the "great tribulation." What would be our approach to our suffering and persecution? I would think we might be tempted to give up. We might be tempted to think we are not Christians. All those temptations might come crashing down upon us and tempt us to turn away. God's Word, however, tells us a different story: it tells us to expect suffering. If Jesus was mistreated and suffered, we should expect to suffer too. That is one example of being on guard against errors that could cause us to fall away from the truth.

This lawless one, this antichrist, will oppose God, will be aligned with Satan, and will deceive people, drawing them away from the truth. Paul does, however, provide us some encouragement in the face of this trial. This lawless one is still under the power and control of God. Paul tells us in verse 6 that God is "restraining him." Of course, again, there are different views of what precisely is restraining the antichrist.[8] Is it the church? Is it the preaching of the gospel? Is it the state and its legal structures? Is it the Holy Spirit? Some have argued that Michael the archangel is the restrainer.[9] According to Daniel 10:13, 20, 21, Michael restrains satanic principalities. This is also consistent with Revelation 12:7, 8: "Now war arose in heaven,

Michael and his angels fighting against the dragon. And the dragon and his angels fought back, but he was defeated, and there was no longer any place for them in heaven." Nicholl explains, "The pre-eminence of Michael in contemporary Jewish thought, especially as *archistrategos*, opponent of Satan and protector of God's people, renders him an especially plausible candidate for the role of restrainer."[10] I think one could even make the case that there are significant parallels between this restraining power described in 2 Thessalonians 2:6, 7 with the angel who restrains Satan's power in Revelation 20, thus interpreting these two passages as the same event.[11] Whatever the precise interpretation is, ultimately we want to say that God is restraining the Antichrist because God is in control of these events, and he will reveal this Antichrist, according to Paul in verse 6, at the appropriate time. Nothing in this passage is outside the scope of God's power.

God's sovereign power over this man of lawlessness is emphasized by the fact that God is even in control of the rebellion on that day. Paul says that God "sends them a strong delusion, so that they may believe what is false, in order that all may be condemned who did not believe the truth but had pleasure in unrighteousness" (vv. 11, 12). Even at that moment, when wickedness is at its peak, God is the one behind the scene orchestrating these events. The Lord sends them a strong delusion in order to condemn wickedness. Perhaps Paul is alluding to the exodus of Israel out of Egypt when, according to the Scriptures, God hardened Pharaoh's heart as Pharaoh hardened his own heart.[12] Paul makes similar statements in Romans when he describes people who refused and suppressed the truth (Romans 1:18–32). This judgment of God in sending a delusion is only the beginning of a judgment that will culminate in the final judgment at the end.[13]

In the midst of this darkness, we should hope in God. We should find comfort in the fact that no matter how dark the description of this man of lawlessness, God is still the King and Ruler of this world. But there is one further description in this passage to notice. The most powerful picture in this passage is not of the Antichrist. In spite of all the descriptions of the Antichrist as taking his seat in the temple and proclaiming himself to be God, the most powerful description in this passage is of Jesus Christ. Paul says that the Lord Jesus will kill the Antichrist "with the breath of his mouth" (v. 8). Can you picture that? Our Lord Jesus Christ can destroy this wickedness and bring it to nothing by the very breath, or literally "spirit," that comes out of his mouth. That is the power of Jesus Christ. Our hope is rooted in him, and one day he will destroy all the rebellion and roll back the curse as he makes all things new.

23

The Steadfastness of Christ

2 THESSALONIANS 2:13–3:5

Does God ever change his mind? Or can you do something to change God's plan?

Each question is a different version of a common concern that many Christians have about God's plan and our roles in that plan. I am referring to the mysterious issue of God's sovereignty and our responsibility.

When I first started preaching, I thought that my preaching and the results from my preaching were dependent upon me. I prayed, but the prayer was more or less to help me do the right thing. I prayed to have the proper words at the right moment. I thought someone's response to my message was dependent upon how well I delivered the message and in particular whether I told the right story at the end of the sermon to produce an emotional response so someone would walk down a church aisle to be saved.

I remember preaching a sermon on bitterness in a church context that needed repentance and healing. At the end of the service it was our custom to invite people forward to demonstrate their response to the Lord. When that time came, several people responded to the message and came forward to pray. I remember struggling with how long to let this continue. I asked the choir director to play another verse of "Just As I Am" or whatever invitation hymn we were using. Since we had already played that hymn four or five times, the choir director was not pleased to do it again, but he played it one more time. I then promptly closed the service.

That whole afternoon I struggled with my decision to close the service. I was weighed down with guilt about being intimidated by the choir director and stopping the invitation before someone else could respond. In my tradition at that time, if I closed the service before someone responded, that person's blood would be on my hands. It was such a heavy feeling that I had a hard time sleeping that night.

Is it true that others' salvation is in my hands? Is it my responsibility to stir up my hearers in such a way that they will respond to the message? Is it up to me? Is it up to you?

In this particular passage Paul explains something important about God's plan, prayer, and the power of God's Word, and although we must affirm that God is in control of everything, we are still responsible to pray. Paul has thus far described some of the difficult situations facing these Thessalonian Christians. In chapter 1 Paul explained that they faced terrible suffering, but Paul had confidence that they would persevere through this suffering and God would demonstrate their faith when Jesus returns. But it was the return of Jesus Christ that was causing them some problems because some of these Christians evidently thought they had missed the second coming. But in chapter 2 Paul explained that they had not missed it because the apostasy had not taken place and the man of lawlessness had not been revealed. Paul then described the wickedness of this man of lawlessness and the fact that many will turn away from Christ during that time. As Christians reading this, we should wonder, if something like this happened in our lifetimes, would we stand firm? We should be on guard against the temptation to turn away from Jesus.

THE POWER OF GOD

What can Paul say to encourage us as we face these trials? Paul appeals to the power of God because it is God who started the process of salvation: "But we ought always to give thanks to God for you, brothers beloved by the Lord, because God chose you as the firstfruits to be saved, through sanctification by the Spirit and belief in the truth" (2:13). Paul makes two strong statements about God's power. First, God started this in the beginning. As Paul says in Ephesians, God "chose us in [Christ] before the foundation of the world" (1:4). What we have here in this early letter of 1 Thessalonians is a short statement that gives us insight into Paul's theology. God has a plan and a purpose, and God's plan will not be stopped. In other letters, notably Ephesians and Romans, Paul gives a more detailed examination of this concept of God's sovereign choice, but in this early letter Paul provides a short, concise statement about God's sovereignty and power in order to encourage these believers as they face evil and wickedness.

Secondly, we should be encouraged by Paul's words because he points out that God has given us his very own Spirit. Not only did God start this process of salvation, but by the gift of his Spirit he will make sure this process reaches its appointed conclusion — our sanctification and belief in the truth. It is the Spirit of God who is at work in us to make our faith grow, our love increase, and our hope remain steadfast. God has loved us and chosen us to be his, and he has demonstrated this by the gift of his Spirit who will sanctify us and reveal the truth to us so that we will obtain an eternal glory. So Paul concludes with this prayer: "Now may our Lord Jesus Christ himself, and God our Father, who loved us and gave us eternal comfort and good hope through grace, comfort your hearts and establish them in every good work and word" (2:16, 17). Paul is confident that the Lord Jesus Christ, who has comforted us, will continue to establish our hearts.

THE TEMPTATION WITH GOD'S POWER

In the midst of examining the power and sovereignty of God, we face a temptation that has been a struggle for many Christians. We are tempted to think this way: *If God is in control, why should I pray? Why should I be worried about my obedience or my perseverance? God has this whole problem under control.* We face a temptation to become slack in our prayer life and in our obedience. Sometimes when we first see that God is in control of all things, our prayer life will often suffer and not remain consistent.

This should not be the case. Notice what Paul does in 3:1: "Finally, brothers, pray for us . . . " Right after talking about God's absolute control over the events that happen in our lives, from the beginning of our salvation all the way to our eternal hope, Paul tells us to pray. Paul sees no contradiction between what he said in chapter 2 about God's power and what he is now saying in chapter 3 about prayer.

This should lead us to several conclusions. First, if we have a struggle with prayer, we are not seeing it rightly. I do not mean that if we struggle with praying, then something is wrong. We all struggle with prayer. Prayer is a hard discipline, but that is not the point of this passage. What I mean is that if we struggle with the concept of prayer, whether we should pray, then we have not understood prayer and the sovereignty of God. Paul sees no conflict between saying that God is in control of everything and that we should pray.

We find it difficult to pull these images together. How is it that God can know all things and plan all things — the beginning, the end, and everything in between — and yet tell us to do certain things? This is certainly a difficult topic, but I fear that the root problem is that our view of prayer and of God is wrong at this point. We have a notion of God as a cosmic servant waiting on our every need, and we have a notion of prayer as the access line to our cosmic servant. Of course we do not want to admit this, but it surfaces when we express our concept of prayer to others in this way: "I know you are having a hard time, but you just need to pray. Prayer changes things."

What do we mean when we say, "Prayer changes things"? This is a common expression, but we never pause to consider what it means. What things? People? Trials? Suffering? What things does prayer change? I fear that we mean this: prayer changes God — our prayer can change God's mind about what is happening in our lives; our prayer can change God's plan. If you do not like what is going on in your life, pray to God. If you pray enough, then things will go better, and that person might get saved or you might be healed of cancer or whatever. But behind those ideas is this notion: we think prayer is a work that forces God's hand, and if we pray, God will get lined up with our plans.

If we believe that about prayer but then discover that the Biblical view of God is one that makes him high and exalted, a King who has a plan that cannot be thwarted, we are going to have a problem with prayer. All of a sudden we realize that prayer is not designed to change God's plan. These two views clash, and the Bible is overwhelming in terms of its description of God's sovereignty and power. As Paul says in Romans,

> Oh, the depth of the riches and wisdom and knowledge of God! How unsearchable are his judgments and how inscrutable his ways! "For who has known the mind of the Lord, or who has been his counselor?" "Or who has given a gift to him that he might be repaid?" For from him and through him and to him are all things. To him be glory forever. Amen. (11:33–36)

This is an all-encompassing description of God's power, and guess what that means? We are not God's counselor when we pray, and if our concept of prayer has this notion of being God's counselor, then we no longer know how to pray — the reason we have been praying is now gone. When we realize that our prayers will not change God or his plan, we will stop praying.

Perhaps we have not had this experience, and in some way we still believe that our prayers can change the way history flows. I do not think this is a Biblical concept, but let's pause and consider what it means. Roger Nicole was one of my professors at Reformed Theological Seminary in Orlando, Florida, and he had something very wise to say about this view of prayer.

> There are people who feel that unless you are prepared to say [that prayer can change God's mind and plan], there is no great value in prayer. . . . If you believe you can change the mind of God through prayer, I hope you are using some discretion. If that is the power you have, it is certainly a most dangerous thing. Surely God does not need our counsel in order to set up what is desirable. Surely God, whose knowledge penetrates all minds and hearts, does not need to have us intervene to tell him what he ought to do. The thought that we are changing the mind of God by our prayers is a terrifying conception.

I will be frank to confess, if I really thought I could change the mind of God by praying, I would abstain. Because I would have to say, "How can I presume, with the limitations of my own mind and the corruptions of my own heart — how can I presume to interfere in the counsels of the Almighty?" No, our minds are too puny to give God advice. It is almost as if you were to introduce somebody who is utterly ignorant of electronics to a nuclear weapons facility and you let that person into the operations room, though they were untrained, and told them to go on and push whatever buttons they thought appropriate. By so doing, you might precipitate an accidental explosion. There is comfort for the child of God in being assured that our prayer will not change God's mind. This is not what is involved in prayer, and we are not in danger of precipitating explosions by some rash desire on our part.[1]

Did you see the point he is trying to get across? It is a comfort for us to know as Christians that our prayers will not change God's mind. How many times have we prayed on the basis of our own desires and whims, only to discover that we did not understand the situation? How terrible would life be if that prayer had changed God's mind! We cannot see the end from the beginning; only God can. Did you catch that one sentence when Nicole said, "If I really thought I could change the mind of God by praying, I would abstain"? How many times have we prayed for something, only in a few months to think, "I am so glad this did not turn out the way I had hoped. Thank you, Lord, for your wisdom"? Prayer is not designed to change God's mind. That is not the purpose of prayer.

THE PURPOSE OF PRAYER

As we examine Paul's words in 3:1, 2, we will understand the purpose of prayer. Paul tells us to pray for two things: 1) the success of the word of the Lord, and 2) deliverance from wickedness. First, he tells us to pray that the word of the Lord will "speed ahead and be honored." The Greek construction here reads, "pray for us . . . that the word of the Lord should run ahead and be honored." The phrase signifies that the Word should move swiftly like a runner and be glorified in the process. But notice that Paul is not talking about himself running the race. The picture is of the gospel itself running forward and accomplishing that which God intended.[2] We are called to pray that God's Word will accomplish what God intends it to accomplish. Our prayer must line up with God's purpose.

The second request is in verse 2: "that we may be delivered from wicked and evil men." This prayer is along the same lines as what Paul said in chapter 2. Remember that Paul described an evil scenario there regarding the man of lawlessness and the wicked deception that would take place. Wicked and evil men were going to rise up and tempt the church with false teaching; so Paul prayed for the Thessalonians to stand firm, resting in the power of God. Now he asked them to pray for him, that he, too, would be delivered from wicked and evil men. Paul had given them an example of this prayer in 2:16, 17, and now he asked them to pray as he did.

These two aspects of Paul's prayer should inform our prayers as well. In other words, our prayers should look like Paul's prayers. First, we should pray that God's will would be done, that the word of God will be successful. Second, we ought to pray that we do not fall into temptation, but that God will deliver us from evil and wickedness so that we will stand firm and persevere. This should sound familiar — it has a pattern similar to the Lord's Prayer. So what are we doing in prayer? Prayer is designed to get us in line with God's plan and God's will and God's kingdom. Prayer puts us in the right place with God. Prayer is not about changing God and his plan. Prayer is about changing us and getting us in line with God's plan and God's will.

You might be wondering where this comes from in our passage. Why would I say that prayer is not about changing God's plan but is about changing us? Notice the very next phrase in verse 3: "But the Lord is faithful." I found it odd that Paul put this right in the middle of these verses. Paul wants us to pray for two things — that the word of God would spread and that we would persevere in the face of evil. Then he writes, "the Lord is faithful."

What is the Lord faithful to do? Is he faithful to change events so they fit our desires and wishes? Not at all. Let's keep reading: "But the Lord is faithful. He will establish you and guard you against the evil one." The Lord is faithful to answer prayer that is in line with his will because he changes us. He will establish us in the faith. He will guard us against the evil one. The Lord is faithful to accomplish his plan, and prayer is designed to draw us into that plan and to conform us to God's will. When we pray, we are asking God's will to be done in our lives as it is done in Heaven. Prayer is getting in line with God's will.

I think that Paul's words right here might provide us one of the clearest definitions of prayer in the entire Bible. What does prayer do? Prayer establishes us and guards us against the evil one. God has designed prayer to function in such a way that it accomplishes that purpose as we seek God and ask for his protection and blessing. The Lord is faithful, and Paul goes on to say, "And we have confidence in the Lord about you, that you are doing and will do the things that we command. May the Lord direct your hearts to the love of God and to the steadfastness of Christ" (vv. 4, 5). There is nothing in those prayers about God changing. Everything after verse 3 is what God is doing for us to change us. He will establish us. He will guard us. He will cause us to obey his Word. He will direct our hearts to his Word and the steadfastness of Jesus Christ.

I began with my own struggle concerning the sovereignty of God and prayer. After that experience on Sunday when I thought someone might end up in Hell because of my failure to keep the invitation going longer, I made an appointment with my college pastor, Dr. Larry Draper, who was then the pastor of West Rome Baptist Church. I described my experience to him, and as I finished the story he was smiling. He explained that he had experienced something similar in his ministry. He asked me to open the Bible to Isaiah 55:8–11 and read it to him:

> For my thoughts are not your thoughts, neither are your ways my ways, declares the LORD. For as the heavens are higher than the earth, so are my ways higher than your ways and my thoughts than your thoughts. For as the rain and the snow come down from heaven and do not return there but water the earth, making it bring forth and sprout, giving seed to the sower and bread to the eater, so shall my word be that goes out from my mouth; it shall not return to me empty, but it shall accomplish that which I purpose, and shall succeed in the thing for which I sent it.

Immediately after reading this passage, I felt as if a weight was lifted from me. Pastor Draper asked me what it meant, and I explained to him basically what I have explained to you in this study. God has a plan, and his plan cannot be stopped. It is not my responsibility to change his plan, and neither is it my responsibility to save someone else. I am called to get in line with God's plan and to faithfully speak and teach God's Word. The results are left up to him.

The Lord is faithful. He will accomplish his plan, and he will direct your hearts to the love of God and to the steadfastness of Christ.

24

The Gospel and Vocation

2 THESSALONIANS 3:6–18

What if I were to predict that Jesus Christ will come back tomorrow? You might think I have lost my mind, and I certainly hope that you would know enough about what we have studied in 1 and 2 Thessalonians to tell me that I have completely forgotten what I have shared in this book. But take a moment and suspend your knowledge of what Paul has told us and consider this question: What would you do if you knew Jesus would return later this week? Would you go to work tomorrow? Would you start calling people? Would you change your life? Would you pray all day? Would you isolate yourself?

Christians have answered that question in different ways throughout history. Early in the church, some people sold all they had, moved to a mountain, and waited for the appearing of Jesus, only to discover that they had to go back down to the city and figure out what to do with their lives when he did not return. We cannot just think that is an extreme view found in the early church. Just ten years ago some Christians sold their homes, cashed in their retirement funds, and moved away from the cities to wait for Jesus to appear in the year 2000 amidst all the excitement and speculation that surrounded the Y2K ordeal.

This response is not the way Paul would tell us to live if Jesus were coming back this week. Paul would tell you to go to work. He would tell you to go to school. He would tell you to continue your life, as a Christian, in your job and responsibilities. We face two difficulties with this type of response. First, we do not live our lives as we are supposed to live them. So we put off apologizing to someone we have wronged, and we put off the areas that we know need to be addressed. If we knew Jesus was coming back this week, we might think of a few things we should do right away to be prepared. But outside of that, Paul's answer would be that we should continue with our lives and go to work.

Perhaps it is difficult to believe that we should continue on with life if Jesus were coming back this week. If so, then we are struggling with the area of calling and vocation. I think this is at the heart of what is taking place in our passage at the end of 2 Thessalonians. This church had a crisis over the issue of work and vocation. We are not exactly sure why this crisis was happening. Some argue that it was a result of the eschatological excitement at this church.[1] In other words, these Christians thought Jesus was coming back, so they sold all they had and were struggling with the consequences. Others have argued that there was social pressure from the rest of the culture in Thessalonica regarding a client-patron relationship.[2] This is the type of relationship where a wealthy person (the patron) would provide for those who were not wealthy (the client) if the client provided certain tasks. Paul might have been addressing Christians who were caught in the client-patron relationship. Because they were both Christians, the wealthy Christian felt an obligation to help the poor Christian, even if the poor Christian was not living up to his or her end of the deal.

We do not have to limit Paul's words to either area. In fact, the speculations range beyond these two concerns to other areas as well. Fee provides a good summary:

> Was it disdain for work itself, because they were people of God's kingdom and thus a cut above needing to work? Was it pressing the gospel of the kingdom a bit too far, *expecting/demanding* the rich to care for the poor? Was it related to their eschatological understanding? Was it an attempt on Paul's part to break up dependencies created by patron-client relationships? Or was it just plain laziness? We simply do not know and in fact getting an answer to this question would hardly affect our understanding of the text at all.[3]

The solution is the same no matter which problem we are facing. Paul is providing a theology of work and vocation in this passage, and he is helping us think about the relationship between work, the benefits that result from it, and its relationship to the peace of our community.

THE QUESTION OF THE DISRUPTIVE-IDLE

In the midst of this section, the obvious issue that is at the surface of this passage concerns these people who are called idlers in the English Standard Version, or those who are "walking in idleness" (vv. 6, 11). The Greek word translated as "idleness" is *ataktos*. This word has other possible translations, and the word *idle* does not get across the broader meaning of the Greek word. Older translations used the words "disorderly" or "unruly," such as the King James Version: "every brother that walketh disorderly" (v. 6). That is actually a good translation that gets across the nuances of the situation. Yes, some brothers who walk disorderly are idle, but the word *idleness* narrows the focus too much.

We can see this within the context. Paul says in verse 11, "For we hear that some among you walk in idleness, not busy at work, but busybodies." Paul describes them as "walking" in this particular manner, and he calls them "busybodies." The picture is not of someone who is sitting around idle, but someone who is working at the wrong things. They are not doing what they are supposed to be doing, and this particular "walk" is at odds with the way they are supposed to be "walking" to please the Lord (1 Thessalonians 4:1), as well as with the tradition received from Paul (2 Thessalonians 3:6).

So our initial concern is this word "idle" or "idleness" that occurs in verses 6, 7, and 11. If you study the translation of this particular word, the history behind it is very odd.[4] The King James Version, which I mentioned earlier, actually had a correct translation in 1 Thessalonians 5:14 with the "unruly." The translation "the idle" first appeared in the Revised Standard Version in 1948 but apparently does not have a strong case. Gordon Fee even says that it is "difficult to fathom" why this meaning took over New Testament translations "despite total lack of evidence for it" as well as the fact that "it does not in fact have a lexical leg to stand on." The word literally means "out of line."[5]

This context is crucial for a proper understanding of what Paul's concern is in our passage. It is important for us to understand this word as meaning "out of line" and not just "idle," in the sense of laziness. To see the importance of this, we need to consider this issue in light of creation. A good theology of work and vocation begins in Genesis before the fall because work is not the result of the fall. We do not work because of sin. Work is part of God's good creation. Paul's words here in response to the Christians in Thessalonica are rooted in the Old Testament because his theology of work and vocation begins with the story of creation.

Notice what Paul says in verse 10: "For even when we were with you, we would give you this command: If anyone is not willing to work, let him not eat."[6] Where did Paul get that command? This command comes from the book of Genesis. Our understanding of work and vocation is rooted in the story of creation. God created the world and called it good, and Adam was called to work. Genesis 1:27–31 explains:

> So God created man in his own image, in the image of God he created him;
> male and female he created them. And God blessed them. And God said
> to them, "Be fruitful and multiply and fill the earth and subdue it and have

dominion over the fish of the sea and over the birds of the heavens and over every living thing that moves on the earth." And God said, "Behold, I have given you every plant yielding seed that is on the face of all the earth, and every tree with seed in its fruit. You shall have them for food. And to every beast of the earth and to every bird of the heavens and to everything that creeps on the earth, everything that has the breath of life, I have given every green plant for food." And it was so. And God saw everything that he had made, and behold, it was very good. And there was evening and there was morning, the sixth day.

This happens in Genesis 1. So before the fall, before sin entered the world, God instructed Adam regarding his service. Adam was to work for his food. Sin is not the reason we work. A healthy view of work and calling is rooted in a right view of creation. We are called to work because that is the way God created the world.

Work, however, is difficult now because of sin. According to Genesis 3, sin caused work to be accomplished only by the sweat of our brows:

> And to Adam he said, "Because you have listened to the voice of your wife and have eaten of the tree of which I commanded you, 'You shall not eat of it,' cursed is the ground because of you; in pain you shall eat of it all the days of your life; thorns and thistles it shall bring forth for you; and you shall eat the plants of the field. By the sweat of your face you shall eat bread, till you return to the ground, for out of it you were taken; for you are dust, and to dust you shall return." (Genesis 3:17–19)

Notice the last phrase. In essence this is, "By the sweat of your face you shall eat until you die." That is, "Since sin has entered the world, you will have pain and toil and labor and sweat. Work does not go the way it is supposed to go. Thorns and thistles will now come forth, and your work will be hard." Before sin there were no thorns and thistles, but because of sin we now face this pain and frustration and toil along with our work. But notice that something does not change: "Your work will produce bread." God was still instructing Adam and the rest of mankind that part of our duty in this world is to work.

Let's tie this back to 2 Thessalonians 3. Paul did not eat anyone's bread without paying for it, but with toil and labor, by the sweat of his face, he worked (v. 8), and that provided them an example for the command, "If anyone is not willing to work, let him not eat" (v. 10). Where did he get that command? It comes from Genesis 3:19: "By the sweat of your face you shall eat bread." We will benefit through our work by eating our bread. Paul's words in 1 Thessalonians 3 are rooted in the language of Genesis 3.

There is a second reason why the background of Genesis 3 is important. Paul did not just get the command about working from there — his whole perspective on life and work started there. Think about it this way: when God created the world, it was good; it was in order; everything was in the right place. Work was orderly and ruled by God's instruction. Adam should have followed God's commands. Everything was supposed to result in peace, which did not just mean the absence of conflict but complete well-being because everything was ordered rightly.

Then sin entered the world. Adam not only broke God's command, but he brought disorder into the whole world, and this disorder disrupted the peace that was part of the original creation. So sin, the breaking of God's commands, brought disorder and disrupted peace; it brought unruly and disorderly behavior. This behavior was "out of line" with God's intent. So God was at work in Genesis 3 to repair the ruins, to bring order and rule and peace.

Do you see how Paul is using this story from the creation narrative as the background of his instructions? One of Paul's central points is that God is repairing the ruins through the church now. That is why is it important to see that the word for "idleness" in 2 Thessalonians 3 is "disorderly" or "unruly." There is more at stake here than simply not doing things. Paul is saying to these Christians in Thessalonica that they were living "out of line" with God. These people were disrupting the work of God in making things right. In Genesis 3 we see God's order: work the ground, receive your bread. We are called to live in such a way that others see the way it is supposed to be, in spite of the struggle and pain.

The Thessalonians were not living in line with God's Word. Instead they were living outside of God's order. It was not simply that they were not working. They had disrupted the way things are supposed to be. Paul was telling them to get back in line with God's order because one of the central purposes of the church is to demonstrate the way reality is supposed to be. But they were not doing that. Their life had created disorder in the church and disorder in the culture. This was a breaking of *shalom*.

PAUL'S INSTRUCTION AND EXAMPLE

In order to address this, Paul did two things: he taught, and he provided an example. To tie this back into the idea that Paul was instructing them along the lines of history, Paul explained that they were not living in accord with "the tradition" (v. 6). When Paul was at the church, he instructed them about Heaven and redemption and salvation and the second coming. He taught them a basic doctrinal outlook on life, and that would have included work and vocation. He explained how they were supposed to live and how their work reflected the glory of God and how as they did their work well and to the best of their ability, they were salt and light to the culture. That is the significance of seeing our vocation properly. Work is missional.

Paul not only instructed them in the truth — Paul also lived out the truth.

He went beyond teaching them by providing them an example in his own life. They observed Paul's labor, and they were even able to see how Paul interacted with Christians and non-Christians as he worked. Paul was not unruly or disorderly, but with toil and labor he worked. By the sweat of his brow he struggled, and he provided for himself with his own hands. He took nothing from them without paying. Was this because teachers and preachers should not take money from a church? That is not the point at all because Paul writes, "It was not because we do not have that right, but to give you in ourselves an example to imitate" (v. 9). It wasn't because he had to work. As a teacher he could have been supported by the church. But Paul chose to live in such a way as to be an example for these young Christians about the importance of hard work so they could imitate him. This example was contrary to many of the traveling teachers of Paul's day who represented philosophical traditions that disparaged manual labor.[7]

THE COMMAND: NO WORK, NO FOOD

Paul, however, was more specific than the appeal to tradition. He gave a straightforward command: "For even when we were with you, we would give you this command: If anyone is not willing to work, let him not eat" (v. 10). We have already seen how Paul was drawing this command from the creation story in Genesis and was instructing this church about the broader concern of vocation and life. This particular command became very important in the history of the church regarding work.[8] An early church document called the *Apostolic Constitutions* (ca. A.D. 375) used this verse as a ground for its instruction regarding the requirement to work for a living. It also provided instruction for ministers concerning how they should help those in need, as well as dealing with the "disorderly" who should not receive help from the church.

After the Protestant Reformation, the concept of one's vocation was revitalized by Martin Luther, who argued that all work and vocation was glorifying to God, not just the role of the minister. Luther also argued that work is not just about what you do but about what God does through you in your calling. Luther believed that the world is God's good creation, and our calling and vocation is to serve Christ in our particular state of life and to watch God work through us for the good of others.[9] The Reformed and Calvinist notions of work and vocation are slightly different, though both emphasize the importance of hard work. Typically the Reformed tradition has been known for its strong work ethic, and this is often related to social action.[10]

POSSIBLE AREAS OF CONCERN

We must pause and consider this command in light of what we face in our culture. Although this is a larger topic than can be covered in one study, I want to at least direct you toward some areas against which we must be on guard as Christians. Part of Paul's central point here is that we have to be on guard against living off other people, which means we have to be on guard against the idea that we have a privileged position as Christians and have a right to be taken care of by others. The Christian ethic concerning work is the opposite of that attitude: we should be generous and sacrificial toward other people. At the heart of this command to work is the notion of providing for yourself so you can be generous toward others.

Let me start with an area that is close to us — the church. We can examine this in two directions. One of the dangers that pastors must be on guard against is the notion that people owe us more than we get. To be very practical, the temptation is that as a minister I might think that someone should always pick up the bill for me at the restaurant. Pastors have to avoid this danger. But this is also a danger related to Christians in general. Christians do not receive a pass in the area of work because the church has a benevolent fund to take care of those who are in need. When the church serves you in this manner, you must be on guard against that service becoming an expectation. The church is not called to continually take care of you. You might need help at a certain time, but the goal is for you to get back on your feet and help others.

The same danger is evident regarding the role of the federal government. I often hear comments in the media to the effect that the federal government is responsible to take care of its people, and I even hear individuals affirm this belief. This is not a Christian position. Yes, the government can play an important role in helping its citizens, but Christians dare not live in such a way as to depend upon the federal government. When national disasters take place, our hope is not in our government. Our hope is in the Lord, the maker of Heaven and earth.

Since I am addressing some areas that might be uncomfortable for us, I should not fail to mention the issue of retirement. The notion of retirement has become "the American dream." The idea is that we are supposed to work hard for forty to fifty years, until we have saved up enough money to retire and play. Maybe you like to golf; maybe you want to travel around the country. Whatever your desire, you get it after you retire. A life of rest and ease. You know what this sounds like to me? It sounds like we have created our own little heaven on earth. John Piper encourages us not to waste our retirement when he writes:

> Live dangerously for the one who loved you and died for you in his thirties. Don't throw your life away on the American dream of retirement. You are as secure as Christ is righteous and God is just. Don't settle for anything less than the joyful sorrows of magnifying Christ in the sacrifices of love. And then in the Last Day, you will stand and hear, "Well done, good and faithful servant. . . . Enter into the joy of your master" (Matt. 25:21, 23).[11]

This does not mean you have to stay at the same job. If you retire, perhaps you can serve God with your time in a way that you were not able to do for the earlier parts of your life. The Bible does not give us any indication that we can stop working or retire this side of Heaven. We are always called to serve God and our neighbor.

Certainly there are qualifications that we must make regarding these concerns. We all face troubles and difficulties, and we should help each other in those times. On the other hand, I should point out that it is dangerous when we do not accept help. That can be a form of pride. So think through these matters and these areas of concern. Be aware of why you work and what you are called to do. But do not get caught in the trap of growing lazy and idle, of being disorderly with your life and thinking that someone else will take care of your problem. That is not the way of the Christian faith. We should not be people who think we will wait and see what happens when we face a problem. The character of our lives as Christians should be a strong work ethic, rooted in creation and the gospel, realizing that we are rendering our work as unto the Lord (Ephesians 6:7) and that he is at work through us.

BUSYBODIES IN THE CHURCH

Paul helps us clarify this situation by explaining that the problem was not just lack of work, but a situation where these Christians chose not to work and to become "busybodies." Paul explains in verse 11, "For we hear that some among you walk in idleness, not busy at work, but busybodies." This is what happens when things are not working the way they are supposed to work. When you are not tending to your own vocation and work, you will face the temptation to poke your nose into business that is not your responsibility. That is what we call being busybodies, and when you call someone a busybody, you are not using that term positively.

The Greek word for "busybodies" (*periergazomai*) is a word for meddling. These Christians who were not working had created disorder in the life of the church because they were meddling in the affairs of other people. This is a consequence of not serving God and neighbor — we are tempted to get into the business of others. We must make sure we see the reason for this: we become "busybodies" because we are not doing what we are called to do. Paul confirms this in verse 12: "Now such persons we command and encourage in the Lord Jesus Christ to do their work quietly and to earn their own living." In other words, we must mind our own business.

Notice the contrast here between the behavior of those who are walking in a way that pleases God by doing their work and those who are not walking according to the tradition but are being disorderly. This contrast is consistent with what we have seen from Paul's argument being rooted in the creation story. Disorderly conduct that disrupts the peace of the church is not the way life is supposed to be lived. It creates busybodies who serve themselves instead of serving others. That kind of self-centered attitude is a direct result of the fall. Instead Paul calls us to be Christians who "do their work quietly and . . . earn their own living" (v. 12). That is a life that is in line with God's intentions and is not self-centered. Busybodies draw attention to themselves and disrupt the life of the church. Those who are working should "not grow weary of doing good" (Galatians 6:9). Not only is work difficult, but dealing with each other in the life of the church is difficult, especially if you are dealing with a busybody.

DEALING WITH THE DISORDERLY

Paul has provided a command about working, and he has explained why this is so important. But what are we to do if the disorderly do not heed Paul's words? How should we respond to those who continue to walk this way? If there is a disruption in the church and someone is being disorderly, our tendency is to ignore it and hope it goes away. If we are honest, we do that in our own lives, and we do it within the church, too. But that is not what Paul tells us to do. Back in verse 6 he told us to "keep away from any brother who is walking in idleness [literally, disorder]." Then at the end of this section Paul commands, "If anyone does not obey what we say in this letter, take note of that person, and have nothing to do with him, that he may be ashamed. Do not regard him as an enemy, but warn him as a brother" (vv. 14, 15). This final command is probably broader than the immediate context. He starts with the words, "If anyone does not obey what we say in this letter . . . " This would probably include some of the earlier commands, but we can apply it to this passage in particular.

Paul gives us two courses of action in response to those who are disorderly: we are to take note of such a person, and we are to have nothing to do with him or her. This is the exact opposite of our tendency to ignore him or her, and that is why this course of action is so difficult. This is one example of church discipline.[12] Discipline is part of the life and ministry of the church, and although it is often neglected today, it is often one of the marks of the church in the tradition that came from the early Protestant churches.[13] For example, *The Belgic Confession* has a section on "The Marks of the True Church," listing three:

> The true church can be recognized if it has the following marks: The church engages in the pure preaching of the gospel; it makes use of the pure administration of the sacraments as Christ instituted them; it practices church discipline for correcting faults. In short, it governs itself according to the pure Word of God, rejecting all things contrary to it and holding Jesus Christ as the only Head. By these marks one can be assured of recognizing the true church — and no one ought to be separated from it.[14]

The three marks include the pure preaching of the gospel, the pure administration of the sacraments (baptism and the Lord's Supper), and the practice of church discipline. This is in line with our current passage as well as with other passages of Scripture such as Matthew 18:15–17, which outlines how to handle sin between brothers, with the final step being that if the offending brother refuses to listen, bring it before the church.[15]

Scripture is clear on this matter. Leaders are charged to watch over the souls of their people, and they will have to give an account. If discipline is not part of the ministry of a church, then a crucial ingredient of growth is missing from the life of that church. Paul is also helping us see that if Christians in a church are disorderly and busybodies, that church will face grief and frustration as a body. In many cases the only way to deal with this is a straightforward approach of rebuke and sometimes disassociation.

THE GLORIOUS CONCLUSION: PEACE

Let us be honest for a moment: these are hard verses. Work and vocation is itself hard because of sin. When it is not functioning properly, which is often, disorder comes into the life of the church. If those who are disorderly do not heed Paul's command and the instruction of the leaders in the church, we could be facing the difficult task of church discipline, hoping to bring a brother back to the proper path. But Paul gives us hope in this process in verse 16. If we follow Paul's commands, if we fulfill our callings and vocations, if we deal with disorderly problems and address them, if we encourage one another, then the Lord will reestablish peace. If disorderliness is taking place to the extent that it becomes a corporate matter, we have lost the peace of the community. If we do not have peace within the community, we have lost one of the central elements of the good news. So Paul explains in verse 16 that by addressing these problems, no matter how hard that may be at the moment, we are on the road to reestablishing peace in the community.

This seems to be a closing word of hope. When we have to face difficult decisions as a church that involve those we love, the path to restoration can be quite difficult. But Paul reminds us with these concluding words that we cannot lose sight of the goal. Our redemption is not simply a ticket to eternal bliss. Our redemption is for the whole world because our redemption is supposed to give the world a picture of the way things are supposed to be. So Paul concludes by reminding us that the Lord will provide peace through these difficult trials, and ultimately he will reestablish peace not only within our community but across the whole world. That is good news indeed.

25

The Gospel Takes Root and Bears Fruit in Thessalonica

1 & 2 THESSALONIANS

What can two letters that were written almost two thousand years ago teach us today? To be more precise, what can we learn from two letters written by a Jew named Paul to people who lived in Thessalonica under the Roman Empire? We all know that our worlds are drastically different. We have cars, planes, television, the Internet, and telephones, to mention just a few differences. There are ethical and political differences (such as the contrast between democracy and kingship). We are certainly more scientifically aware than the Christians who lived back then, so surely we have to figure out a way to understand the Bible in light of our own world.

We should not overestimate our scientific advancements and knowledge. These differences are superficial; they are not at the core of who we are as humans. We must not drive a wedge between our world and Paul's world. We live within the realm of the New Testament in the same way that Paul did because we are participants in the New Covenant. This means that we live in fundamentally the same age as those Christians living in Thessalonica because we still face fundamental issues in life — sin, redemption, holiness, idolatry, hope, death. In spite of the differences between then and now, we all still die, and we all need the gospel when we face death. Facing the same types of struggles and trials, we must understand the gospel.

WHAT IS THE GOSPEL?

Paul explains "that Christ died for our sins in accordance with the Scriptures, that he was buried, that he was raised on the third day in accordance with the

Scriptures" (1 Corinthians 15:3, 4). The word *gospel*, which means "good news," has two primary aspects. The first aspect is *news*. This message is an announcement of an event that happened in history. It is not merely something that happened to us but is a historical event that took place in the life, death, and resurrection of Jesus Christ. Secondly, this news is *good*. This event that happened in history is good because through God's infinite wisdom, he applies that historical event to us. In particular, this good news is that Jesus died on the cross in order to solve our biggest problem — the issue of sin.

We are not preaching the gospel if our message is, "Do this." Instruction concerning a certain way of life or conduct is not the gospel. We are called to live and walk a particular way as Christians, and the gospel has a bearing on our lives. But ethical instructions and moral commands are not the gospel. The gospel is not our faith. The gospel is not our repentance. The gospel is not the way we live our lives. Paul provides a distinction for us between what God has done, often called the indicative, and what God calls us to do, often called the imperative. This distinction is crucial to a proper understanding of the gospel.

THE GOSPEL CAME TO THESSALONICA

Paul brought this good news of God's work through his Son Jesus Christ to cities and regions within the Roman Empire, and in Acts 17 we read of Paul's bringing this good news to Thessalonica. He explained to the Jews and God fearers in that great city that all the promises of God have been answered through Jesus Christ. The fall of Adam and Eve, the entrance of sin into the world, the wickedness during the flood, the evil idolatry at the Tower of Babel, the failure of Israel — all these "falls" have been redeemed in the gospel of Christ. Christ died for our sins, and through his death he will remake the world.

The gospel is indeed the specific message about how Christ died for our sins, but it is also a cosmic message about the Lordship of Jesus Christ. Isaiah proclaims, "How beautiful upon the mountains are the feet of him who brings good news, who publishes peace, who brings good news of happiness, who publishes salvation, who says to Zion, 'Your God reigns'" (Isaiah 52:7). The good news is not only the forgiveness of our sins. It is the complete obliteration of sin when Jesus makes all things new.

Luke's report of this church plant is a testimony to the power of the gospel: "some of [the Jews] were persuaded and joined Paul and Silas, as did a great many of the devout Greeks and not a few of the leading women" (Acts 17:4). Paul himself says that the "gospel came to [them] not only in word, but also in power and in the Holy Spirit and with full conviction" (1 Thessalonians 1:5). But Paul had to leave the church suddenly because of conflict and opposition in that city. There were false charges against him, but one charge was true, and this charge will always be true against Christians: "These men who have turned the world upside down have come here also . . . and they are all acting against the decrees of Caesar, saying that there is another king, Jesus" (Acts 17:6, 7). The Christians were claiming to serve a king other than Caesar. Because Jesus is Lord, they had a different loyalty and a different citizenship, and so do we.

This is what the gospel does. The gospel changes our status. In the case of the Christians in Thessalonica, they were no longer merely citizens of Rome, and they could no longer give Caesar their complete loyalty. They had become citizens of Heaven, and they awaited a Savior who is the King — Jesus Christ the Lord. They were first of all Christians, and so are we. We are not first of all citizens of any earthly kingdom. We are first of all citizens of Heaven, and the gospel changes the way we approach life in the church and in the world.

1 THESSALONIANS

Now that we have finished our study of these two letters, we can see the overall picture of how the gospel took root in the life of this early church. This gospel was not only the power of God that caused these early Christians to believe, but the gospel was also the power of God that kept them firm in the faith. In other words, the message and power of the gospel is as relevant for Christians as it is for non-Christians. We never move beyond the gospel as Christians. What we have in 1 Thessalonians is an example of the gospel plowing through the life of these Christians in various ways. I want us to see the big picture of how the gospel took root and shaped a church under Paul's ministry.

GOSPEL TRANSFORMATION: CHRISTIAN LIFE AND MINISTRY (1:1–2:16)

Paul's first letter to the Thessalonians highlights the transformation that took place in the life of these people. He addresses them as the church in God the Father and the Lord Jesus Christ. They have been baptized into the name of the Father, the Son, and the Holy Spirit, and thus they have a new identity. Paul is thankful for this transformation that is demonstrated in their "work of faith and labor of love and steadfastness of hope in our Lord Jesus Christ" (1:3). These three areas — faith, love, and hope — are the fundamental virtues of the Christian faith. Not only does the gospel bring about this change in regard to our faith, love, and hope, but the gospel continues to supply the power for these virtues to grow and mature.

This growth, however, takes place through suffering. The gospel came to them "not only in word, but also in power and in the Holy Spirit and with full conviction" (v. 5). When Paul says the gospel came to them "in power," he means that they received the Word "in much affliction" (v. 6). We see this in Acts 17 where we see that they believed the truth about Jesus and continued to believe even after Jason was taken to jail. They did not deny Jesus. That is conviction empowered by the gospel through the Holy Spirit.

Notice how Paul ties this particular area of suffering back to the gospel. He writes, "And you became imitators of us and of the Lord, for you received the word in much affliction" (1 Thessalonians 1:6). Paul explains that their suffering was following a pattern. They were imitating Paul, and Paul was imitating Jesus. This is a proper perspective on suffering in light of the gospel — picking up our cross and following Jesus Christ. But notice that Paul adds another phrase at the end of that verse: "with the joy of the Holy Spirit." Paul brings together two experiences that we often keep separated — affliction and joy. The gospel allows us to have a confident and steadfast joy in the face of our suffering because this world is not our home.

One of our greatest struggles in the midst of suffering is that we often have no explanation of its purpose. In our darkest moments we cry out, "Why are you doing this, God?" But when the gospel comes into our lives, our suffering takes on a different perspective. How does the gospel change our suffering? Think about the heart of the gospel: an innocent man named Jesus died upon a cross, and it meant something. His suffering was not pointless; it had a purpose. And his suffering redeems our suffering. The message of the gospel helps us understand that as we embrace Christ and trust him, we suffer along with Christ.

To see suffering in light of the gospel means that we will not view our suffering as God's wrath but as God's redemptive work of refining us. We see this at the end of 1 Thesssalonians 1. These Christians had turned from idols to God, and now they were waiting for the Son to return from Heaven. What will Jesus do when he returns? He "delivers us from the wrath to come." Our suffering is working for us an eternal weight of glory. If we trust Christ, we are not suffering because of God's anger against us. On the cross Jesus took the full force of God's wrath. He didn't take half of it so we could suffer under part of God's wrath in our lives. He didn't take 99 percent of it. As the hymn "It Is Well with My Soul" says, "My sin, not in part but the whole, / Is nailed to the cross, and I bear it no more, / Praise the Lord, praise the Lord, O my soul!" Jesus took it all so we would be delivered from the wrath to come. Note how this good news of what Jesus did took root in the lives of these Christians and how it changed the way they lived.

The Transformation of Paul. As we move into 1 Thessalonians 2, we see that this gospel also transformed the Apostle Paul and continued to provide what he needed to minister. Paul explains, "For you yourselves know, brothers, that our coming to you was not in vain. But though we had already suffered and been shamefully treated at Philippi, as you know, we had bold-ness in our God to declare to you the gospel of God in the midst of much conflict" (vv. 1, 2). Remember that Paul had just left Philippi, where he had been shamefully treated and thrown into jail. After he was released, what did he do? I would be tempted to go back to Jerusalem and find another way to minister. Maybe I could stop in Antioch for a while and heal — I would certainly need a break. Thankfully Paul was living in line with the gospel, and he continued his mission. When he got to Thessalonica, we know what happened. He faced more suffering and more affliction. In spite of those trials, Paul was still confident and bold to speak the gospel, consciously bearing his cross.

It seems that some accused Paul of having wrong motives in his work of ministry, but he denied that he was ministering out of "error or impurity or any attempt to deceive" (v. 3). Instead he continued to minister because he had been "approved by God to be entrusted with the gospel" (v. 4). Paul was concerned about God's approval; so he spoke to please God, not men (v. 4). That is why Paul could describe his ministry as being gentle, like a mother taking care of her children (v. 7). He was affectionate and was willing to share not only the gospel of God but also his own life (v. 8).

We need to see the connection between the root of the gospel and its fruit. When Paul came to preach the gospel, he was able to endure much affliction and suffering because his confidence was in God. Since he trusted Christ, since he had been approved by God, he was no longer under God's wrath, and he saw his afflictions through the cross of Christ. So he was will-ing not only to share the gospel but to share his own life. He gave of himself. The gospel called forth this sacrificial behavior because that was the way Christ lived for us. As the gospel took root in Paul's life, he not only taught the gospel, he imitated Jesus Christ.

Paul also reminds us that the gospel empowers the preaching of God's Word: "And we also thank God constantly for this, that when you received the word of God, which you heard from us, you accepted it not as the word of men but as what it really is, the word of God, which is at work in you believers" (v. 13). When the gospel comes to us through the preaching of God's Word, we no longer receive it as just another sermon — it is God's message. So the gospel transforms preaching, both from the perspective of the minister and from the perspective of the hearer.

Paul connects the importance of the word of God to the suffering of the church. In other words, when that church accepted the message of the gospel as God's word, they became participants in the work that God was doing across the whole world. Paul explains, "For you, brothers, became imitators of the churches of God in Christ Jesus that are in Judea" (v. 14). The gospel has the ability to transform churches across different cultures. The same gospel that transformed Judea was transforming Thessalonica, and evidence of this was in their suffering.

> For you suffered the same things from your own countrymen as they did from the Jews, who killed both the Lord Jesus and the prophets, and drove us out, and displease God and oppose all mankind by hindering us from speaking to the Gentiles that they might be saved — so as always to fill up the measure of their sins. But God's wrath has come upon them at last! (vv. 14–16)

This is another avenue by which we see the power of the gospel. In the life, death, and resurrection of Jesus we have the demonstration of good news: we have been forgiven through his sacrifice. But we also have a calling to pick up our crosses and follow Jesus. When the gospel takes root in the life of a church, its people will be conformed to Jesus Christ, and that means bearing a cross. That is a gospel-centered approach to suffering.

GOSPEL TRANSFORMATION: SACRIFICE (2:17–3:13)

A new section begins in 1 Thessalonians 2:17, and this section conveys Paul's great concern for these Christians. Paul had been torn away from them, and he longed to go back and minister to them, but Satan hindered him. So Paul figured out a solution to this problem: he would send Timothy to minister to them. We see here another example of how the gospel bears fruit — in this case by spurring Paul on to be sacrificial. Timothy is described as Paul's "brother and . . . coworker in the gospel" (3:2).

When I read about Paul's decisions in the ministry, especially his decision to send Timothy back to Thessalonica, I get the impression that Paul was consciously living in light of the gospel as evidenced by his actions and ministerial choices. Paul looked at this situation and wanted to demonstrate his love for this church. He had shared the gospel with them, he had given himself as much as he could while he was there, but he had to leave quickly. Now they were struggling and confused, and they needed to be encouraged. So Paul was thinking about how to demonstrate the depth of his love for them. Since Paul could not go to them, he decided to send perhaps his most precious gift — his brother and fellow coworker, Timothy. That decision was a result of a life centered on the gospel. We do not make that kind of decision if we are self-centered persons. It is a decision filled with sacrificial love.

It is important to note the nature of Paul's sacrifice. There are two ways to approach sacrificial living. The first way is the "gut it out" type of sacrifice. We are all too familiar with that model. Just give it up, gut it out, and sacrifice all you can. That way of life is not based on the gospel. It has no power. The alternative is a gospel-centered type of sacrifice. In Paul's ministry to this church, he chose to live sacrificially for them. He gave them Timothy instead of keeping Timothy with him. That sacrifice was rooted in the reality of the gospel of God the Father giving his only begotten Son. When we express our love for others, are we expressing that love sacrificially? Is it in line with the gospel? Does it bring us joy to sacrifice for others? We must find our joy in God and Christ so we can live sacrificially. We are called to live a life that is rooted in the gospel and is in line with the gospel.

GOSPEL FRUIT: A LIFE THAT PLEASES GOD (1 THESSALONIANS 4, 5)

After overflowing with thanksgiving and demonstrating a life of sacrifice, Paul now turns his attention to specific areas of life where we must walk in a manner that pleases God. First, he explains that we must demonstrate a life of love (4:1–12). Paul calls us to love God, follow his will, and grow in holiness, but these commands are to be obeyed within our community, too, as we love one another. The command that we are to abstain from sexual immorality is a command to be loving toward those around us because we are to honor one another with our bodies. The positive side of the command is an expression of brotherly love. We are called to help others in need and to encourage each other in this journey.

Second, Paul calls us to a life of hope (4:13–18). One of the struggles we face in the Christian life is the issue of death. Friends and loved ones die. One day we will die too. There is no way to avoid death, and there is no way to avoid grief. But there is hope. The gospel provides hope in the face of death because death does not have the last word. Those who have died in Christ will be raised from the dead on the last day. In spite of our grief, we can face death with hope, and that is a life that pleases God.

Third, we are called to a life of patience (5:1–11). Paul provides instructions for us regarding the second coming of Jesus Christ. We cannot know the precise time or the season of Christ's return, but we can be confident that he will come back and fulfill his promise. A life of patience draws from the gospel by realizing that God kept his promise and sent his Son in the first advent and that God will keep his promise and send his Son in the second advent. We have this knowledge, and we are called to walk in the light of it during these dark days, demonstrating our confidence in God as we patiently wait for him to fulfill his promises.

Finally, we are called to a life of community (5:12–28). The last section of this letter is a reminder to us about the way we are to live together in Christ's church until he returns. The church is our most significant community. Our life together in Christ's church is the training ground for our growth, and this is a crucial component of a life that pleases God. Paul provides instructions for leaders, church members, and the life of worship.

Paul covers a lot of ground in this first letter. So as he comes to a conclusion, what can he possibly say to encourage these Christians (and us) regarding the future that God intends? Paul concludes with these words: "Now may the God of peace himself sanctify you completely, and may your whole spirit and soul and body be kept blameless at the coming of our Lord Jesus Christ. He who calls you is faithful; Paul will surely do it" (5:23, 24). I personally find it encouraging that as Paul gets near the end of this book, he reminds us of the beginning. God started this whole process, and God will finish it. He will keep us holy and blameless until Christ returns. That is good news . . . but it is not the end of our story.

2 THESSALONIANS

Paul had to write a second letter to this church. It would be a nice, clean ending if the first letter was the final letter, especially with its glorious ending. But the gospel allows us to be honest and face the fact that life do not always go the way we plan. God promises he will keep us until the return of Christ, but more work needed to be done in this church, just as more work is needed in our churches.

Since we have a second letter, we can see some of the areas where the Thessalonians were confused, even after the first letter. I think this is a picture of the Christian life. There is no quick-fix solution. There is no silver bullet. The gospel is a seed that takes root in our lives and over a period of time produces fruit. So the Thessalonian believers needed two letters, many sermons, numerous worship services, and lots of Bible studies, and they still struggled with their faith, as do we. This second letter is instructive because of the Thessalonians' areas of confusion, which are areas we struggle with today as well. Paul addresses three primary concerns — suffering, true doctrine, and patience. In fact, these areas are connected. God was developing a patient faith in their lives as they struggled with their suffering and future judgment, struggles that are often caused by false teaching.

GOSPEL CONFIDENCE: STAND FIRM

Don't Be Discouraged by Suffering (1:1–12). Paul's second letter is straightforward and to the point. In his first letter, we have five chapters that span eighty-nine verses of encouraging words to a struggling church. But in this second letter we have only three chapters that span forty-seven verses. The two themes of suffering and doctrine are woven throughout the book, and Paul immediately gets to the point when he says, "We ourselves boast about you in the churches of God for your steadfastness and faith in all your persecutions and in the afflictions that you are enduring" (v. 4). But he wants to remind them that their own suffering is "evidence of the righteous judgment of God, that you may be considered worthy of the kingdom of God, for which you are also suffering — since indeed God considers it just to repay with affliction those who afflict you, and to grant relief to you who are afflicted as well as to us, when the Lord Jesus is revealed from heaven with his mighty angels" (vv. 5–7). Paul helps them see that this suffering is working toward their future salvation. The ungodly will be punished, and the godly will be saved on that great and glorious day when Jesus returns.

Don't Be Deceived by False Teaching (2:1–3:5). When he moves into chapter 2, Paul has to address the issue of false teaching. It is crucial for the church to understand that the devil is trying to sway us away from the truth by the constant temptation to engage in apostasy and lawlessness. So we must be on guard and not be deceived by false teaching. This false teaching will reach a climax at the end, right before Jesus returns, but evil and lawlessness will attack the church throughout her history. In the midst of these attacks and the temptation to fall away, we can still have confidence in the sovereign power of God, who "chose you as the firstfruits to be saved, through sanctification by the Spirit and belief in the truth" (2:13). That is precisely why God called us through the gospel: he will work to establish us so that we will obtain the glory of the Lord Jesus Christ. The Lord is faithful, and he will establish us and guard us against the evil one (3:3).

Don't Grow Weary in Doing Well (3:6–18). As we wait for the day of Christ's return, we must not grow weary in doing good. We will face temptation to practice unruly behavior that will show itself in laziness and meddling. But that is not the way God created and designed the world. To live like that is to give in to the false teaching. We are called to do our work quietly and to earn our own living. By living that way, we will be a witness not only to our own community but to the whole world. It is through these small actions that God has determined to reestablish his *shalom*, his peace, and to make things the way they are supposed to be.

A GOSPEL-CENTERED LIFE

How can we end this study? Is there a way to provide a helpful summary to Paul's teaching? In both letters Paul opened with the three Christian virtues of faith, love, and hope. These virtues are consistent throughout some of Paul's other letters also, although they appear in different order. Through church history, theologians and pastors have realized that these virtues provide a summary of the Christian life. St. Augustine's *Enchiridion*, which means "small manual" or "booklet," is a summary of the Christian faith that is organized according to the three graces that are necessary for a life that pleases God — faith, love, and hope. After reflecting on Paul's instructions in these two letters, I do not think it was an accident that he began his letters with these graces.

Paul calls us toward *a gospel-centered faith* that is focused upon Jesus Christ, our Redeemer and King. We are called not only to believe on him at the beginning of the Christian life but to trust him throughout the Christian life. Our faith should never move beyond Christ and his cross, and because our faith is fixed upon Jesus Christ, we are judged worthy of the kingdom. Do not buy into a "gospel" that changes that focus. Fix your eyes upon Jesus, the author and perfecter of our faith.

Paul also calls us to *a gospel-centered love.* We are called to love God and our neighbor, and that love flows out of the reality that God has accepted us. If God is for us, who can be against us? Because we are accepted, we can love and care for others without any expectation. In both letters Paul emphasized the area of work and vocation as an expression of this love. By working, we are not placing a burden on others, and through our work we can be generous toward others. Our work and calling is the central way that God works through us and uses us for his kingdom.

Finally, Paul also called us to *a gospel-centered hope.* We are called to remain steadfast in the face of trials and afflictions, believing that God is at work in those trials to conform us to the image of Christ. We should see our suffering through the cross, realizing that the power of God at work in his Son is the same power at work through us. Our hope is not based on the promise of a safe life in this world but on the promise that Christ will come back one day and vindicate his people, bring justice, and make all things new.

These virtues are the fruit of a gospel-centered life. Paul is calling us to live within the reality of our union with Christ. We need to see ourselves in Christ, believe we have been accepted and pardoned so we can love others, and remain steadfast in the hope of the promises of God. That is a life that pleases God and a life centered upon the gospel.

Soli Deo gloria!

Notes

CHAPTER ONE: LISTENING TO PAUL'S CONVERSATION

1. Calvin J. Roetzel, *The Letters of Paul: Conversations in Context*, 4th ed. (Louisville: Westminster John Knox, 1998). J. Christian Beker, in his important work *Paul the Apostle: The Triumph of God in Life and Thought* (Philadelphia: Fortress, 1980), called a letter from Paul a "word on target" (p. 12).
2. For an overview of theological themes, see I. Howard Marshall, *New Testament Theology: Many Witnesses, One Gospel* (Downers Grove, IL: InterVarsity Press, 2004), pp. 238–245. Marshall highlights the following themes: mission and apostleship, the gospel, conversion, steadfastness, sanctification, the resurrection, and the *parousia*. See also Karl P. Donfried and I. Howard Marshall, *The Theology of the Shorter Pauline Letters*, New Testament Theology (New York: Cambridge University Press, 1993), pp. 28–63.

CHAPTER TWO: CHRISTIANITY AT THESSALONICA

1. The discussion of background, unless specifically noted, comes from the following sources: Gordon D. Fee, *The First and Second Letters to the Thessalonians*, NICNT (Grand Rapids, MI: Eerdmans, 2009), pp. 3–8; G. K. Beale, *1–2 Thessalonians*, IVPNT (Downers Grove, IL: InterVarsity Press, 2003), pp. 13–37; Gene L. Green, *The Letters to the Thessalonians*, PNTC (Grand Rapids, MI: Eerdmans, 2002), pp. 1–74; Jeffrey A. D. Weima, "1 Thessalonians: From Text to Sermon," Kerux 2004 Summer Pastor's Institute (cassette tapes); Jeffrey A. D. Weima, "1 & 2 Thessalonians," in *The Zondervan Illustrated Bible Backgrounds Commentary*, vol. 3. *Romans to Philemon*, ed. Clinton Arnold (Grand Rapids, MI: Zondervan, 2002), pp. 405–410; Ben Witherington, III, *The Acts of the Apostles: A Socio-Rhetorical Commentary* (Grand Rapids, MI: Eerdmans, 1998), pp. 486–511; David G. Peterson, *The Acts of the Apostles*, PNTC (Grand Rapids, MI: Eerdmans, 2009), pp. 475–483; Darrell L. Bock, *Acts*, BECNT (Grand Rapids, MI: Baker, 2007), pp. 548–554; D. A. Carson and Douglas J. Moo, *An Introduction to the New Testament*, 2nd ed. (Grand Rapids, MI: Zondervan, 2005), pp. 532–553.
2. Weima, "1 Thessalonians: From Text to Sermon."
3. Weima, "1 & 2 Thessalonians," p. 406.
4. For what follows see Green, *Letters to the Thessalonians*, pp. 20–24.
5. Weima, "1 Thessalonians: From Text to Sermon."
6. K. P. Donfried, "The Cults of Thessalonica and the Thessalonian Correspondence," *New Testament Studies* 31 (1985): 336–356.
7. Weima, "1 & 2 Thessalonians," pp. 406–407.
8. Peterson, *Acts*, p. 483.
9. It is hard to gauge this type of statistic, but some missiologists believe that more Christians died for their faith during the twentieth century than during all previous centuries combined. See James C. Hefley and Marti Hefley, *By Their Blood: Christian Martyrs of the Twentieth Century* (Grand Rapids, MI: Baker, 1996); Robert Royal, *The Catholic Martyrs of the Twentieth Century: A Comprehensive World History* (New York: Crossroad Publishing, 2000).
10. See David Aikman, *Jesus in Beijing: How Christianity Is Transforming China and Changing the Global Balance of Power* (Washington, D.C.: Regnery, 2006). Although

Aikman documents the persecution of believers in China, he also demonstrates the power of the gospel in spite of these threats. This is precisely what happened in the Roman Empire as the gospel eventually overcame all opposition.

11.   Abraham Kuyper, "Sphere Sovereignty," in *Abraham Kuyper: A Centennial Reader*, ed. James D. Bratt (Grand Rapids, MI: Eerdmans, 1998), p. 488.

CHAPTER THREE: WHAT IS IN A GREETING?

1.   David E. Aune, *The New Testament in Its Literary Environment* (Philadelphia: Westminster, 1987), pp. 162–163; and Michael J. Gorman, *Apostle of the Crucified Lord: A Theological Introduction to Paul & His Letters*, Chapter 3, "Paul's Letters: Apostleship in Absentia" (Grand Rapids, MI: Eerdmans, 2004), pp. 74–97.

2.   Jeffrey A. D. Weima, "1 & 2 Thessalonians," in *The Zondervan Illustrated Bible Backgrounds Commentary*, vol. 3. *Romans to Philemon*, ed. Clinton Arnold (Grand Rapids, MI: Zondervan, 2002), p. 411.

3.   R. Laird Harris, Gleason L. Archer Jr., Bruce K. Waltke, *Theological Wordbook of the Old Testament* (Chicago: Moody Press, 1980), 2:930–931.

4.   See Cornelius Plantinga Jr., *Not the Way It's Supposed to Be: A Breviary of Sin* (Grand Rapids, MI: Eerdmans, 1995).

5.   Some early manuscripts have the Greek text as "grace and peace to you from God our Father and the Lord Jesus Christ," but Gordon D. Fee, *The First and Second Letters to the Thessalonians*, NICNT (Grand Rapids, MI: Eerdmans, 2009) observes that this addition is secondary on every account: "(1) it is missing in all the earliest and best evidence across the board, both East and West; (2) these words are found in 2 Thessalonians in all known manuscripts without variation; and thus (3) there is no way to account for such an early and widespread 'omission' in this letter alone in the Pauline corpus" (p. 12, note 13). Fee goes on to say that "in all subsequent appearances, beginning with 2 Thessalonians, Paul adds the source already assumed here, but not expressed: 'from God our Father and the Lord Jesus Christ.'"

CHAPTER FOUR: THE IMPORTANCE OF THANKFULNESS

1.   J. L. White, *Light from Ancient Letters* (Philadelphia: Fortress Press, 1986), p. 39; quoted in Jeffrey A. D. Weima, "1 & 2 Thessalonians," in *The Zondervan Illustrated Bible Backgrounds Commentary*, vol. 3. *Romans to Philemon*, ed. Clinton Arnold (Grand Rapids, MI: Zondervan, 2002), p. 411.

2.   Weima, "1 & 2 Thessalonians," p. 411.

3.   See *Shorter Catechism*, Question 86.

4.   Yong Kim, "Biblical Theology and Hebrews 11," 1999 Kerux Conference. Cassette tape.

5.   John Calvin, *Calvin's Commentaries* (Grand Rapids, MI: Baker, 1993), 21:239.

6.   Gordon D. Fee, *The First and Second Letters to the Thessalonians*, NICNT (Grand Rapids, MI: Eerdmans, 2009), p. 26.

7.   Ibid.

8.   See ibid., pp. 20–26 and Robert J. Cara, *1 & 2 Thessalonians* (Darlington, UK: Evangelical Press, 2009), pp. 34–35.

9.   For these two theological positions, see Chad Owen Brand, ed., *Perspectives on Election: Five Views* (Nashville: Broadman & Holman, 2006); Robert A. Peterson and Michael D. Williams, *Why I Am Not an Arminian* (Downers Grove, IL: InterVarsity Press, 2004); Jerry L. Walls and Joseph Dongell, *Why I Am Not a Calvinist* (Downers Grove, IL: InterVarsity Press, 2004). My own view is similar to Sam Storms, *Chosen for Life: The Case for Divine Election* (Wheaton, IL: Crossway, 2007).

10. Fee, *First and Second Letters to the Thessalonians*, pp. 30–31; see also Hans K. LaRondelle, *The Israel of God in Prophecy* (Berrien Springs, MI: Andrews University Press, 1983) for the argument that the church is the new Israel.

CHAPTER FIVE: THE CHRISTIAN DOCTRINE OF IMITATION

1. Daniel Schorn, "Tom Brady: The Winner," *60 Minutes* CBS, November 6, 2005, http://www.cbsnews.com/stories/2005/11/03/60minutes/main1008148.shtml.

2. Paul uses the notion of imitation, or *imitatio Christi*, in 1 Corinthians 4:16; 11:1; Ephesians 5:1; Philippians 3:17; 1 Thessalonians 1:6; 2:14; 2 Thessalonians 3:7, 9. Interestingly, Paul's use of the verb in 1 Thessalonians 1:6 ("became imitators") is in the passive voice. This means they are not doing it — God is doing it.

CHAPTER SIX: ALL OF LIFE IS REPENTANCE

1. Tim Keller, "Talking about Idolatry in a Postmodern Age," http://www.monergism.com/postmodernidols.html.

2. Anselm, *Why God Became Man*, in *A Scholastic Miscellany: Anselm to Ockham*, ed. Eugene R. Fairweather (Philadelphia: Westminster Press, 1956), p. 138. The quote is a translation of the Latin phrase, *"Nondum considerasti quantum ponderis sit peccatum."* The emphasis here is on the weight of our sin. I first read the phrase in Michael Horton, *Putting Amazing Back into Grace* (Grand Rapids, MI: Baker, 1991), p. 159.

CHAPTER SEVEN: UNION WITH CHRIST AND THE CHRISTIAN LIFE

1. John Piper, Mark Driscoll, and Sinclair Ferguson, "Panel Discussion—Piper, Driscoll, and Ferguson," Desiring God 2008 National Conference, September 26, 2008, http://www.desiringgod.org/resource-library/resources/panel-discussion-piper-driscoll-and-ferguson.

2. John Murray, *Redemption Accomplished and Applied* (Grand Rapids, MI: Eerdmans, 1955), pp. 201, 205.

3. See G. Adolph Deissmann, *The New Testament Formula "In Christ Jesus,"* originally *Die Neutestamentliche Formel "in Christo Jesu"* (Marburg: N. G. Elwert, 1892), p. 3. Deissmann's conclusion was that Paul was the originator of the formula as a technical religious expression (p. 70).

4. For example, Herman N. Ridderbos, "In Christ, with Christ: The Old and the New Man," in *Paul: An Outline of His Theology*, trans. John Richard De Witt (Grand Rapids, MI: Eerdmans, 1997), pp. 57–64; Richard B. Gaffin Jr., *By Faith, Not by Sight: Paul and the Order of Salvation* (Waynesboro, GA: Paternoster, 2006); Richard B. Gaffin Jr., *Resurrection and Redemption: A Study in Paul's Soteriology* (Phillipsburg, NJ: P&R, 1987); Anthony A. Hoekema, "Union with Christ," in *Saved by Grace* (Grand Rapids, MI: Eerdmans, 1994), pp. 54–67; Mark A. Garcia, *Life in Christ: Union with Christ and Twofold Grace in Calvin's Theology*, Studies in Christian History and Thought (Milton Keynes, UK: Paternoster, 2008); Michael S. Horton, *Covenant and Salvation: Union with Christ* (Louisville: Westminster John Knox, 2007); William B. Evans, *Imputation and Impartation: Union with Christ in American Reformed Theology*, Studies in Christian History and Thought (Milton Keynes, UK: Paternoster, 2008); Walter Marshall, *The Gospel Mystery of Sanctification* (Grand Rapids, MI: Reformation Heritage Books, 1999); John Murray, "Union with Christ," in *Redemption Accomplished and Applied*, pp. 161–173.

5. Sinclair B. Ferguson, *In Christ Alone: Living the Gospel Centered Life* (Lake Mary, FL: Reformation Trust, 2007).

CHAPTER EIGHT: PREACHING THE WORD OF CHRIST

1. See Edwin C. Dargan, *A History of Preaching*, 2 vols. (Grand Rapids, MI: Baker, 1968); O. C. Edwards Jr., *A History of Preaching* (Nashville: Abingdon, 2004).

2. Dawn DeVries, "Calvin's Preaching," in *The Cambridge Companion to John Calvin*, ed. Donald K. McKim (New York: Cambridge University Press, 2004), p. 108.

3. See Peter Adam, *Speaking God's Words: A Practical Theology of Preaching* (Vancouver, BC: Regent College Publishing, 2004).

4. Although I only examine Romans 10 and John 10 in this context, several texts within the Pauline epistles in particular demonstrate the way God speaks through preaching: Romans 10:17; 2 Corinthians 2:17; 2 Corinthians 5:18–21 (note especially v. 20 where God/Christ speaks through preaching). We also have texts that emphasize the preacher as a spokesman for another — 1 Corinthians 15:9–11; 2 Corinthians 4:2, 5; 11:4; and Galatians 1:12; 2:2. Finally we have passages that describe ministers as saving those who hear them: Romans 11:13, 14; 1 Corinthians 9:22; 1 Timothy 4:16. C. E. B. Cranfield even compares Paul's statement of Christ speaking through ministers to what is said concerning prophetic authority in Jeremiah 14:14; 23:21; 27:15 (*Romans*, ICC, vol. 2 [New York: T & T Clark, 2002], p. 534). One could also make a case for the use of Philippians 1 as emphasizing the distinction between the person of the proclaimer and the proclamation itself (hence Paul rejoices in the gospel being preached by those who are trying to harm him). Contrast this perspective with Paul's condemnation of the Judaizers in Galatians because they are preaching a different gospel.

5. John Murray, *The Epistle to the Romans*, NICNT, vol. 2 (Grand Rapids, MI: Eerdmans, 1965), p. 58.

6. John Piper, *Let the Nations Be Glad! The Supremacy of God in Missions*, 2nd ed. (Grand Rapids, MI: Baker, 2003), pp. 55, 151, 183.

CHAPTER NINE: THE GOSPEL AND YOUR SUFFERING

1. See www.desiringgod.org/Blog/1405_Preparing_for_Sudden_Suffering/.

2. M. Barth, "Was Paul an Anti-Semite?" *Journal of the Evangelical Theological Society*, 5 (1969): 98, quoted by Frank Gillard, "The Problem of the Anti-Semitic Comma Between 1 Thessalonians 2.14 and 15," *New Testament Studies*, 35 (1989): 481. For the evangelical perspective, see the discussion by Greg Beale, *1–2 Thessalonians*, IVPNT (Downers Grove, IL: InterVarsity Press, 2003), pp. 82–89.

3. For example, see Daryl Schmidt, "1 Thess. 2:13–16: Linguistic Evidence for an Interpretation," *Journal of Biblical Literature* 102/2 (1983): 269–279.

4. Beale, *1–2 Thessalonians*, p. 84.

5. Hans K. LaRondelle, *The Israel of God in Prophecy* (Berrien Springs, MI: Andrews University Press, 1983) argues convincingly that Jesus was the true Israel of God, and as such, all those who believe upon Jesus are the true Israel of God.

CHAPTER TEN: LIVING IN LIGHT OF THE GOSPEL

1. This is referenced in Acts 17:15 as well as in 1 Thessalonians 3:1, 2.

2. This insight regarding the nature of the covenant comes from Charles G. Dennison, "Thoughts on the Covenant," in *Pressing Toward the Mark: Essays Commemorating Fifty Years of the Orthodox Presbyterian Church*, ed. Charles G. Dennison and Richard C. Gamble (Philadelphia: The Committee for the Historian of the Orthodox Presbyterian Church, 1986), pp. 7–21.

3. These reflections come from a sermon by Charles G. Dennison, "Philippians 2:17–30," Sermon 36 (Sewickley PA: Grace OPC, 1991), Cassette tape.

4. Ibid.

5. Ibid.

6. G. K. Chesterton, *Orthodoxy* (London: Jane Lane, 1909), pp. 34, 35.

CHAPTER ELEVEN: BECOME WHAT YOU ALREADY ARE IN CHRIST

1. John Murray, *Principles of Conduct: Aspects of Biblical Ethics* (Grand Rapids, MI: Eerdmans, 1957), p. 11.

2. Jeffrey A. D. Weima, "1 & 2 Thessalonians," in *The Zondervan Illustrated Bible Backgrounds Commentary,* vol. 3. *Romans to Philemon*, ed. Clinton Arnold (Grand Rapids, MI: Zondervan, 2002), p. 419.

3. See William D. Dennison, "Indicative and Imperative: The Basic Structure of Pauline Ethics." *Calvin Theological Journal,* XIV (April 1979): 55–78 and Herman Ridderbos, "Indicative and Imperative," chap. 7, sect. 42 in *Paul: An Outline of His Theology*, trans. John Richard De Witt (Grand Rapids, MI: Eerdmans, 1975), pp. 253–258.

4. Charles G. Dennison, "Thoughts on the Covenant," in *Pressing Toward the Mark: Essays Commemorating Fifty Years of the Orthodox Presbyterian Church*, ed. Charles G. Dennison and Richard C. Gamble (Philadelphia: The Committee for the Historian of the Orthodox Presbyterian Church, 1986), p. 10. I first heard this expression from some of Dennison's sermons. Dennison would often say that you cannot get to Heaven unless you start in Heaven, and you cannot pursue holiness unless you are already holy.

5. John Murray's *Principles of Conduct* contains one reference to sex in the index of subjects. Outside the discussion of marriage, it just does not come up for discussion.

6. What follows is from Weima, "1 & 2 Thessalonians," "Sexual Conduct in the Greco-Roman World," p. 419.

7. Demosthenes, *Against Neaera*, in *Orations*, vol. 6, Loeb Classical Library, trans. A. T. Murray (Cambridge, MA: Harvard University Press), p. 122, quoted in Gordon D. Fee, *The First and Second Letters to the Thessalonians*, NICNT (Grand Rapids, MI: Eerdmans, 2009), p. 143.

8. F. F. Bruce, *1 & 2 Thessalonians*, Word Biblical Commentary, vol. 45 (Dallas: Word, 1982), p. 82. Interpreters should be aware that until about thirty years ago the idea of cultic prostitution was viewed as a historical fact. Recently, however, critical scholars have argued against the notion of cultic prostitution. See Karel van der Toorn, "Prostitution, Cultic," in *The Anchor Bible Dictionary*, vol. 5, ed. David Noel Freedman (New York: Doubleday, 1992), pp. 510–513; and more recently Stephanie Budin, *The Myth of Sacred Prostitution in Antiquity* (Cambridge: Cambridge University Press, 2008).

9. Weima, "1 & 2 Thessalonians," p. 420.

10. Greg Beale, *1–2 Thessalonians*, IVPNT (Downers Grove, IL: InterVarsity Press, 2003), p. 116.

11. Greg Beale outlines four primary views: 1) Paul is commanding us to control our own bodies; 2) Paul is commanding males to control their sexual organ; 3) Paul is instructing Christian men on how to take a wife in an honorable manner, a view represented by the translation of the RSV: "that each one of you know how to take a wife for himself in holiness and honor"; 4) Paul is referring to a Greek law regarding the inheritance of a daughter that Christians should not observe. See ibid., pp. 116–120 for a full explanation.

12. Ibid., p. 116. Also in agreement with this interpretation are the following translations and commentators: ESV, NEB, NIV; John Calvin, *Calvin's Commentaries*, (Grand Rapids, MI: Baker, 1993), 21:274; Bruce, *1 & 2 Thessalonians*, p. 83; Weima, "1 & 2 Thessalonians," p. 420; Robert J. Cara, *1 & 2 Thessalonians* (Darlington, UK: Evangelical Press, 2009), p. 108; I. Howard Marshall, *1 and 2 Thessalonians*, New Century Bible Commentary (Grand Rapids, MI: Eerdmans, 1983), p. 109; Leon Morris, *The First and Second Epistles to the Thessalonians*, NICNT (Grand Rapids, MI: Eerdmans, 1959), p. 124; and Charles Wanamaker, *The Epistles to the Thessalonians*, NIGTC (Grand Rapids, MI: Eerdmans, 1990), p. 152.

13. J. I. Packer, *Growing in Christ* (Wheaton, IL: Crossway, 1994), pp. 264, 265.

14. See: Barna Group, "New Marriage and Divorce Statistics Released," March 31, http://www.barna.org/barna-update/article/15-familykids/42-new-marriage-and-divorce-statistics-released. Like the overall divorce rate, the Christian divorce rate is a complex issue that includes the following problems: a proper definition of "Christian," fear of being honest because of the religious stigma associated with divorce, and issues that involve legal marriages or common-law relationships.

CHAPTER TWELVE: THE FRUIT OF THE GOSPEL: LOVE

1. Tertullian, *Apology*, 39.6.
2. Justin Martyr, *First Apology*, Chapter 14.
3. John R. W. Stott, *The Message of 1 and 2 Thessalonians* (Downers Grove, IL: InterVarsity Press, 1991), p. 90.
4. Gordon D. Fee, *The First and Second Letters to the Thessalonians*, NICNT (Grand Rapids, MI: Eerdmans, 2009), p. 162.
5. Stott, *Message of 1 and 2 Thessalonians*, p. 88.
6. Bruce Winter, "'If a man does not wish to work . . .': A Cultural and Historical Setting for 2 Thessalonians 3:6–16," *Tyndale Bulletin*, 40.4 (1989): 303–315.
7. See R. F. Hock, "The Workshop as a Social Setting for Paul's Missionary Preaching," *Catholic Biblical Quarterly*, 41 (1979): 438–450; A. J. Malherbe, *Paul and the Thessalonians* (Philadelphia: Fortress, 1987), pp. 7–20.
8. Jeffrey A. D. Weima, "1 & 2 Thessalonians," in *The Zondervan Illustrated Bible Backgrounds Commentary*, vol. 3. *Romans to Philemon*, ed. Clinton Arnold (Grand Rapids, MI: Zondervan, 2002), p. 408.

CHAPTER THIRTEEN: THE SECOND ADVENT OF CHRIST

1. John R. W. Stott, *The Message of 1 and 2 Thessalonians* (Downers Grove, IL: InterVarsity Press, 1991), pp. 106, 114.
2. Theocritus, *Idyll*, 4.42, quoted in Jeffrey A. D. Weima, "1 & 2 Thessalonians," in *The Zondervan Illustrated Bible Backgrounds Commentary: Volume 3, Romans to Philemon*, ed. Clinton Arnold (Grand Rapids, MI: Zondervan, 2002), p. 422.
3. Stott, *Message of 1 and 2 Thessalonians*, p. 106.
4. Ibid., p. 114.

CHAPTER FOURTEEN: RESURRECTION HOPE IN THE FACE OF DEATH

1. C. S. Lewis, *The Silver Chair* (New York: HarperCollins, 1994), p. 212.
2. See John Piper, "Job: Reverent in Suffering," sermon preached on July 7, 1985; http://www.desiringgod.org/resource-library/resources/job.reverent-in-Suffering/.
3. See Thomas G. Long, *Accompany Them with Singing: The Christian Funeral* (Louisville: Westminster John Knox, 2009), pp. 57–76.
4. Colin R. Nicholl, *From Hope to Despair in Thessalonica: Situating 1 and 2 Thessalonians*, Society for New Testament Studies Monograph Series (New York: Cambridge University Press, 2004). One should also consult Nicholl's notes on "1 & 2 Thessalonians" in the *ESV Study Bible* (Wheaton, IL: Crossway, 2008), pp. 2301–2320.
5. Theocritus, *Idyll*, 4.42, quoted in Jeffrey A. D. Weima, "1 & 2 Thessalonians," in *The Zondervan Illustrated Bible Backgrounds Commentary*, vol. 3. *Romans to Philemon*, ed. Clinton Arnold (Grand Rapids, MI: Zondervan, 2002), p. 422.
6. John Calvin, *Calvin's Commentaries*, (Grand Rapids, MI: Baker, 1993), 21:363.
7. Long, *Accompany Them with Singing*, p. vi.
8. Robert J. Cara, *1 & 2 Thessalonians* (Darlington, UK: Evangelical Press, 2009), p. 126.
9. Seyoon Kim, *The Origin of Paul's Gospel* (Grand Rapids, MI: Eerdmans, 1982). Kim argues that Paul's Damascus road experience is crucial for the development of his theological perspectives.
10. Greg Beale, *1–2 Thessalonians*, IVPNT (Downers Grove, IL: InterVarsity Press, 2003), p. 138.
11. Cara, *1 & 2 Thessalonians*, p. 132.
12. Beale, *1–2 Thessalonians*, p. 138
13. Anthony A. Hoekema, *The Bible and the Future* (Grand Rapids, MI: Eerdmans, 1979), p. 92.

14. For example, see Ernest Best, *The First and Second Epistles to the Thessalonians*, Harper's New Testament Commentaries (Peabody, MA: Hendrickson, 1986), pp. 194–196.

15. Cara, *1 & 2 Thessalonians*, p. 129.

CHAPTER FIFTEEN: WHAT ABOUT THE RAPTURE?

1. These views are presented in Darrell L. Bock, ed., *Three Views on the Millennium and Beyond*, (Grand Rapids, MI: Zondervan, 1999).

2. The premillennial view breaks into different perspectives on how Christ will return before the Millennium. Historic premillennialists believe Christ will come back right at the beginning of this thousand-year reign. Dispensational premillennialists believe that Christ will secretly rapture his saints at the start of a seven-year period before the beginning of the thousand-year reign. Dispensationalists have continued to develop their theology to the point of a new perspective called Progressive Dispensationalism. See Darrell L. Bock and Craig A. Blaising, *Progressive Dispensationalism* (Grand Rapids, MI: Baker, 2000) and Herbert W. Bateman IV, ed., *Three Central Issues in Contemporary Dispensationalism: A Comparison of Traditional and Progressive Views* (Grand Rapids, MI: Kregel, 1999).

3. For a brief history of the usage of this word in English, consult *The Oxford English Dictionary*, which can now be consulted online: http://dictionary.oed.com/. See also, R. G. Clouse, "Rapture of the Church," in *Evangelical Dictionary of Theology*, ed. Walter A. Elwell (Grand Rapids, MI: Baker, 1984), pp. 908–910. The Latin Vulgate renders 1 Thessalonians 4:17 as follows: "*deinde nos qui vivimus qui relinquimur simul rapiemur cum illis in nubibus obviam Domino in aera et sic semper cum Domino erimus.*" Jerome's translation of the Greek word transliterated *harpazō* is in bold italics. *Harpazō* is used only in 1 Thessalonians 4:17 and Acts 8:39. In Acts 8:39 it describes the transporting of Philip suddenly from Gaza to Azotus.

4. See Robert H. Gundry, *The Church and the Tribulation* (Grand Rapids, MI: Zondervan, 1973), pp. 100–111.

5. Gordon D. Fee, *The First and Second Letters to the Thessalonians*, NICNT (Grand Rapids, MI: Eerdmans, 2009), pp. 178, 179.

6. F. F. Bruce, *1 & 2 Thessalonians*, Word Biblical Commentary, Vol. 45 (Dallas: Word, 1982), p. 101.

7. Robert J. Cara, *1 & 2 Thessalonians* (Darlington, UK: Evangelical Press, 2009), p. 130. Cara also suggests the following passages in regard to the trumpet: Joel 2:1; Zephaniah 1:15, 16; Zechariah 9:14; Matthew 24:31; 1 Corinthians 15:52; Revelation 11:15.

8. Fee, *First and Second Letters to the Thessalonians*, p. 176. Fee's observations on this passage are very rich in regard to the connections between the coming of Yahweh and the coming of Christ. Very few commentators make the connection between Psalm 47:5 and 1 Thessalonians 4:16. See also C. A. Evans, "Ascending and Descending with a Shout: Psalm 47:5 and 1 Thessalonians 4:16," in *Paul and the Scriptures of Israel*, eds. C. A. Evans and J. A. Sanders, JSNTSS 83 (Sheffield: Sheffield Academic Press, 1993), pp. 238–253. This interpretation has implications regarding Christ as fully divine as well as the significance of this event in 1 Thessalonians 4 as being the final coming.

9. See Jeffrey A. D. Weima, "1 & 2 Thessalonians," in *The Zondervan Illustrated Bible Backgrounds Commentary*, vol. 3. *Romans to Philemon*, ed. Clinton Arnold (Grand Rapids, MI: Zondervan, 2002), pp. 422, 423; Cara, *1 & 2 Thessalonians*, pp. 131–133; and Gene L. Green, *The Letters to the Thessalonians*, PNTC (Grand Rapids, MI: Eerdmans, 2002), pp. 226–228. Gordon Fee, however, does not think this is Paul's point in using this term. He explains, "a recent investigation of the word has demonstrated that this is unlikely, and that all the other accoutrements of such ceremonial receptions are altogether missing from this passage" (*First and Second Letters to the Thessalonians*, p. 180).

10. Cara, *1 & 2 Thessalonians*, p. 133.

Chapter Sixteen: The Day of the Lord

1. Meredith G. Kline, *Images of the Spirit* (Eugene OR: Wipf & Stock, 1999), p. 101.
2. Ibid., p. 97.
3. Kline writes, "God's Glory-Presence was the executor of both the dual sanctions. Thus, in Israel's exodus history, the same Glory that functioned to bless Israel was the divine Agent to inflict God's curse on the Egyptians. The Glory-cloud was a protective shade to one, a bewildering darkness to the other. The Glory-fire was a guiding light to one, but to the other a blinding, consuming blaze. So it was from the beginning." See Meredith G. Kline, *Kingdom Prologue: Genesis Foundations for a Covenantal Worldview* (Eugene, OR: Wipf & Stock, 2006), p. 103.
4. For an evaluation of the day of the Lord in connection with the work of Jesus Christ, see J. Bergman Kline, "The Day of the Lord in the Death and Resurrection of Christ," *Journal of the Evangelical Theological Society*, 48/4 (December 2005): 757–770.

Chapter Seventeen: Concerning Times and Seasons

1. John R. W. Stott, *The Message of 1 and 2 Thessalonians* (Downers Grove, IL: InterVarsity Press, 1991), p. 107.
2. Ibid.
3. Edgar Whisenant, *88 Reasons Why the Rapture Will Be in 1988/On Borrowed Time* (Nashville: World Bible Society, 1988). Wikipedia claims that 4.5 million copies of this book were sold; http://en.wikipedia.org/wiki/Edgar_C._Whisenant.
4. "They went so far as to alter regular programming on September 11–13. Instead of airing their nightly *Praise the Lord* television talk show, they ran videotapes of pre-recorded shows dealing with the rapture. For non-Christians who might be watching, the revised programming included specific instructions on what to do in case Christian family members or friends disappeared and the world was thrust into the tribulation." Richard Abanes, *End-Time Visions: The Doomsday Obsession* (Nashville: Broadman & Holman, 1998), p. 93.
5. "Rapture Seer Hedges on Latest Guess," *Christianity Today*, October 21, 1988, p. 43.
6. See also Robert G. Clouse, Robert N. Hosack, and Richard V. Pierard, *The New Millennium Manual: A Once and Future Guide* (Grand Rapids, MI: Baker, 1999). For a study related to American culture in particular, see Paul Boyer, *When Time Shall Be No More: Prophecy Belief in Modern American Culture* (Cambridge: Harvard/Belknap, 1992).
7. See "The Rapture Index," *Rapture Ready*, accessed November 15, 2010, http://www.raptureready.com/rap2.html.
8. Stott, *Message of 1 and 2 Thessalonians*, p. 109.
9. Beverly Roberts Gaventa, *First and Second Thessalonians*, Interpretation (Louisville: Westminster John Knox, 1998), p. 72.
10. Greg Beale, *1–2 Thessalonians*, IVPNT (Downers Grove, IL: InterVarsity Press, 2003), p. 151.

Chapter Eighteen: A Gospel Community

1. Leon Morris, *The First and Second Epistles to the Thessalonians*, NICNT (Grand Rapids, MI: Eerdmans, 1959), p. 166.
2. See chapter 24 of this book, "The Gospel and Vocation," on 2 Thessalonians 3:6–18, for a more detailed examination of church discipline.
3. John L. Dagg, *Manual of Church Order* (Harrisburg, PA: Gano Books, 1990), p. 274.
4. Greg Beale, *1–2 Thessalonians*, IVPNT (Downers Grove, IL: InterVarsity Press, 2003), p. 164.
5. See Gordon D. Fee, *The First and Second Letters to the Thessalonians*, NICNT (Grand Rapids, MI: Eerdmans, 2009), pp. 208–210 for an evaluation of this word and a short

translation history of the term. Beale states that Fee suggested the term "unruly" for the revision of the NIV (Beale, *1–2 Thessalonians*, p. 164).

6. Beale, *1–2 Thessalonians*, p. 165

7. Commentators interpret the term "weak" here in three different ways (or a combination of these views): physically weak (health or economic distress), spiritually weak (spiritual immaturity), and morally weak (threatened by temptations). Those who see "weak" from a physical perspective include Gene L. Green, *The Letters to the Thessalonians*, PNTC (Grand Rapids, MI: Eerdmans, 2002), p. 254; Beale, *1–2 Thessalonians*, p. 166; Robert J. Cara, *1 & 2 Thessalonians* (Darlington, UK: Evangelical Press, 2009), p. 153; and Charles Wanamaker, *The Epistles to the Thessalonians*, NIGTC (Grand Rapids, MI: Eerdmans, 1990), p. 198.

8. The basis of this command being applied to the church is the distinction Paul makes at the end of verse 15: "do good to one another and to everyone." The "one another" statement seems to apply to the church, and the "to everyone" category seems to include those outside the church.

9. Abraham J. Malherbe, *The Letters to the Thessalonians*, ABC (New Haven, CT: Yale University Press, 2004), p. 328.

10. Fee, *First and Second Letters to the Thessalonians*, p. 214.

11. See ibid., pp. 213–225 and John R. W. Stott, *The Message of 1 and 2 Thessalonians* (Downers Grove, IL: InterVarsity Press, 1991), pp. 123–131.

12. For these reasons, see Stott, *Message of 1 and 2 Thessalonians*, p. 124.

13. Ralph Martin, *Worship in the Early Church* (Grand Rapids, MI: Eerdmans, 1964), pp. 135, 136. Martin explains: "When the passage is set down in lines, it reads as though it contained the 'headings' of a Church service. The note of glad adoration is struck at the opening: 'Rejoice always' (verse 16). Prayer and thanksgiving are coupled — a trait which comes into the Church from the synagogue assembly. Christians are counseled to give the Spirit full rein, especially as He opens the mouths of the prophets (verses 19, 20); but cautioned (verse 21) that they must test the spirits (cf. 1 John iv, 1). Above all, nothing unseemly must enter the assembly (verse 22), but all should be done 'decently and in order' (1 Corinthians xiv, 40). And the closing part of this 'Church order' — if this description is correct — contains a comprehensive prayer for the entire fellowship (verse 23), expressed in the confidence that God will hear and bless (verse 24)."

14. Fee, *First and Second Letters to the Thessalonians*, p. 214.

15. Stott, *Message of 1 and 2 Thessalonians*, p. 126.

16. Fee, *First and Second Letters to the Thessalonians*, p. 214.

17. See Wayne Grudem, ed., *Are Miraculous Gifts for Today? Four Views* (Grand Rapids, MI: Zondervan, 1996).

18. William Perkins, *The Art of Prophesying* (Carlisle, PA: Banner of Truth, 1996).

19. See Richard B. Gaffin Jr., "A Cessationist View," in *Are Miraculous Gifts for Today? Four Views*, p. 42ff. and his more developed argument in *Perspectives on Pentecost: New Testament Teaching on the Gifts of the Holy Spirit* (Philipsburg, NJ: P&R, 1979), pp. 89–116.

20. See Wayne Grudem, *The Gift of Prophecy in the New Testament and Today* (Wheaton, IL: Crossway, 2000) and Grudem, *Systematic Theology: An Introduction to Biblical Doctrine* (Grand Rapids, MI: Zondervan, 1994), chapter 52, "Gifts of the Holy Spirit (1): General Questions," pp. 1016–1048 and chapter 53, "Gifts of the Holy Spirit (2): Specific Gifts," pp. 1049–1090.

21. See C. Samuel Storms, "A Third Wave View," in *Are Miraculous Gifts for Today? Four Views*, pp. 175–223. I became aware of these developments through the influence of John Piper and the 1991 Desiring God Pastors Conference titled "Spiritual Gifts and the Sovereignty of God." Wayne Grudem was the keynote speaker, and Piper did a biographical presentation on Martyn Lloyd-Jones.

22. I think Vern Poythress makes the best case for this perspective: Vern S. Poythress, "Modern Spiritual Gifts as Analogous to Apostolic Gifts: Affirming Extraordinary Works of the

Spirit within Cessationist Theology," *Journal of the Evangelical Theological Society*, 39/1: 71–101.

23. This is Gaffin's point in *Perspectives on Pentecost*.

24. The King James Version translates verse 22 as, "Abstain from all appearance of evil." Although it was outside of the purpose of this particular sermon, I did address this with my congregation when preaching through 1 Thessalonians. Part of the reason for this is the whole view of the Christian life that developed out of that verse regarding Christian ethical conduct. The idea was that you should back off from evil so far that there would not even be any appearance of evil, even if what you were doing was not actually sinful. At one point in American religious history this would have been applied to drinking, smoking, dancing, movies, and a whole host of other possible scenarios that *appeared* evil. Whatever wisdom there is in developing hedges around our ethical lives, it should not be based on a mistranslation of this verse or on taking the verse out of its context in regard to the particular point Paul is addressing.

CHAPTER NINETEEN: THE RIGHT PERSPECTIVE ON SUFFERING

1. Jonathan Edwards, *Memoirs of Jonathan Edwards*, in *The Works of Jonathan Edwards*, vol. 1 (Carlisle, PA: Banner of Truth, 1992), pp. xii, xiii.

2. Greg Beale, *1–2 Thessalonians*, IVPNT (Downers Grove, IL: InterVarsity Press, 2003), p. 182.

3. Although this is not the majority interpretation, it is argued for by Beale, *1–2 Thessalonians*, pp. 183–185; Leon Morris, *The First and Second Epistles to the Thessalonians*, NICNT (Grand Rapids, MI: Eerdmans, 1959), pp. 197–199; I. Howard Marshall, *1 and 2 Thessalonians*, New Century Bible Commentary (Grand Rapids, MI: Eerdmans, 1983), pp. 172, 173; Henry Alford, *The Greek New Testament*, vol. 3 (Grand Rapids, MI: Baker, 1980), p. 285; and John Eadie, *Commentary on the Greek Text of the Epistles of Paul to the Thessalonians* (Birmingham, AL: Solid Ground Christian Books, 2005), pp. 234–237.

4. Geerhardus Vos, "The Structure of Pauline Eschatology," in *The Pauline Eschatology* (Philipsburg, NJ: P&R, 1994), pp. 1–41. See in particular his chart on p. 38. Vos's work was ahead of its time and has subsequently influenced a host of recent scholars, including Greg Beale, who applies this insight to his commentary on 1 Thessalonians. See Beale, *1–2 Thessalonians*, pp. 18–23. Oscar Cullmann, *Christ and Time* (London: SCM Press, 1952), pp. 84–87, used an illustration from World War II to explain the already/not yet structure. D-day was the phrase used to describe the victory at Normandy, which is usually referred to as the beginning of the end of World War II. This battle was the *decisive* battle for that war. However, Vday was the phrase used to describe the final victory in the war. Cullmann described Jesus' first coming as "D-day," since this is when Satan was decisively defeated. "V-day" is the second coming, when Jesus' enemies will totally surrender and bow down to him. Cullmann explains, "The hope of the final victory is so much more vivid because of the unshakeably firm conviction that the battle that decides the victory has already taken place" (p. 87).

5. Leon Morris, *First and Second Epistles to the Thessalonians*, p. 198: "The second point we must bear in mind is that in this verse the 'manifest token' is probably not suffering simply, but the whole of the previous clause. That is to say, it includes also the bearing of the Thessalonians under suffering." For more details, see Marshall, *1 and 2 Thessalonians*, pp. 172, 173.

6. Marshall, *1 and 2 Thessalonians*, p. 173: "Although commentators generally take judgment as future, it does not make good sense of the passage; moreover, elsewhere Paul uses a different Greek word (*krima*, not *krisis* as here) for the future judgment. Rather the thought is of God's present process of judgment on his people which has the aim of judging them to be worthy of the kingdom. This understanding of the word gives good sense. The trials and the way in which the readers are enduring them . . . constitute evidence of a righteous process of judgment which God is carrying out in order that he may see that they are worthy of the kingdom, granted that he will repay those who suffer with future reward."

CHAPTER TWENTY: ETERNAL DESTINIES

1. See J. Gresham Machen's sermon on the text of Matthew 10:28 in *God Transcendent* (Carlisle, PA: Banner of Truth, 1998). Sinclair Ferguson utilized this at the 1990 Desiring God Pastors Conference in the lecture "Universalism and the Reality of Eternal Punishment: The Biblical Basis of the Doctrine of Eternal Punishment."

2. Greg Beale, *1–2 Thessalonians*, IVPNT (Downers Grove, IL: InterVarsity Press, 2003), p. 186.

3. Walter Marshall, *The Gospel Mystery of Sanctification* (Grand Rapids, MI: Reformation Heritage Books, 1999), p. 42.

4. For example, see Philip E. Hughes, *The True Image: The Origin and Destiny of Man in Christ* (Grand Rapids, MI: Eerdmans, 1989), pp. 405–407; Clark H. Pinnock, "The Destruction of the Finally Impenitent," *Criswell Theological Review*, 4 (1990): 246, 247; E. Fudge, "The Final End of the Wicked," *Journal of the Evangelical Theological Society*, 27 (1984): 325–334; David L. Edwards and John R. W. Stott, *Evangelical Essentials: A Liberal-Evangelical Dialogue* (Downers Grove, IL: InterVarsity Press, 1988), pp. 275, 276, 312–321.

5. John R. W. Stott, *The Message of 1 and 2 Thessalonians* (Downers Grove, IL: InterVarsity Press, 1991), p. 149.

6. I. Howard Marshall, *1 and 2 Thessalonians*, New Century Bible Commentary (Grand Rapids, MI: Eerdmans, 1983), p. 179.

7. Beale, *1–2 Thessalonians*, p. 189.

8. Wayne Grudem, *Systematic Theology: An Introduction to Biblical Doctrine* (Grand Rapids, MI: Zondervan, 1994), p. 1148.

9. Robert J. Cara, *1 & 2 Thessalonians* (Darlington, UK: Evangelical Press, 2009), p. 288 references the following: *Baltimore Catechism, No. 3,* 185; *Catechism of the Catholic Church*, 1035, 1861; *Orthodox Confession of the Catholic and Apostolic Eastern Church*, 68; *Augsburg Confession*, 17; *Belgic Confession*, 37; *Westminster Confession of Faith*, 33.3; *Westminster Larger Catechism*, 29, 89.

CHAPTER TWENTY-ONE: JESUS WILL NOT COME UNTIL . . .

1. See Clarence Larkin, *Dispensational Truth, or God's Plan and Purpose in the Ages* (Glenside, PA: Clarence Larkin Estate, 1918) and *Rightly Dividing the Word* (Glenside, PA: Clarence Larkin Estate, 1920).

2. Robert J. Cara, *1 & 2 Thessalonians* (Darlington, UK: Evangelical Press, 2009), pp. 197, 198 provides a summary of the views: "1) One is that the Second Coming includes a complex series of events; hence, people were claiming that aspects of it had occurred, though not the final portions. 2) A second possibility is that the events of the Second Coming had been internalized or "spiritualized;" hence, there is in reality no future resurrection of the dead or new heavens and earth (cf. 2 Timothy 2:18; 2 Peter 3:4–10). 3) A third suggestion is that the Second Coming involves events that are not visible; hence, major things have happened, even though they are not seen."

3. John R. W. Stott, *The Message of 1 and 2 Thessalonians* (Downers Grove, IL: InterVarsity Press, 1991), p. 157; Anthony Hoekema, *Jehovah's Witnesses* (Carlisle, UK: Paternoster, 1973), pp. 90, 91.

4. Greg Beale, *1–2 Thessalonians*, IVPNT (Downers Grove, IL: InterVarsity Press, 2003), pp. 203, 204 goes on to explain four observations that confirm this interpretation: "(1) A 'falling away' assumes some sort of prior turning to God. (2) This is consistent with the above-noted usage of *apostasia* in the Old Testament. (3) It is also consistent with the immediate context of deception within the church. (4) It is supported by the closest verbal parallel to this passage, namely, *Martyrdom of Isaiah* 2:4, 5, where 'the angel of iniquity' empowers evil Manasseh 'in causing apostasy [*apostasia*], and in the lawlessness [*anomia*] that was disseminated in Jerusalem,' that is, among God's people." This is further evidence that *apostasia* should not be translated as "departure" and used as evidence for a rapture and resurrection.

5. See Robert L. Thomas, "1 and 2 Thessalonians," in *The Expositor's Bible Commentary*, ed. Frank E. Gaebelein (Grand Rapids, MI: Zondervan, 1978), 11:318, 319.

CHAPTER TWENTY-TWO: REBELLION AND HOPE

1. I will use the terms *apostasy* and *rebellion* interchangeably here. The following summary was drawn from John R. W. Stott, *The Message of 1 and 2 Thessalonians* (Downers Grove, IL: InterVarsity Press, 1991), p. 162ff.

2. The most comprehensive recent survey is Kim Riddlebarger, *The Man of Sin: Uncovering the Truth about the Antichrist* (Grand Rapids, MI: Baker, 2006). For shorter surveys, see Geerhardus Vos, "Man of Sin," in *The Pauline Eschatology* (Philipsburg, NJ: P&R, 1994), pp. 94–135; F. F. Bruce, "Excursus on Antichrist," in *1 & 2 Thessalonians*, Word Biblical Commentary, vol. 45 (Dallas: Word, 1982), pp. 179–188.

3. St. Augustine describes the view that some interpreters were taking in regard to this passage: "Some people would have it that Antichrist means here not the leader himself but what we may call his whole body, that is of those who belong to him, together with himself, their leader." But then he cautions: "For myself I am much astonished at the great presumption of those who venture such guesses" (*The City of God*, 20.19.2), quoted in Peter Gorday, "1–2 Thessalonians," in *Ancient Christian Commentary on Scripture, New Testament*, ed. Thomas C. Oden (Downers Grove, IL: InterVarsity Press, 2000), 9:110.

4. This summary is dependent upon Stott, *Message of 1 and 2 Thessalonians*, pp. 165–167; Bruce, "Excursus on Antichrist," pp. 182–188; Riddlebarger, "Know Your Enemy-The Antichrist in Church History," in *Man of Sin*, pp. 135–166.

5. For a summary of these views, see Greg Beale, *1–2 Thessalonians*, IVPNT (Downers Grove, IL: InterVarsity Press, 2003), pp. 207–211.

6. See 1 Corinthians 3:16, 17; 6:19; 2 Corinthians 6:16; Ephesians 2:19–21; 1 Peter 2:4–7; Revelation 3:12; 21:22.

7. Those who argue that "temple" is figurative for the church include the following: John Calvin, *Epistles to the Philippians, Colossians, and Thessalonians*, Calvin's Commentaries, (Grand Rapids, MI: Baker, 1993), 21:330, 331; George C. Findlay, *The Epistles of Paul the Apostle to the Thessalonians* (Grand Rapids, MI: Baker, 1982), pp. 170–174; R. C. H. Lenski, *The Interpretation of St. Paul's Epistles to the Colossians, to the Thessalonians, to Timothy, to Titus, and to Philemon* (Minneapolis: Augsburg Fortress Press, 2008), pp. 414, 415; William Hendriksen, *Thessalonians, Timothy and Titus* (Grand Rapids, MI: Baker, 1992), p. 178; Beale, *1–2 Thessalonians*, pp. 206–211; Robert J. Cara, *1 & 2 Thessalonians* (Darlington, UK: Evangelical Press, 2009), pp. 200, 201.

8. I. Howard Marshall, *1 and 2 Thessalonians*, New Century Bible Commentary (Grand Rapids, MI: Eerdmans, 1983), pp. 196–200 provides a helpful summary of the views.

9. Beale, *1–2 Thessalonians*, pp. 216, 217 and Colin R. Nicholl, "Appendix 1: Michael, the Restrainer Removed" in *From Hope to Despair in Thessalonica: Situating 1 and 2 Thessalonians*, Society for New Testament Studies Monograph Series in (New York: Cambridge University Press, 2004), pp. 225–249.

10. Nicholl, "Appendix 1," p. 232.

11. G. K. Beale, *The Book of Revelation*, NIGTC (Grand Rapids, MI: Eerdmans, 1999), pp. 973–1028. See also Sydney H. T. Page, "Revelation 20 and Pauline Eschatology," *Journal of the Evangelical Theological Society*, 23.1 (1980): 31–43.

12. N. T. Wright, *Paul for Everyone: Galatians and Thessalonians* (Louisville: Westminster John Knox, 2004), pp. 146, 147. See Exodus 4:21; 7:13; 9:12.

13. Beale, *1–2 Thessalonians*, p. 222.

CHAPTER TWENTY-THREE: THE STEADFASTNESS OF CHRIST

1. Quoted in Greg Beale, *1–2 Thessalonians*, IVPNT (Downers Grove, IL: InterVarsity Press, 2003), pp. 242, 243.

2. Ibid., p. 237.

CHAPTER TWENTY-FOUR: THE GOSPEL AND VOCATION

1. Leon Morris, *The First and Second Epistles to the Thessalonians*, NICNT (Grand Rapids, MI: Eerdmans, 1959), p. 251; and Greg Beale, *1–2 Thessalonians*, IVPNT (Downers Grove, IL: InterVarsity Press, 2003), p. 249.

2. See Gene L. Green, *The Letters to the Thessalonians*, PNTC (Grand Rapids, MI: Eerdmans, 2002), p. 342; and Charles Wanamaker, *The Epistles to the Thessalonians*, NIGTC (Grand Rapids, MI: Eerdmans, 1990), p. 282.

3. Gordon D. Fee, *The First and Second Letters to the Thessalonians*, NICNT (Grand Rapids, MI: Eerdmans, 2009), pp. 324, 325.

4. For what follows, see ibid., p. 209ff.

5. Ibid., p. 209. Fee also has a note connected to that comment that continues: "See the two entries in BDAG ἀτακτέω / ἀτάκτως who, regarding the verb, note that 'the trans[lation] *be idle, lazy* does not take adequate account of Gr[eco]-Rom[an] social history.' In fact, there is no known evidence of any kind in its favor" (note 19).

6. I am viewing this command in its broader Biblical-theological framework, but some argue that Paul's command applies to the issue of discipline and who should eat the Lord's Supper. See Abraham J. Malherbe, *The Letters to the Thessalonians*, ABC (New Haven, CT: Yale University Press, 2004), p. 460; Green, *Letters to the Thessalonians*, p. 355. I doubt this is the case since Paul reminds them that he did not eat anyone's bread without paying for it (2 Thessalonians 3:8).

7. Abraham J. Malherbe, *Paul and the Thessalonians* (Philadelphia: Fortress, 1987), pp. 100, 101.

8. What follows is dependent upon Robert J. Cara, *1 & 2 Thessalonians* (Darlington, UK: Evangelical Press, 2009), pp. 237, 238.

9. See Gustaf Wingren, *Luther on Vocation*, trans. Carl C. Rasmussen (Eugene, OR: Wipf & Stock, 2004) and Gene Edward Veith Jr., *God at Work: Your Christian Vocation in All of Life*, Focal Point Series (Wheaton, IL: Crossway, 2002).

10. See John Murray, *Principles of Conduct: Aspects of Biblical Ethics* (Grand Rapids, MI: Eerdmans, 1957), pp. 82–106. Max Weber, in his well-known book *The Protestant Ethic and the Spirit of Capitalism*, argued that certain theological principles bound up in the Protestant doctrine of vocation allowed capitalism to develop in the West. Although Weber realizes the importance that Protestants placed on seeing all vocations as existing for God's glory, he also argues that Calvinism in particular stirred the development of this type of ethic with its doctrine of predestination. Work became the way to know whether one was predestined.

11. John Piper, *Rethinking Retirement: Finishing Life for the Glory of Christ* (Wheaton, IL: Crossway, 2009), p. 29.

12. Church discipline is a controversial issue in the life of the church, but it has both a positive perspective (discipleship and perseverance) and a negative perspective (rebuke and withdrawal). Discipline has a clear Biblical precedent not only in our passage but also in the overall instructions in the New Testament. See Everett Ferguson, "The Church and Her Teacher: The New Way of Life" in *The Church of Christ: A Biblical Ecclesiology for Today*, in (Grand Rapids, MI: Eerdmans, 1996), pp. 349–410. Ferguson covers the areas of Christian ethics, fellowship, discipline, liberty, society, and unity. For a popular treatment in light of the ministry of the church, see Mark Dever, "Mark Seven: Biblical Church Discipline" in *9 Marks of a Healthy Church* (Wheaton, IL: Crossway, 2004), pp. 167–193 and Jay Adams, *Handbook of Church Discipline* (Grand Rapids, MI: Zondervan, 1986).

13. See Edmund Clowney, "The Marks of the Church," *The Church*, in Contours of Christian Theology (Downers Grove, IL: InterVarsity Press, 1995), pp. 99–115.

14. Article 29. See also John Calvin, *Institutes of the Christian Religion*, ed. John T. McNeill, trans. Ford Lewis Battles, The Library of Christian Classics, vol. 21 (Philadelphia: Westminster, 1960), IV.2.1–4.

15. Daniel E. Wray, *Biblical Church Discipline* (Carlisle, PA: Banner of Truth, 2001) provides a helpful chart demonstrating the significance of Matthew 18 for church discipline.

Scripture Index

General Index

Aaron, 126
Abel, 162
Abraham, Abram, 40, 77, 128
Adam and Eve, 30, 117, 129, 130, 142, 180, 184, 197, 198, 199, 206
Advent, 107, 108, 109
Affliction see *Tribulations*
"All of Life Is Repentance" (Keller), 54
Ames, William, 9
Amillennialism, 123
Anselm, 53
Antichrist, the, 172, 174, 175, 180, 181, 182, 183, 184, 185, 188
Antiochus IV (Epiphanes), 181
Apostasy, 174, 176, 177, 180, 184, 188, 213
Apostolic Constitutions, 200
Aristotle, 45, 83
Armageddon, Oil and the Middle East Crisis (Walvoord), 109
Arminianism, 39
Athens, 83, 84
August, Emperor, 91
Augustine, 39, 120, 161, 213

Babylon, 130, 131, 180, 182
Baptism, 40, 47, 49, 96, 146, 204, 207
Barna, George, 95
Barna Group, the, 95
Beale, Greg, 77, 119, 142, 148, 167, 174
Belgic Confession, The, 203
Brady, Tom, 44
Brainerd, David, 71
Brooks, Phillips, 9
Busybodies, 37, 102, 148, 197, 202, 203, 204

Cabiri of Samothrace, cult of, 92
Cain, 162
Calvin, John, 36, 51, 69, 70, 117, 161
Calvinism, 39, 200
Cara, Robert, 118, 120, 125
Carey, William, 71
Chesterton, G. K., 86
China, 27
Church, the, 32, 40, 47, 59, 82, 85, 95, 133, 145, 146, 152, 154, 203, 211
    in Thessalonica, 15, 16, 32, 33, 47, 102, 103, 116, 148, 155, 196
Church discipline, 147, 203, 204
Church planting, 17, 21, 206
Covenant with God, 82, 119, 128, 174
    New Covenant, the, 205
    old covenant, 82
Cur Deus Homo (*Why God Became Man*) (Anselm), 53

Dagg, John L., 147
Day of Pentecost, 133
Day of the Lord, 125, 126, 129 (chapter 16 *passim*), 137, 138, 139, 143, 152, 173, 175
Death, 50, 115, 116, 117, 121, 128, 134, 137, 148, 205, 211
Demosthenes, 91
Desiring God, 59
Disorderliness, 37, 46, 102, 146, 147, 148, 197, 199, 200, 202, 203, 204
Dispensationalism, 123, 124, 172
Divorce, 95
Draper, Larry, 193

Edwards, Jonathan, 153, 154
Egypt, 24, 40, 51, 77, 90, 131, 185
88 Reasons Why the Rapture Will Be in 1988 (Whisenant), 138
Election, doctrine of, 39, 40, 41, 46
Elijah, 134
Endurance see *Steadfastness*
Ethics, 89, 90, 146

Faith, 28, 36, 38, 41, 47, 69, 70, 107, 152, 155, 160, 207, 214
Faithfulness, 156, 157, 158, 159, 201
Fall, the, 156, 162, 179, 197, 198, 203, 206
Fee, Gordon, 37, 101, 125, 126, 148, 149, 150, 151, 196, 197
Ferguson, Sinclair, 59, 60, 61, 162
Flood, the, 206
Forgiveness of sin, 33, 36, 57, 58, 60, 78, 165, 206, 210

God,
    faithfulness of, 20, 152, 192, 193, 212, 213
    Father, 28, 31, 32, 33, 47, 59, 63, 74, 87, 154, 173, 207, 211
    grace of, 30, 31, 32, 33, 41, 96, 154, 159
    judge, 30, 76, 78, 125, 129, 130, 131, 132, 157, 158, 164, 185
    mercy of, 54, 133
    sovereignty of, 28, 37, 153, 154, 185, 187, 188, 189, 190, 213
    wrath of, against sin, 18, 19, 30, 52, 54, 57, 58, 68, 74, 75, 78, 130, 132, 138,

Index of
Sermon Illustrations

King Nebuchadnezzar's pride, fall, and then submission to the true God illustrates all of our spiritual rebellion, 181

Love

G. K. Chesterton: "How much larger your life would be if your self could become smaller in it," 86

Sacrificing with clenched fists, not open hands, is not love, 86

Tertullian: "See how they love one another," 99

Justin Martyr: "because of Christ, we live together with such people and pray for our enemies," 99

John Stott: sometimes love means supporting ourselves so others don't have to support us, 101

St. Augustine's *Enchiridion* reminds us of the three graces of the Christian life—faith, hope, and love, 213

Marriage/The Family

J. I. Packer: "Our benighted society urgently needs recalling to the noble and ennobling view of sex which Scripture implied and the seventh commandment assumes," 94–95

Barna Group: no difference in the divorce rate among unbelievers and among believers, 95

Persecution/Opposition

The dazzling opening ceremonies of the Beijing Olympics made a stark contrast to the conflicts between the Chinese government and the persecuted church, 27

Communications technology and media constantly bombard us with a message opposed to the gospel, 43

On TV, in the movies, at the mall, at the grocery store—everywhere—we are bombarded with sexually objectionable images, 91

Prayer

Even pagans in the ancient world prayed, but not to the true God, 35

Roger Nicole: "There is comfort for the child of God in being assured that our prayer will not change God's mind," 191

Preaching

John Calvin: "The Word of God is not distinguished from the word of the prophet. God wishes to be heard through the voice of his ministers," 70

Second Helvetic Confession: "The preaching of the Word of God is the Word of God," 70

John Murray: "Christ speaks in the gospel proclamation," 71

John Piper: John 10 ("other sheep" need to hear about the Good Shepherd) is the great missionary text of the Bible, 71

The Puritans called preaching prophecy, 150

Pride

King Nebuchadnezzar's pride, fall, and then submission to the true God illustrates all of our spiritual rebellion, 181

The Rapture

There is an ongoing temptation to figure out the date when Christ will come back for his church, 138, 139

The Rapture Index seeks to identify activities or events that indicate the Rapture is near, 139

Repentance

The first of Martin Luther's Ninety-five Theses: "Our Lord and Master Jesus Christ . . . willed the entire life of believers to be one of repentance," 54

Tim Keller article, "All of Life Is Repentance," 54

Westminster Shorter Catechism. Question 87: "a saving grace, whereby a sinner, out of a true sense of his sin . . . doth . . . turn from it unto God," 54

Resurrection of Christ and of Believers

Funerals were once called "witnesses to the resurrection," 116

Robert Cara: "Paul's antidote to the grief of the Thessalonians is to remind them . . . [about] the reality of the death and resurrection of Christ," 118

Salvation

Augustine and Pelagius debated the doctrine of election, 39

Sinclair Ferguson: "You begin to learn to interpret your life in terms of what God says about you because you are united to Christ," 59

John Murray: "Union with Christ is . . . the central truth of the whole doctrine of salvation," 60

The hymn "It Is Well with My Soul" reminds us that God forgave us for all of our sins, not just some of them, 208

About the Cover

The design of the book jacket brings together the talents of several Christian artists. The design centers around the beautiful banner created by artist Marge Gieser. It is photographed on the jacket at around one-twentieth of its original size.

Concerning the Biblical message behind the banner for *1 & 2 Thessalonians*, Marge Gieser writes:

> The Thessalonian church had been "blessed . . . in Christ with every spiritual blessing in the heavenly places" (Eph 1:2) in spite of the trials and persecutions they were enduring. Inspired by the Holy Spirit (top of banner) they were known for their labor of love and their endurance. Paul teaches them not to fear the future or the evil one and to encourage each other with the knowledge they have. First Thessalonians speaks of being "caught up together . . . in the clouds" at Christ's return (4:17), the blessed hope of all believers.

The other artists contributing their talents to the creation of the jacket were: Bill Koechling photography; Paul Higdon, design and typography; and Josh Dennis, art direction.